T H E
LEAP

THE
LEAP

HOW TO SURVIVE AND THRIVE
IN THE SUSTAINABLE ECONOMY

CHRIS TURNER

RANDOM HOUSE CANADA

PUBLISHED BY RANDOM HOUSE CANADA

Copyright © 2011 Chris Turner

www.randomhouse.ca

Random House Canada and colophon are registered trademarks.

Library and Archives Canada Cataloguing in Publication

Turner, Chris, 1973–
The leap : how to survive and thrive in the sustainable economy / Chris Turner.

Issued also in electronic format.

ISBN 978–0-307–35922–3

1. Environmental economics. 2. Sustainable development. 3. Economic history—21st century. I. Title.

HC79.E5T87 2011 338.9'27 C2011–901728–8

Text design by Leah Springate

Cover images: © Swim Ink 2, LLC/CORBIS, yxowert/Shutterstock.com

The author gratefully acknowledges the financial support of the Alberta Foundation for the Arts, the Canada Council for the Arts, and the Banff Centre. A comprehensive list of the author's source materials is located online at www.randomhouse.ca

Printed on paper that contains FSC certified 100% post-consumer fibre.

Printed and bound in the United States of America

10 9 8 7 6 5 4 3 2 1

This book is dedicated to the memory of
Hermann Scheer (1944–2010)

This book is for Alexander

"Delays are the refuge of weak minds, and to procrastinate
on this occasion is to show a culpable intention to the bounties
of nature; a total insensibility to the blessings of Providence,
and an inexcusable neglect of the interests of society . . .
The overflowing blessings from this great fountain of public
good and national abundance will be as extensive as our
country, and as durable as time."

—DeWitt Clinton,
*Memorial of the Citizens of New York, in Favour of a
Canal Navigation Between the Great Western Lakes
and the Tide-Waters of the Hudson, 1816*

< CONTENTS >

< PROLOGUE >

TO FURNISH MORE CERTAIN CONVEYANCE

TWO TRACKS AND THE CHASM IN BETWEEN

THIS BOOK BEGINS from a simple but fundamental premise: that business as usual has ceased to be. The norms of twentieth-century prosperity have become the instruments of twenty-first century collapse. The track that brought us to this place, functional and stable as it might seem from certain vantage points, cannot lead us any further. Moreover, the engine of our success to date—that great, roaring internal combustion engine that powered the Industrial Revolution—is fast becoming obsolete. The best evidence from energy analysts, economists and climate scientists alike all indicates the necessity of a wholesale transformation, a complete redesign and rebuilding of the socioeconomic foundations of our societies.

There are any number of pronouncements on the urgent need for this shift. Maybe the most succinct and unequivocal one appeared in a recent International Energy Agency report. "Current global trends in energy supply and consumption," it read, "are patently unsustainable—environmentally, economically, socially."

Here's the American sustainability pioneer Paul Hawken, speaking to the graduating class of the University of Portland in

2009: "Civilization needs a new operating system, you are the programmers, and we need it within a few decades."

"The choice we face"—this is how US president Barack Obama put it—"is not between saving our environment and saving our economy. The choice we face is between prosperity and decline."

Such is the scale of the challenge and the urgency of change. This is not a situation calling for gradual, incremental tweaks. We need a decisive jump from one structural foundation to another inside a single generation. This is a broad lateral shift, a change not in final destination but in the path we use to get there. I call it The Leap—in this case, the Great Leap Sideways.

What do I mean by a great leap? And why sideways? To explain, let's take a brief survey of The Leap's metaphorical landscape.

First, imagine our hypermodern, speed-of-light digital society as a train on a long, transcontinental track, bound—so goes the eternal promise—for some brighter future. The engine, fed for 150 years by energy-dense fossil fuels, is staggering in its speed and power. (It devours more than eighty million barrels of oil every single day.) The amenities on board are impossibly lavish and sophisticated—instant worldwide communication with virtually anyone anywhere; the contents of seemingly all the world's libraries available at the tap of a keyboard or the touch of a handheld screen; the entertainment omnipresent and widely varied and provided, often as not, by actors on 3D stages more lush and vibrant than real life. There are machines to do all the heavy lifting, medicines to treat nearly every disease that afflicts humankind. The food is elaborately prepared, drawn effortlessly from every corner of the globe and available on an instantaneous whim any time of year, and so plentiful the very idea of scarcity-induced hunger has been all but eradicated. The level of comfort in nearly every class of compartment is at least a few rungs up from that enjoyed only by royalty in the dark centuries prior to the industrial age.

There is, on the surface, no reason at all to seek out other means of transport.

But as you lean back into your contoured seat, you gaze out the window to your side and notice some sort of depression on the horizon. The train, you realize, is veering slowly but steadily in that direction. For the first time you can remember, you notice bumps and jiggles in the ride. The tracks have evidently begun to deteriorate beneath you, rails warping and ties splitting. The threat of a derailment, which seemed impossible when you boarded, now seems terrifyingly imminent each time the train makes a particularly intense shudder across another hump in the track.

Back out the window, the depression is now close enough to the side of the train to reveal the chasm's full measure: it is broad and impossibly deep, stretching far below you. It's difficult to tell exactly how steep and long the drop is, but there's no way the train would survive the plunge, and you certainly wouldn't, either. At this speed, in such comfortable environs, it's difficult to tell for certain how quickly the tracks are closing the ground between them and the lip of the chasm—the train sometimes seems to pull away from the precipice for stretches of time—but as you pay closer attention it becomes harder and harder to convince yourself you're headed anywhere but over a cliff.

Let's imagine that a sort of preternatural clarity pervades the scene at this moment, and a wide horizon comes into view under improbably clear skies. Let's imagine you can see the faint spectre of another train zipping along on the far side of the chasm.

This other vehicle, you notice, is headed in the same direction. It's pointed at the same station, bound for roughly the same place you were already going—a place with the same goals, if you will, similar values and institutions and standards of living. What's more—here a fellow passenger who's had a chance to ride on this new conveyance pipes up—the train in the distance boasts the same amenities, similar levels of comfort and service and sophistication, a quality of life that's fundamentally better in many ways than the one you've always known. The track beneath its wheels is gleamingly new, and it's veering away from the chasm even more sharply than your track is headed toward it. There's no stopping that other train—in fact, it appears to be picking up speed even as your fellow passenger starts to explain how it works. And to hop aboard, he insists, would not be a total change in direction or a jump ahead into some unrecognizable future. It would be a sideward move to a parallel track. A better way to get where we're already going.

He can't help himself, this guy, he's out of his seat now, ranting. We've got to jump, he says. We've got to go now, while there's still enough momentum left in this vehicle to launch us over the chasm. Some of the passengers are aghast, a few others begin to nod and whoop in agreement; a couple, their jaws firmly set, insist it's pure madness. Someone tries to shout the guy down, while another passenger hands him a megaphone.

He's seen it done, he insists. There's less to it than you think. We could simply change trains.

I'm that guy, that ranting passenger. And the jump over that chasm is The Leap—our vital Great Leap Sideways.

In the coming chapters, I'll show you what I've seen, the evidence that convinces me beyond any doubt that we can make this shift. Around the world and in our backyards, communities and businesses, cities and industries, energy regimes and economies, even entire nations have made this Leap to arrive at a place of reinvigorated community, renewed industrial might and greater economic health and social well-being. I'll also explain how to make these Leaps—the common tactics and techniques, the best engines and preferred fuels, as well as the greatest hurdles.

Change of the magnitude required for a Great Leap Sideways, however, can be a difficult thing to apprehend fully in the present tense. Our vantage point is too close to the enormous apparatus of the status quo. Our attachments to the fine details of the coaches we're riding in and our habituation to even the sharpest of lurches along the failing track are too strong. We find it hard to see the full depth of the chasm, harder still to recognize the sturdier track on the far side as the better path to our destination.

So I'd like to begin making my case for The Leap with the example of one completed long ago, one whose execution and outcome should be beyond dispute. Let's journey first to the streets of New York City at the dawn of the last industrial age to demonstrate the surprisingly modest ways in which a leap of epochal magnitude can be launched.

THE HIDDEN LEGACY OF THE BLACK BALL LINE

If you survey Lower Manhattan from its eastern edge along Pearl Street today, the primacy of New York might seem preordained. With one of the world's most perfectly sculpted deepwater harbours at your back, you gaze west at a great spiking wall of wealth and power sheathed in steel and stone and glass, preposterous in its dimensions and concentrated here as no place else on earth. The New York Stock Exchange, the Federal Reserve Bank and offices bearing the nameplates of practically every financial and commercial titan you can think of reside within a ten-block radius. Expand the circle in concentric rings, and it soon encloses mainstays of the global publishing and entertainment industries, the headquarters of the United Nations, the residences, galleries, performance spaces and stomping grounds of intellectuals and artists who collectively set much of the modern world's cultural agenda. New Yorkers have long been notorious for their belief that there is nothing that truly matters in the world unless it matters to New York, and on Pearl Street you can feel the immutable weight that gives the place such a deep sense of its own centrality.

There are, of course, a great many practical explanations for New York's ascendancy. There is its physical location, midway along the densely populated northeastern coast of the United States, astride that excellent harbour. The audacious Erie Canal project of the 1820s linked the city to America's Midwestern breadbasket and turned its port into the nation's predominant commercial centre, which in turn made it the first port of call for the majority of the young nation's immigrants. The railroad boom later in the nineteenth century not only deepened those links but transformed Wall Street into one of the world's major financial hubs. America's position in world affairs was further bolstered by Europe's two crippling twentieth-century wars, and a disproportionate share of the new wealth and importance of the United States naturally accrued to its primary city.

Before any of that could happen, though, there was a single merchant in a Pearl Street counting house with a great notion, modest on its surface but revolutionary in its impact—a new way of thinking about commerce that set the stage for all that came after. It was not a new kind of boat or engine, not a technological advance at all. It was an idea. A cognitive shift. A way of organizing a business that elevated it from the handmade, informal world of the pre-industrial merchant trade to the speed and precision of industrial-scale shipping.

—

On a blustery winter morning in January 1818, a small crowd of New Yorkers gathered in the swirling snow down at the wharf where Pearl Street's merchants sent and received their shipments. They were there to witness the launch of an innovation that many of them believed was pure folly. The piers were piled high as always with great bales of cotton, crates of Chinese tea and sacks of flour from upstate New York farms. The waterfront taverns and coffee houses overflowed with would-be passengers. People and produce alike waited indefinitely like this, sometimes for weeks, until the right mix of wind, weather and full cargo holds emerged to sanction the long sail to Europe. Sometimes, ships even waited for a guarantee of return cargo before setting off across the Atlantic. It was frustrating and woefully inefficient, this interminable waiting, but how else could you hope to cross the ocean? As long as there had been shipping, this was simply the *only* way people and their stuff travelled. Which is what made the launch of the swift, three-masted *James Monroe* scheduled for ten o'clock that morning at Pier 23 remarkable enough to attract a crowd, even in the snow.

The previous October, a curious notice had appeared in the *New York Evening Post*, announcing plans for the creation of a "line of American packets"—ships that carried packets of transatlantic mail and thus ran on less variable schedules than regular merchant ships. There would be four ships in the line, the notice declared, and the intention was for one of them to set sail for Liverpool and another to embark on the return journey on a certain day each month. A similar notice in the *Liverpool Mercury* was unequivocal on this matter. "In order to furnish more certain Conveyance for Goods and Passengers," it read, "a regular succession of Vessels . . . will *positively sail, full or not full*, from

Liverpool on the 1st, and from New York on the 5th of every month, throughout the year."

The deceptively simple innovation here was this: the replacement of the standard merchant ship's departure plan—*on or about*, when the fates were properly aligned—with a firm date to set sail, *full or not full*. The conventional mercantile wisdom of the day suggested that setting a fixed date virtually assured frequent departures by half-empty boats in the face of unfavourable winds—a guarantee of financial ruin.

This new packet line was the brainchild of a Yorkshire Quaker immigrant named Jeremiah Thompson, and he knew as well as the tutting skeptics in the coffee houses just how much risk was involved in his plan. But he was also uniquely aware of the potential reward.

Thompson had come to New York in 1801 to trade the woollens produced in his family's factory in England, working out of his uncle's warehouse on Pearl Street. He'd been repeatedly frustrated back in Yorkshire by the irregular delivery of raw materials from the US, and he'd grown equally exasperated by the unpredictable arrival of the family firm's manufactured goods in New York. So he convinced another uncle in the mercantile trade and two other prominent New York merchants to join him in a new kind of shipping venture, along with two Liverpool firms to handle the traffic at the English end of the line.

The partnership was well positioned for success from the start, with plenty of money and a steady flow of shipments from its own offices. And New York had just emerged from the embargoed doldrums of the War of 1812 with a flurry of ambitious new enterprise. In March 1817, the New York Stock and Exchange Board had been formally established on Wall Street. And then on the Fourth of July, the state's new governor, the legendary DeWitt Clinton, had launched his brazen plan to dig a 360-mile canal from the Hudson River to Lake Erie. New York City seemed poised for a mercantile boom. "There can be but little doubt of the success of the under-taking," Thompson wrote to his English partners.

As he surveyed the *James Monroe* at anchor on the morning of January 5, 1818, however, Thompson surely felt more doubt than he let on. If New York was an ambitious, forward-looking and increasingly bustling commercial hub, its claim on a leading position in American trade was far from secured. Philadelphia, Baltimore and New Orleans were all ports of at least equal impor-tance, and all three had better connections with the cotton and wheat fields of the interior already in place. And there in the water, the *James Monroe*'s undersized cargo seemed to testify to the folly of Thompson's plan. Just eight of the boat's twenty-eight luxurious berths were filled with paying passengers, and the ship's hold con-tained a middling cargo of cotton, flour, apples and wool. As pre-dicted, the packet line was preparing to make its first departure more than half-empty.

Thompson, though, was a forthright Quaker through and through. He stood by his word. When the bells of St. Paul's Chapel rang out ten o'clock, the *James Monroe* hoisted its anchor and set sail. Its bow was broader and blunter than those of most ships, its hull shallower, sacrificing carrying capacity for speed. Extra-wide sails further boosted its chances of reducing the time of an Atlantic crossing. It flew a broad flag, a bold black ball on a red field that gave the new enterprise its common name: the Black Ball Line.

Twenty-five days later, the *James Monroe* reached the Liverpool harbour; its sister ship, the *Courier*, sailed into the port of New York forty-nine days after its New Year's Day departure from Liverpool. By the time it arrived, a new notation had already begun to appear in the city's shipping news. The extensive tables of "Vessels up for Foreign Ports" in those lists were a sea of uniformity, the column under the heading "To Sail" reading either "soon" or "first wind." The listings for the Black Ball's boats, however, bore clear dates—"Feb. 5, posit."—accompanied by an asterisk that told the story of a fundamental shift in the baseline of the shipping business. "This is one of the Line of Packets," the asterisk's explanatory text read, "and will positively sail as advertised." The firm's notoriety—if not its success—was already assured.

Black Ball ships struggled to fill their holds for the first few years as the marketplace adjusted. Meanwhile, a flurry of speculation in real estate and canal stocks incited a financial panic that paralyzed New York's commercial sector through much of 1819. But Thompson and his partners stayed the course, and by the early 1820s they'd emerged as the first name in the transatlantic shipping business. Competitors soon launched new packet lines of their own, and Thompson expanded the Black Ball fleet to keep pace, switching to biweekly departures. By the mid-1830s, there were fourteen packet lines operating out of New York, with as many as thirty transatlantic departures each month, ushering in an era of American predominance in global shipping that would continue until the Civil War and not be equalled again until the end of the Second World War.

The full impact of the Black Ball innovation, however, stretched far beyond the port of New York. Packets were instrumental in establishing the lucrative "cotton triangle"—the trade engine of America's first radical post-colonial phase of growth. Southern cotton had been Jeremiah Thompson's intended prize all along, and it found perfect symbiosis with several other kinds of freight whose traffic boomed in the years after the opening of the Erie Canal. Packet ships carried cotton from the south to New

York, took on flour and other produce shipped down the canal from the Midwest, and brought it all to Liverpool for manufacture and sale in Europe. They returned laden with processed goods, including the woollens manufactured by firms like the Thompson family's—and with immigrants.

In 1820, the year the Black Ball Line really started to take off, the port of New York welcomed 3,800 new Americans. In 1837—the peak of the packet era—60,000 new arrivals landed in New York, accounting for 75 percent of all American immigration that year. They arrived by all manner of seafaring conveyance, but the most common berth was the cramped, reeking steerage compartment of a packet ship. Thus did New York become not just America's most important city, but its most populous and dynamic one.

There were, to be sure, many players in New York's meteoric nineteenth-century rise to global stature, legendary names like Astor and Vanderbilt among them. But the less storied name of Jeremiah Thompson was, at the time, considered just as vital. As one New York newspaper put it in 1836: "Credit is due him for that which has done more for the prosperity of this city than any other project in our day."

Which is why it's important to recognize *how* Thompson contributed to this transformation. His was an age of furious innovation: New technologies arrived on the scene—in shipping and far beyond—faster than the political and commercial elites of the day could figure out how to implement them. The steam engine and cotton gin, canals and then railroads, the newspaper and later the telegraph—all fundamentally transformed the nature of business and of society itself in the 1800s. After many centuries of slow, incremental advancement, the Industrial Revolution reimagined human society wholesale, all but overnight.

Thompson's hidden legacy was his *structural* change of the shipping business, making it capable of adjusting to all this turmoil. He did not make minor changes to established practices; there was no way to function in both the old order and the new one, no way to expand production and sales to industrial scale while continuing to ship raw materials and finished products according to the exigencies of pre-industrial trade. So Thompson set the entire enterprise on a new foundation of clockwork efficiency and steadfast reliability. The Black Ball Line was a jump from one set of rules and priorities to an entirely different set—all of it, all at once, without caveats or second guesses or backtracks. It was a bold lateral leap from one set of assumptions, practices and priorities to another. A Great Leap Sideways—the kind of jump that must now become our own.

THE GREAT LEAP SIDEWAYS

The Black Ball Line continued to run until the 1870s, by which time great oceanic steamers and swift clipper ships had come to dominate seafaring trade out of New York. But the structural innovation Thompson had pioneered long outlived the company itself. Indeed, it still provides the logistical backbone of global shipping today.

This is a critical point about The Leap as we find ourselves again in a time of unprecedented technological change and enormous turmoil. Great Leaps—and industrial revolutions—may be powered by new machines, but they are not *defined* by them. Their trajectories are determined instead by the thinking behind the innovations, the question of what a society's priorities are and what a nation dreams of becoming. In the long run, the shipping schedule is more important than the ship or its contents, the commitment to the leap more important than the tools to lay the new track or the design specs on the new engines.

So what is this Great Leap Sideways?

Like Jeremiah Thompson's simple, transformative idea of scheduled departures, The Leap is first and foremost a cognitive jump, a shift in perspective and priorities. There is new technology and infrastructure involved—some of it fresh from the lab, some ancient in design—but it is not fundamentally about the tools. Whereas technological revolutions like the one that has reshaped telecommunications in the last twenty years are driven by new kinds of tools—"disruptive technologies," in the preferred lingo of the digital world—The Leap is propelled by disruptive *techniques*. New kinds of policy, new metrics, new design parameters for vehicles and homes and whole cities, new ways of solving problems and thinking through challenges. It is not about material wealth or technical know-how but about creating the social and political will to commit to making the jump.

And finally—critically—The Leap is not just about *escaping from* but also *moving toward*, not motivated solely by the avoidance of disaster but also, even principally, by the desire to pursue our brightest possible future. The track on the other side leads not just somewhere safer but somewhere *better*.

The reason I can state this so baldly is because, as I said, I've been there. And what follows is, in one sense, a travel guide to the places where we arrive upon landing. I've seen first hand the exhilaration the Great Leap Sideways inspires, and I can see no good reason why anyone wouldn't want to be where this Leap lands us. These are not allegorical scenarios like the train ride I described but real communities, cities, businesses, even whole nations—places that are already thriving in the sustainable twenty-first-century world order, all of them as real as Jeremiah Thompson's New York and the yellowed pages of an 1818 shipping list. The Leap does not take us to a place of hardship or deprivation. It's not about sacrifice, not a world predicated on going without or getting by. Quite the opposite: it's a leap from a failing system to one that works, from decline and imminent peril to a new kind of prosperity with a healthy future stretching far out in front of it.

The Leap brings us to communities of ultra-efficient homes that produce substantially more energy than they consume over the course of a year, houses that function as power plants and make tidy profits for their owners (see Chapter Three: The Leap in the Nation). The Leap places businesses and their hometowns at the front ranks of the second industrial revolution (see Chapter Four: The Leap in the Economy). The Leap can involve nothing more daunting than a casual bike ride through an elegant city with the best cycling infrastructure on the planet (see Chapter Five: The Leap in the City). And it can provide a more effective template for entrepreneurship on a small-town scale as well as a new model for suburban development (see Chapter Six: The Leap in the Community). On the far side of a Leap, the electricity grid, powered primarily and reliably by the wind and sun, feeds fuel to the electric car you drive to work, which then offsets the cost of the power by selling it back to the grid while it's parked (see Chapter Seven: The Leap on the Grid).

Before we can proceed to the finer details of all this innovation, though, I first have to establish the necessity of The Leap and examine what we've learned to date about the physics of making the jump and landing safely on the other side. This will be the subject of Chapters One (The Necessity of The Leap) and Two (The Mechanics of The Leap).

So let's return to our allegorical train—the one we're on now with its engine running low on fuel and the track falling apart beneath us, edging ever closer to that precipice out the window. Let's take a full look at the depth and breadth of the chasm carved out by our unsustainable way of life.

< ONE >

THE NECESSITY OF THE LEAP

THE PRECIPICE & THE FALL OF 2008

ON MONDAY MORNING, September 15, 2008, Wall Street traders awoke to the startling news of the bankruptcy of Lehman Brothers, one of New York's oldest and most respected investment firms. Merrill Lynch had avoided the same fate only by selling itself off to Bank of America at a deep discount the night before. More than $20 billion in investment capital vanished from Morgan Stanley's books over the ensuing forty-eight hours of financial chaos, forcing that venerable firm to issue a warning on Wednesday that it might well run right out of cash before the weekend. General Electric, meanwhile, worried publicly that it was in danger of having to cease operations for lack of credit to pay its employees and its bills, and insurance giant AIG's midweek plummet toward insolvency was slowed only after the Federal Reserve strung out a multibillion-dollar safety net beneath it.

US Treasury notes were soon trading at less than 1 percent interest—a guaranteed investment in the future of the world's largest economy valued essentially the same as cash, an alarmingly clear sign of the wholesale flight of confidence from the American financial system. Money began to flee from mighty Goldman Sachs the next day, at which point the US government intervened directly with its unprecedented $700-billion bailout. (All figures here and throughout the book are in US dollars unless otherwise noted.) Still, it was only the Sunday night intervention by a Japanese bank that saved Morgan Stanley from total collapse the following Monday morning.

Over the next few weeks, practically the whole of Iceland's banking sector was nationalized to prevent the ruin of the country's economy. Not long after that, the British government rolled out its own bailout to avoid the failure of two of its biggest banks. Around the world, mortgages went sour and banks went begging. Jobs disappeared, homes emptied and credit vanished. Construction cranes fell idle worldwide. Contracts and orders were cancelled, retail and advertising space left vacant. Even the assembly of new oil-drilling rigs in the deep seas off the coast of Brazil and the wilderness of northern Alberta, essential to the steady chug of the global economy, ground to a halt for want of a loan.

There was of course no bigger news in the fall of 2008 than the global financial meltdown. It so fully dominated headlines and the public discourse worldwide that other stories, some freighted with consequences just as dire for the economy's (and the planet's) long-term health, passed with little notice at all.

There were in particular two other emerging calamities, less publicized but just as awesome in scale—energy scarcity and climate chaos—that are now converging with our economic woes to form the defining crisis of the twenty-first century. If you were watching carefully among the fragments of smashed-mirror information in those chaotic months of 2008, you could piece together a picture that made it clear these were not random, disjointed events. These were tightly interconnected, born of a single unsustainable system in imminent danger of complete failure. Together, they form the chasm that we all must cross as soon as possible. They define the necessity of The Leap.

—

The sudden halt in our frenzied hunt for more fuel, buried though it was in the news of broader economic chaos, should've been more alarming. It came, after all, just a few months after oil prices had reached all-time highs in response to skyrocketing and seemingly insatiable demand. This was a dramatic indication of our proximity to the precipice and the hazardous scale of our possible fall. And if you were keeping careful watch, the chasm's floor seemed to fall away even further before your eyes in November 2008, with the publication of the International Energy Agency's (IEA) annual World Energy Outlook—the bellwether of the energy crisis looming in the shadows of the banking disaster.

In conventional energy circles, the IEA's World Energy Outlook is a document whose importance resides somewhere between essential field guide and holy writ. A comprehensive report on the entire planet's proven conventional energy reserves—especially the fossil-fuel trinity of oil, coal and natural gas—the Outlook provides the benchmarks used by governments and energy companies alike to set their priorities, make investments and draft policy. The 2008 edition contained an unprecedented admission: For the first time ever, the IEA acknowledged that peak oil was a fixed reality on the horizon. Beyond the peak—the all-time high in global production—the price of oil will climb upward in volatile spikes, availability steadily downward, and competition for the oil that remains only more ferocious.

It was, to be sure, a backhanded admission, easily lost amid the banner headlines of the ongoing economic crisis. The IEA report simply stated that "global oil production in total is not expected to peak before 2030," implying that it would do so sometime around then. Still, for an organization whose top officials dismissed the very idea of peak oil as mere doomsaying as recently as 2005, it was a startling reversal. So much so that George Monbiot, the influential *Guardian* columnist and author of *Heat*, pressed IEA chief economist Fatih Birol for clarification. How, Monbiot wondered, had this remarkable shift in position occurred? Birol replied that the 2008 *Outlook* was the first one ever to replace "assumptions" about global oil production with actual data from the world's eight hundred largest oil fields. Whereas the 2007 *Outlook* had estimated that the global oil supply was dwindling by 3.7 percent each year due to drying wells and slower flows (meaning that production from new sources had to increase by at least that amount simply to keep global supply steady), the 2008 report revised the rate of decline to 6.7 percent. Under repeated questioning from Monbiot, Birol revealed that the IEA now believed that oil production would reach its global peak by 2020.

"The world's energy system is at a crossroads"—so read the opening sentence of the 2008 *Outlook*'s Executive Summary. The next line we've seen already: "Current global trends in energy supply and consumption are patently unsustainable—environmentally, economically, socially." A factsheet accompanying the 2009 *Outlook* stated the problem even more baldly. "The days of cheap energy are over," it read, in italicized, oversized type. Another passage, in boldface this time: "Without a change in policy, the world is on a path for a rise in global temperature of up to 6°C, with catastrophic consequences for our climate."

The conventional energy business—particularly the fossil-burning part of it—is the IEA's primary subject and raison d'être. Owing to this cozy relationship, the IEA is not in the habit of dismissing the status quo of that industry as "patently unsustainable," nor of describing its path as one barrelling toward catastrophe. Most remarkable, though, is that the IEA was now making unambiguous and emphatic links between fossil fuel dependency and environmental disaster.

This direct connection between the coming energy supply crunch and the climate crisis was just as apparent when viewed from the precipice in the fall of 2008, but again only if you were watching carefully. Few of us were, of course—in the midst of burst housing bubbles and collapsing banks, a press release like the one issued on August 14, 2008, on behalf of the world's leading coral reef researchers was almost entirely ignored. (*The New York Times*, for example, didn't catch up with the story until January 2009.) When it comes to long-term consequences and global scale, though, nothing that happened in the second half of 2008 was as vital to the health of our collective future as "The Honolulu Declaration on Ocean Acidification and Reef Management." If the chasm that yawned wide in those months has a bottom, it is a place first mapped by the Honolulu Declaration.

The full import of the declaration is easy to miss, shrouded as it is in the technical language of marine science and public policy. The eight-page document, signed by a dozen of the world's top coral reef scientists, begins with a detailed explanation of the nature and extent of the acidification problem. Ocean acidification is a phenomenon only recently uncovered but as old as the oceans themselves, governed by a process in which excess carbon dioxide in the earth's atmosphere is absorbed by the world's oceans and turned into weak carbonic acid, increasing their overall acidity. Roughly a quarter of the carbon dioxide generated by human industry ends up in the oceans this way.

The Honolulu Declaration was inspired by recent measurements of the mean pH level of the world's oceans, which has declined from 8.2 to less than 8.1 since the dawn of the Industrial Revolution. The declaration noted that by midcentury our current emissions trajectory would lower the oceans' pH to a level not seen in "tens of millions of years" and cause "major changes" in marine habitat. "Such changes compromise the long-term viability of coral reef ecosystems and the associated benefits that they provide." This was an oblique and measured way of saying that the world's coral reefs—*all* of them—were on the verge of extinction.

Anyone watching news coverage of the economic meltdown understood immediately what hundreds of billions of dollars in losses meant, but it took some specialized knowledge to understand the enormity of the Honolulu Declaration. You needed to know, for starters, that the pH scale is logarithmic, meaning that a change of 0.1 indicates a 30 percent increase in the acidity of the world's oceans. You needed to understand as well that a pH of 8.1 is less than 0.1 away from the point at which corals can no longer make reefs, and that the world's foremost expert on corals—Charlie Veron, former chief scientist of the Australian Institute of Marine Science and a Honolulu Declaration signatory—believes that we are as little as a decade away from that "commitment" point on the pH scale, *beyond which there will be no way to save the world's coral reefs.* Furthermore, it helped to know that there have been five mass extinctions of the world's coral reefs in the distant geological past, all of them caused by overly high concentrations of carbon dioxide in the earth's atmosphere. And that a quarter of everything that lives in the ocean is dependent on coral reefs for its survival, and that hundreds of millions of people are dependent on all of that marine life for their livelihoods. And ultimately that the discovery of the fact of ocean acidification, through a simple and irrefutable litmus test, a scientific measurement so tried and true it is taught to millions of children in science classrooms around the world, is the strongest piece of evidence yet uncovered of the threat to humanity posed by the climate change crisis. In short, if there's a canary in the global climate coal mine, its name is ocean acidification, and the Honolulu Declaration is the tune the sick bird is singing on its deathbed.

It is a terrible thing to lose a home or a job; the human costs of the financial collapse of 2008, measured in ruined lives and collapsed communities and multivalent social decay, will surely outweigh even those catastrophic trillion-dollar losses in the long term. The prospect of permanently rising oil prices threatens not only to amplify such problems at every gas pump but also to fundamentally alter the economic equations by which we feed and clothe and house ourselves using goods delivered to us over immense distances by oil's grace (and often made from the byproducts of its refining). The disastrous BP oil spill in the Gulf of Mexico in 2010 provided a graphic illustration of the staggering size of the modern energy economy and the profound risk involved in its everyday operations. Still, these problems remain comprehensible in human terms. Losses can be calculated, compensation paid out, leaking wells sealed. But there is simply no tabulating the cost of the loss of an entire ecosystem and the permanent alteration of the chemistry of every drop of sea water on the planet—and all the money in the world can't begin to repair the damage.

The extinction of the world's coral reefs would be the defining disaster of a less turbulent age all by itself, and the cascade of interlinked calamities that will be visited on the world by climate change will come to define the ultimate boundaries of crisis in the twenty-first century. The real kicker, though, is that all of these crises are deepening more or less simultaneously. Almost in lockstep, actually. This is not an accident or a coincidence. The crises in our economic system, our energy supply and our climate are *converging*—not just in the sense of separate trajectories pulling together, but also in the way that an optical illusion of multiple images will converge into a singular reality in our field of vision. What appeared to be a patch of scattered ruts in the path ahead is in fact a single gaping hole. The basic logic of the easy-credit bubble that precipitated the economic meltdown is as much a petrochemical creation as plastic or pesticide, a byproduct of oil's miraculous energy and the unprecedented rewards reaped by burning it at industrial scale. Another petrochemical byproduct— carbon dioxide—is the primary engine of climate change.

In broad strokes, the three-headed crisis maps out like this. Starting in the nineteenth century, fossil fuels became the chief fuels of industry's engines. Oil—exponentially denser in energy and far easier to transport than any other fuel source humankind had ever harnessed—was particularly crucial to this new industrial order, and it ushered in an era of seemingly boundless expansion. Wall Street emerged as the most important financier of this expansion, replacing the more modest mercantile system with the frenetic wizardry of corporate high finance. The sheer pace of innovation and growth fuelled by the oil economy supplied the logic for a whole system based on the idea that economic growth could be limitless on a finite planet. This idea found its ultimate expression in an era of credit so abundant it was handed out by the billions without collateral, through financial instruments so complex and obscure that not even the people buying and selling them understood what they were. And the entire process played out under a steadily expanding cloud of carbon dioxide and other greenhouse gases that were slowly but irreversibly changing the earth's climate on the epochal scale of geologic time. Fossil fuels fed a rapacious economic order driven by the pursuit of growth at all costs, which in turn produced a global environmental catastrophe.

There is only one crisis, just a single deep chasm. And now there is the necessity of crossing it.

THE AGE OF FAIL

At the peak of the economic crisis in late September 2008, US Treasury Secretary Henry Paulson and Federal Reserve Board Chairman Ben Bernanke were called before a Senate committee to defend the massive bank bailout they'd ordered. In a widely distributed press photo of the Senate hearing room in Washington that day, Bernanke and Paulson can be seen sober-suited and downcast in the foreground, their faces slightly out of focus. They form a sort of living frame for the real focus of the picture—a sheet of paper held aloft several rows behind them so that it floats between the two men like the caption in a political cartoon. A single word has been scrawled across the page in block capitals: FAIL.

This was the high-water mark, in terms of visibility, for one of the most prevalent internet memes of 2008: the FAIL meme. (For the uninitiated, urbandictionary.com offers this concise definition of a *meme*: "A pervasive thought or thought pattern that replicates itself via cultural means.") The FAIL meme began as a simple photo-captioning trend. Internet users had taken to digging up the most blatant examples of incompetence and miscalculation they could find—images of poorly worded public notices and accidentally scatological icons, home videos of people and animals alike wounded by their own idiocy or hubris—and posting them online with the simple caption FAIL embossed on them. Sign FAIL. Logo FAIL. Running FAIL. Fetch FAIL.

The FAIL meme seemed to speak with unique clarity to its time, providing an all-encompassing catchphrase. Failure might be as universal as life itself, but this was a time of extraordinarily prominent and sophisticated and devastating failure. The same system that produced such lofty heights of wealth and technological complexity that the trade in baroque, inscrutable financial instruments became one of society's most lucrative professions had also dug out the chasm that now threatens society's ruin. This was the Age of FAIL.

There were three critical system failures that ushered in the Age of FAIL. The first is, in a sense, simple human error. The train's engineer, overconfident in the reliability of free-market autopilot, was lulled into contented sleep at the controls. Let's call this Steering FAIL. This was the FAIL indicated by the sign raised at Bernanke and Paulson's Senate hearing, and it referred to a problem even deeper and more corrosive than the trade in toxic assets that had nearly toppled all of Wall Street.

For a generation or more, the global economy had been guided by a model predicated on an almost absolute faith in the infallible reason of free markets—an ideology referred to in some quarters as "market fundamentalism." This model in turn stood on the foundational notion that economic growth was an end in itself. And both of these—unfettered markets and limitless growth—were understood to be synonymous with the greater good. Market-driven engines could mostly steer themselves, and the public sector—the collective expression of everything in society that existed outside the marketplace—was at best an irrelevant distraction and at worst a dangerous obstacle to be shrunk (if not eliminated). The meltdown of 2008 was, among other things, an epic FAIL of market fundamentalism.

The extraordinary scale of this failure was widely noted. In the thick of the bailout in September 2008, Treasury Secretary Paulson himself called it an "economic 9/11." At a roundtable discussion about the crisis a few months later, financier George Soros invoked the broader scope. "Markets were seen basically as self-correcting," he said. "That paradigm has proven to be false. So we are dealing not only with the collapse of a financial system, but also with the collapse of a worldview." Perhaps most dramatically, former Federal Reserve chairman Alan Greenspan, the single actor most responsible for the structure of the collapsed system, admitted to Congress that the crisis revealed "a flaw in the model" he'd been using to guide his work for forty years. "Greenspan's 'flaw' has profound repercussions," Raj Patel noted later in his book *The Value of Nothing*. "To understand it fully would mean a complete reappraisal of the way we conduct our lives. We would need not only a new way of mooring our expectations of our society and our economy . . . but also a different ideology governing the exchange of goods and services."

So thorough was this Steering FAIL that some of its critical assumptions were revealed to be the exact inverse of economic reality. "The belief that markets can take care of themselves and therefore government should not intrude has resulted in the largest intervention in the market by government in history"—so noted the economist and Nobel laureate Joseph Stiglitz in *Freefall*, his 2010 post-mortem of the meltdown.

Stiglitz argues that there were two key reasons for this market failure, two intractable defects in the system spawned by market fundamentalism. The first was a problem of *agency*—the separation of actor from owner and of risk from reward in the modern financial system. Because the managers of investment firms were by and large not the owners of those firms, their vested interest was not in long-term viability but in short-term profit. Overnight successes, however fleeting or dubious, boosted stock prices and improved quarterly analyst ratings, both of which padded salaries and bonuses for those managers.

Another consequence of this agency failure was the ascent of *securitization*—the transformation of debt into bundles of securities that could be bought and sold by parties unrelated to the original transactions—and it presented an even bigger problem. This introduced an artificial separation between lender and borrower—a fundamental breach of hundreds of years of banking convention. Stiglitz: "Those buying a mortgage-backed security are, in effect, lending to the homeowner, about whom they know nothing. They trust the bank that sells them the product to have checked it out, and the bank trusts the mortgage originator. The mortgage originators' incentives were focused on the quantity of mortgages originated, not the quality."

In just one year of the housing bubble's ascendancy, American lenders handed out about one *trillion* dollars in "mortgage equity withdrawals" alone to American homeowners. This meant 7 percent of American GDP that year consisted exclusively of loans to debt-ridden American homeowners whose only collateral was the theoretical profit made on presumed increases in the value of the mortgaged homes themselves. This was a mathematical formula for FAIL.

The second core defect in the market fundamentalist model that led to the 2008 economic failure, Stiglitz argues, is the problem of *externalities*. The banks trading all this bad credit did not take into account the millions of foreclosures, job losses and other social calamities they could cause when they calculated the risk involved in trading them. Instead, they removed many of the biggest risks from their equations and coerced the much-maligned public sector into covering the costs of those risks as they emerged. "In short"—this is Stiglitz's summary—"America's financial markets had failed to perform their essential societal functions of managing risk, allocating capital, and mobilizing savings while keeping transaction costs low. Instead, they had created risk, mis-allocated capital, and encouraged excessive indebtedness while imposing high transaction costs."

High finance is sometimes likened to a kind of rigged, high-stakes gambling ring, and there was an implicit assumption embedded in the trillions of dollars in wildly risky bets that were being made on bad debt. That assumption was that the economy was an unstoppable engine of limitless growth, a perpetual money-generating machine. Short-term risk was ultimately mean-ingless, because in the long term there would be more money in the coffers to cover the worst bets. It's an assumption that points to the essential way in which the game was presumed to be rigged, the market fundamentalist equivalent of the inviolable casino law that the house always wins.

During the years of the housing bubble, this assumption expressed itself in the willingness to hand out bad mortgages in the false certainty that real estate values across the board would continue to grow, but the implications of this misplaced faith run deeper than that. The very measure of a nation's economic health —GDP growth—expresses complete trust in the assumption of limitless growth, in effect turning the finite nature of the planet itself into an externality. Of course there are *physical* limits to the earth's bounty, but they are far away in some distant, irrelevant future, some time and place eons beyond what the financial sector means when it says *long term*. And so it's reasonable—and profit-able—to carry on under the assumption that growth is inevitable and neverending.

Nowhere is that faith more absolute than on the question of energy. And our firm belief in the boundless availability of more fossil fuels is the second key contributor to our epic failure: Engine

FAIL. Limitless growth, after all, is only a reasonable expectation because there is assumed to be no practical limit to the amount of energy we can generate, and this is deemed reasonable because there is assumed to be no limit to the amount of fuel we can find to feed those engines of growth. This points to the ultimate reason why the solution to Steering FAIL is not simply to replace the incompetent driver with a more skilled and alert pilot. We have reached the ultimate limit of our ability to increase the amount of energy we procure from fossil fuels. Regardless of who is driving, we are also in imminent danger of Engine FAIL.

This ultimate limit is often generally described as *peak oil*, which indicates oil's pride of place among the holy trinity of fossil fuels. Coal and natural gas are widely employed in electricity generation and heating, but there are many other ways to do those jobs, and each fuel has its intrinsic limitations. (Coal is uniquely dirty and inefficient; the transportation of natural gas across long distances—and especially across seas—is expensive and technologically complex; etc.) The primary engines of the industrial age run on oil, from internal combustion motors in cars and trucks and tractors to jet fuel in airplanes and heavy oil in ships, not to mention oil's role as an essential raw material at manufacturing plants making fertilizer, pesticide and plastic around the world.

From the moment we slip on our Lycra-waisted underwear in the morning to the moment we blearily drop our plastic-handled, plastic-bristled toothbrush back into its plastic cubby before bed, we exist in a world provided by oil's bounty. Oil goes into nearly every morsel of food we eat—a full ten calories of fossil fuel energy are needed to produce just one calorie of energy in most processed foods. Oil provides the basic materials for hip replacements and sterile insulin syringes, for carpeting and paint, for laptop computers and mobile phones. And above all else it is the benefactor of our unprecedented mobility, the gas that keeps modern society roaring and soaring across the country and around the world with ease. In the summer of 2008, when oil reached an all-time high of $147 per barrel, humanity was producing about 86 million barrels of the stuff per day. That's the equivalent of more than 3.5 *billion* gallons of gasoline extracted daily from beneath the earth's surface.

Despite oil's ubiquity—or maybe because of it—we rarely stop to consider the true value of our preferred fuel. It is a staggeringly dense package of easily transported, easily harnessed energy, a thick syrup of prehistoric solar power concentrated over hundreds of millions of years and extracted from deep underground using millions of dollars in equipment. It is then processed and refined, hauled from the other side of the world to a storage tank up the block, kept there in ample supply for our around-the-clock convenience. And we are outraged when its price approaches the cost of an equivalent amount of bottled water.

As the age of oil scarcity dawns, then, it's worth asking what, after all, is the *real* price of a barrel of oil? Not the price it's trading for on any given day, mind you, but its replacement cost in human labour. Well, a barrel of oil is six gigajoules of energy— that's six billion joules. Empirically speaking, a joule is the amount of energy needed to lift a one-pound weight to a height of nine inches, but the replacement cost is better understood anecdotally, at human scale. So imagine an average healthy adult male on a treadmill. Wire the treadmill up to a generator and start him running. After an hour, he'd have produced about 360,000 joules of energy—enough to light a 100-watt light bulb for the length of his run. To get a barrel of oil's worth out of this system—operating it eight hours a day, five days a week, weekends and holidays off like any other production line—you'd need to put the guy to work for about 8.6 years. And at minimum wage where I live, you'd owe him $138,000 or so for his labours.

This was the revolutionary power of the discovery of fossil fuels, this radical expansion in the scale of human industry. Oil's impact has been perhaps the most dramatic and its price the most carefully tracked, but coal and natural gas have been just as vital. (You could get the equivalent of those 8.6 years of treadmill-generated energy out of a quarter-ton of coal for a quarter the price of a barrel of oil, at current market rates.) At the dawn of the nineteenth century, the world's farms were worked by human hands and the harnessed energy of horses and oxen. In the 1840s, wheat cut by hand using scythes on the American plain would require four transfers en route to the port of New Orleans, and at each transfer point it would take a crew working all day to hand-load a single barge with seven thousand bushels; just ten years later, a single worker at the port of Chicago could do the same job operating a steam-powered loader in about an hour. In the half-century that followed, the percentage of Americans tilling the land would plummet from 90 percent to 40 percent, and by the late twentieth century it would decline to just 2 percent or less, as gas-fuelled tractors and threshers and combines almost completely supplanted human labour. And so it has gone for the mining of minerals and the harvesting of lumber, the manufacture and shipment of goods, and the transport of human populations. The Industrial Revolution may have been born in a cotton gin or a steam engine, but its global-scale, high-speed modern phase began with the dawn of the age of oil in the late nineteenth century.

What's more, the *logic* of modern economics is a fossil fuel logic. The investment banks that financed the miraculous expansion in human industry around the turn of the century were founded in an era of unprecedented, seemingly instantaneous growth fed by fossil fuels. After the near-death experience of the Great Depression, they emerged from the Second World War—the first fully oil-fuelled war—convinced that an economy could predicate its success on the limitless growth of its bottom line. The wartime exigencies of rapid expansion, measured by GDP growth, became the permanent measure of economic health. This was a fossil-fuelled euphoria, wedded to the logic of petroleum and coal just as wholly as the internal combustion engine and the steam turbine were. And it was dependent on the premise that the growth of the global fuel supply is potentially as limitless as the economy itself. Our economy remains dependent on this fundamentally false assumption, which is what the IEA was getting at when it labelled the global energy supply system *patently unsustainable*. Unsustainable, that is, not in its transient details but in its core structure.

Perhaps the most alarming thing about the IEA's loss of faith in our current energy regime is that the agency is, if anything, understating the case. The IEA's 2008 estimate for a peak in global oil production, for example—around 2020, followed by an "undulating plateau" of ten to fifteen years supplied by new, unconventional sources—is an outlier at the rosy end of the spectrum (and the IEA has since acknowledged that *conventional* oil production likely peaked in 2006).

A Canadian geologist named J. David Hughes, who has spent his life mapping conventional coal resources for the Canadian government, embarked in recent years on a second career as a tireless energy data cruncher and globetrotting bearer of inconvenient truths about those numbers. Hughes presents his findings in a meticulously detailed PowerPoint slideshow he calls "The Energy Sustainability Dilemma." The presentation is dense with charts and graphs, including one that aggregates estimated dates of the global peak in oil production. The twenty-three different sources of estimates range from the US Army to the Association for the Study of Peak Oil and Gas (ASPO) to the oil industry's own analysts. The aggregate estimate is between 2012 and 2014, depending on whether you discard the wildest outliers. Either date, as Hughes likes to tell his audiences, is "tomorrow in geological terms." And indeed there are some experts, ASPO founder and former oil-company geologist Colin Campbell among them, who would argue that the actual answer is actually *yesterday*—the summer of 2008, when oil prices flirted with $150 per barrel and the most dramatic period of new investment in exploration and drilling the world's ever seen pushed the global supply to eighty-six million barrels per day.

The IEA's faith in our ability to supply ourselves adequately with oil until 2030 or so is predicated on daily production levels growing to at least 105 million barrels—a volume more than 20 percent greater than the all-time global peak fed by easily accessible conventional oil fields. In a startlingly frank US Energy Information Administration (EIA) presentation from the spring of 2009, a graph of the global "liquid fuels" supply assigns the following label to the yawning gap between the demand for those 105 million barrels and the dwindling conventional reserves: "Unidentified Projects." *Damned if we know*, is what they mean. In the EIA's estimation, that gap will be ten million barrels wide— roughly equivalent to all of Saudi Arabia's current production—by 2016, expanding to more than fifty million barrels per day by 2030. In effect, then, we will have to replace nearly two-thirds of our current oil supply with new and as-yet-unidentified sources in the next twenty years.

The crux of the peak oil problem is not just that half of all the oil in the world is gone, but that the *nature* of the half that remains is fundamentally different from the stuff that's drying up.

We will be replacing conventional sources like the vast Middle Eastern oil fields with petroleum mined from the thick sludge of northern Alberta or drilled from five miles beneath a seabed in water more than a mile deep in the Gulf of Mexico. "It's not a resource issue," Hughes tells his audiences. "It's a deliverability issue. Bottom line is we've gone through the easy stuff." To explain this more thoroughly, Hughes's presentation includes a series of charts dealing with obscure but crucial figures like "Energy Return on Energy Invested" (EROEI). Conventional, gusher-type crude oil—the kind of light sweet crude seen in the opening credits of *The Beverly Hillbillies* and discovered under the desert sands of Saudi Arabia as the limitless-growth logic came into favour in the late 1940s—comes to market at an EROEI ratio of 100:1. For every barrel of oil's worth of energy invested in a drilling project, in other words, the return is a hundred barrels of fuel. "New conventional" oil sources—the kind found by drilling miles under the sea floor, for example—is produced at an EROEI of 25:1, and arrives freighted with the staggering risk that came to horrific reality in BP's catastrophic 2010 blowout in the Gulf of Mexico. In the oil sands of northern Alberta, which now supplies more than 20 percent of America's oil, the EROEI is between 3:1 and 6:1, depending on the location of the deposit. In general, the cost, effort, risk and environmental impact all increase dramatically as the value of the EROEI ratio ratchets down toward parity. (Corn ethanol, darling of the American farm states, is somewhere near 1:1, and in its first boom phase in 2007 and 2008 it sent the global price of corn skyrocketing, triggering food shortages worldwide.)

When Hughes and other analysts look beyond oil, they foresee similar limits emerging across the spectrum of conventional energy sources. A 2008 report in Britain's *New Scientist*, for example, outlined the parameters of what it dubbed "The Great Coal Hole."

As the report noted, the benchmark "reserves-to-production ratio" for coal worldwide—the number of years humanity could continue consuming the fuel at current rates of production—had declined from 277 in 2000 to 144 in 2006. This was not because 133 years' worth of coal went up in smoke in those 6 years but because, as in the IEA's oil estimate, analysts have begun using more accurate methods of reporting and projection. Germany's Energy Watch Group now estimates that *peak coal* could be a worldwide reality by 2025. Hughes, meanwhile, observes that conventional natural gas production is already past peak in many parts of the world, including all of North America—a reality masked by a huge continental boom in shale gas production (a practice involving a substantial increase in environmental and human health risks, which I'll come back to). Hughes's ballpark estimate for what he calls the *hydrocarbon peak*—the point at which energy production from all fossil fuel sources, which currently provide about 88 percent of all the energy used in the world, reaches its global maximum—is 2021. Again: that's tomorrow in geological terms.

Now, the prospect of a global hydrocarbon peak within a decade or so would be a grave, paradigm-shifting kind of problem even if combusted oil and coal and shale gas emerged from the world's engines and smokestacks in great clouds of lilac-scented fairy dust. Which of course they don't, which brings us to the third and ultimately most catastrophic FAIL we face.

The steering has failed, but drivers can be replaced or retrained. The engine has failed, but engines can be retooled or redesigned for new types of fuel. But when the track fails, there's no avoiding calamity. And that is what the condition of the earth's natural environment amounts to—a fundamental breakdown in the infrastructure upon which the entire vehicle depends. Track FAIL, in other words.

By far the most monumental sign of impending Track FAIL, although far from the only one, is *anthropogenic* (i.e., manmade) climate change. As I've already noted, the consequences of just one aspect of the climate crisis, ocean acidification, would be cataclysmic all by themselves. Carbon dioxide levels in the earth's atmosphere, meanwhile, have reached the highest concentration seen in fifteen million years, causing the steady uptick in global mean temperature known as "global warming." (Though the terms *global warming* and *climate change* are often used interchangeably, it's more accurate to think of global warming as one of many manifestations of anthropogenic climate change.)

The impact of climate change is just as grave at microcosmic scale, where even the most seemingly trivial alterations attest to emerging catastrophe. The ski season in the eastern United States has shortened by as much as a third, and wine production has begun to fall off at legendary French vineyards that have been carefully and reliably cultivated for centuries. The species of ash tree used to make baseball bats is endangered, and the California avocado crop will likely shrink in size by as much as 40 percent in the coming years. In one region of Australia, a twelve-year drought has combined with record high temperatures to produce the most ferocious bushfires on record; another region has seen the worst flooding in the country's history. In western Canada, pine beetles are surviving warmer winters to reproduce in epidemic numbers, devastating vast swaths of irreplaceable alpine forest. By 2020 or so, there will be no glaciers left in Glacier National Park in Montana. As glaciers and ice caps continue to melt and sea levels continue to rise, there will likely be at least one or two fewer island nations on the planet as well. And so on.

Even where climate change isn't the primary culprit, the

global ecological picture is a grim monotone panorama of decline and devastation. Populations of the majestic bluefin tuna are on the verge of total collapse due to overfishing. Half the planet's wetlands have vanished, and water levels in many of its most vital rivers—the Colorado, Indus and Nile among them—have been reduced to the point where water often fails to reach their mouths in the driest months. The water crisis is particularly acute in Australia's Murray-Darling Basin, which no longer carries near enough water to support the AUD$30-billion agriculture industry that employs 60,000 growers along its banks. (The Australian government has begun offering farmers cash incentives to quit farming forever and leave the water that remains for the region's parched cities.) A vicious strain of wheat stem rust is ruining vital grain crops across Asia and Africa in greater volume each season. The entire agricultural industry in Punjab—India's breadbasket—is at imminent risk of failure; three times as much fertilizer is now required to maintain yields, which are further threatened by unprecedented soil erosion and reduced soil fertility, new strains of pesticide-resistant insects, and a water table dropping a metre per year.

Thirty percent of the planet's amphibians, 23 percent of its mammals and 12 percent of its birds now face extinction from one cause or another or all of the above, amounting to the most profound wave of extinction the earth has seen in millions of years. All told, the estimated cost of the damage wrought by human activity on the biosphere's vital infrastructure is somewhere between $2 and $4.5 *trillion* per year, *every* year—equal to the cost of the two worst years of the recent financial meltdown. This is the cost of Track FAIL, renewed annually.

To properly measure the scale of this extraordinary upheaval in the biosphere and identify its main cause, the atmospheric chemist and Nobel laureate Paul Crutzen proposed the term "Anthropocene Era" as a label for this new period in geological time. Back in 1998, this was a rhetorical flourish, but Crutzen was wrong only about the semantics—the Anthropocene is likely not a new era but a new *epoch*. (Epochs, which ordinarily last for tens of millions of years, are intervals of geological time two steps shorter in scale than eras.) In a 2008 essay entitled "Are we now living in the Anthropocene?" twenty-one members of the Stratigraphy Commission of the Geological Society of London— the body responsible for naming and dating geological time— recommended considering the term for official recognition.

The Holocene Epoch—the one that humanity's greenhouse-gas emissions appear to have ended sometime between the dawn of the Industrial Revolution and today—began 12,000 years ago, at the end of the last ice age. Its most distinctive trait was an exceptionally stable climate, producing seasonal predictability of temperature and precipitation and a paucity of extreme climate phenomena—factors essential to the success of agriculture, industry and civilization itself. The hard fact of the Anthropocene is that this stability is gone, and the takeaway lesson is that *none* of the systems that brought us here— not our economic model or our fossil-powered energy regime, not the agricultural practices we've honed over generations, not our once-vaunted banking and financial systems, *none of it*—can be relied upon to carry us forward. This is an across-the-board FAIL— "total system failure," as it's sometimes called—and it compels a fundamental reimagining of the human project.

Recall Paul Hawken's advice to the graduating class of the University of Portland: *Civilization needs a new operating system, you are the programmers, and we need it within a few decades.*

IMAGINATION FAIL

For a wide range of reasons (which I'll return to in more detail in the next chapter), the predominant response to these crises by business and political elites has consisted mostly of elaborate efforts to prolong business as usual by any and all means. No scheme has been deemed too grandiose, no hypocrisy too glaring and no system too riddled with the pockmarks of previous failure, so long as it avoids the hard work of reconceiving the foundations of the whole system in the way Paul Hawken suggests. In the aggregate, it amounts to a global case of Imagination FAIL.

The most prominent Imagination FAIL is of course the Herculean effort made since 2008 to preserve the basic structures of our crumbling economic system. Not a dime of the $700-billion-plus handed to banks and other financial institutions by the US government—nor any of the bailout money handed out anywhere else—has been earmarked for a reconfiguration of the way bottom lines are counted or a critical analysis of the doctrine of limitless growth. Almost every nation on earth still measures its success or failure by the changes in its GDP, and every bank receiving bailout money still lives or dies by the distorted short-term scale of its daily stock price and quarterly earnings statement. Every sage who predicted the collapse has called for a top-to-bottom reconfiguration of the entire system—"wholesale reform" is the term used by Nouriel Roubini, the New York University economist mocked as "Dr. Doom" until his grave forecasts of imminent collapse came to pass, after which he's been treated like an infallible prophet. Such reform has not been forthcoming, to say the least.

The measures taken to extend the age of oil another few decades have been even more extravagant. The blowout at a BP rig 5,000 feet (about 1,500 metres) underwater in the Gulf of Mexico may have brought unprecedented attention to the baroque engineering feats required to keep our gas tanks full, but the collective response to date has ignored the more far-reaching implications of the disaster. Especially at the leadership level, the disaster has been treated as a bad-apple anomaly or the cost, dire as it may be, of doing business at eighty-six million barrels per day.

At the peak of media interest in the Gulf disaster, voices that attempted to bring broader context to the discussion were treated in the same marginal, condescending manner that Roubini and his pessimistic colleagues once were. *Fortune* magazine, for example, actually used Roubini's pre-collapse nickname to describe energy analyst Matt Simmons, labelling him "the Gulf Coast oil spill's Dr. Doom." One of the only prominent energy experts to predict the $147 oil-price spike in 2008, Simmons likes to point out that the "replacement cost of incremental oil"—the price, for example, of replacing a barrel of oil from a conventional deposit found somewhere like Saudi Arabia with a barrel from four miles beneath the surface of the Gulf of Mexico—is much more than $147 per barrel. That added cost vanishes into a (for now) miniscule uptick in the aggregate price, and its deeper implications remain conspicuously absent from the mainstream conversation about our energy future, with potentially catastrophic consequences.

It's the same story of a status quo overextended to the fraying point for the other conventional fuel sources. Both the US and Canadian governments, for example, have invested billions of dollars in carbon capture and storage (CCS) technology. The promise of this feat of engineering wizardry is that the great fog of emissions from coal-fired power plants and energy-intensive mining operations in the Alberta tar sands will one day be re-injected forever into reservoirs beneath the earth's surface. (This is the core technological breakthrough behind the notion of "clean coal.") The first successful commercial application of this technology on earth has been up and running for years at an off-shore natural-gas platform in the North Sea, operated by the Norwegian oil company Statoil. It covers its costs—barely—because it presents a unique business case for CCS: the carbon dioxide in the natural gas stream had to be removed anyway to prepare the gas for sale, the storage reservoir is directly underneath the platform, and the Norwegian government imposes the world's steepest tax on carbon dioxide emissions.

The track record for CCS at conventional power plants, meanwhile, has thus far shown nowhere near the kind of success needed to justify its hype. The most elaborate CCS test project at a coal-burning facility, for example, came into operation at a power plant in West Virginia in late 2009. The first phase of the project has managed to successfully capture about 1.5 percent of the plant's emissions, at a cost of nearly $13 million. The second phase, which if all goes well will be up and running in 2014 and bring the total price tag to $673 million, will bury about 18 percent of the plant's emissions. Two billion-dollar CCS projects in Canada, meanwhile, promise to sequester carbon dioxide at a cost of CAD$761 per tonne (or roughly forty times the price of sequestering a tonne of carbon dioxide via the European Climate Exchange). A study by the German Parliament's Office of Technology Assessment determined that CCS won't be viable at a commercial power plant until 2020 at the earliest.

The skewed reasoning behind CCS is worth underscoring. Billions have been invested in the unproven technical feat of burying carbon dioxide emissions from coal-fired power plants underground, which will take many more billions of dollars and a minimum of a decade or two to bring to market (if ever). All of this merely to continue to rely on a fuel source whose emissions are known to cause tens of thousands of deaths worldwide each year, and the mining of which in the US now involves the literal decapitation of entire mountains—not to mention the human and environmental costs of climate change. This is deemed a more rational, economical response to the energy crisis than switching to clean, abundant renewable fuel sources, which are already technically feasible and commercially viable all over the world. Even as concerns remain about the leakage of carbon dioxide decades or even centuries after its capture, the CCS concept receives billions in public funding, while the same fossil fuel companies touting clean coal spend millions on lobbying efforts pushing for moratoriums on wind-farm construction, citing specious health risks. (The province of Ontario recently suspended offshore wind development in response to such a lobbying campaign, which was based in part on the unsubstantiated health hazards pointed out by a pediatrician named Nina Pierpont and also by widely debunked economic data peddled by the American Energy Alliance, a "think tank" established on the largesse of ExxonMobil and the oil-and-gas magnates the Koch brothers.) And this is but one piece of an elaborate global subsidy apparatus that according to the IEA pumped $312 billion into fossil fuels in 2009 alone—almost ten times the total global subsidy for renewable energy. We spend ten dollars propping up mature "free market" fuel sources, in other words, for every dollar we spend on "uncompetitive" renewables. This is the illogical calculus of Imagination FAIL.

The natural gas business, meanwhile, has brought volatile prices under control through a massive production boom in shale gas. This new, unconventional gas source is locked inside tiny pockets of hard, porous shale bedrock. The sedimentary stone has to be first cracked apart by injecting it with a proprietary mix of highly pressurized water, sand and chemicals—a process known as hydraulic fracturing, or *fracking*—after which the gas can be pumped to the surface. A significant portion of the shale gas boom in the US operates in the Marcellus Shale deposit across a broad rural stretch of West Virginia, Pennsylvania and New York, a region from which cities like Philadelphia and New York City draw their water supplies. The industry insists its wells are tightly sealed and present no hazard to public health or the environment, but residents and environmentalists have expressed alarm at the potential for catastrophe if a well were to leak its toxic fracking stew into the water supply. And in any case, the shattering of ancient rock to pump out a greenhouse-gas-emitting fuel is neither an ecologically sound use of fresh water nor a long-term solution to the energy crisis.

Dealers in the "hard" truth about our energy future, including several prominent environmentalists, have pointed instead to nuclear power as our best long-term option. (Indeed it is often referred to as the *only* long-term option.) Nuclear power, its newfound boosters point out, is free of greenhouse gas emissions (at least at the site of power generation, though the mining, refining and transport of radioactive materials are far from emissions-free) and "scalable," by which they mean that each generating unit is very large, and so it would take a far smaller number of 1000-megawatt nuclear plants—as opposed to, say, 5-megawatt wind turbines—to replace the world's current stock of coal plants. Nukes thus scale up to our current needs more rapidly, or so the reasoning goes.

To accept this argument, however, requires us to ignore the fact that a nuclear plant proposed in most jurisdictions today couldn't possibly be up and running until ten years from now at the very earliest. (The Fukushima catastrophe in Japan is likely to extend this commissioning process for new nuclear plants in many jurisdictions.) What's more, nuclear plants habitually take longer to build than originally promised, invariably overrun their budgets, and often require refurbishments more expensive than initial estimates predict, sooner than initially predicted. As J. David Hughes points out in his "Energy Sustainability Dilemma" talk, it would take the greatest construction boom in the history of nuclear energy simply to replace all the aging nuclear plants that will have to be shuttered in the next twenty years. What's more, that first generation of nuclear power fell short of its initial promise, scale-wise, by a factor of about thirty worldwide, and it never solved its nagging waste problem in any convincingly risk-free way. Meanwhile, the much-ballyhooed next generation of nuclear plants—particularly the heavily hyped "fast breeder" reactors— has run into technical obstacles so implacable that even France, the most nuclear-friendly jurisdiction on the planet, has begun shifting its focus to renewables. And the bottom line? As *The Economist* put it, "Not one [nuclear plant], anywhere on earth, makes commercial sense."

What's appealing about nukes in some quarters is the same thing that justifies bank bailouts: they oblige no fundamental change in the *structure* of the system. A nuclear-powered energy grid (or one powered by carbon-sequestering coal plants, if you prefer) is still highly centralized and organized around the extraction, processing and consumption of a scarce, commodified fuel source, producing a toxic waste stream. (As I'll explain in more detail in Chapter Two, renewable energy reconfigures every aspect of this energy equation.) Which is to say that deepwater drilling, clean coal, fracked shale gas and more nukes make intrinsic sense to the same energy bureaucrats and industry leaders whose logic created the crisis. It shouldn't surprise us at all that the minds that dug the chasm lack the imagination to find ways to get out of it. All they've ever known is the shovel.

The most bizarre strain of Imagination FAIL, though, has to be the concept of *geoengineering*. The term refers to the intentional large-scale alteration of the climate in order to temporarily mitigate some of the worst consequences of anthropogenic climate change. It's a perverse sort of logic (if oddly symmetrical): Because human industry has changed the climate so drastically, we now face a crisis of such terrifying scale that the only way to guard against its impact may be to alter the climate even further and much more deliberately. The grandiose schemes and technological marvels bounced around under the guise of geoengineering demonstrate that imagination itself is not the problem. We have no shortage of wildly inventive ideas and audacious plans—we simply direct them disproportionately at dreaming up ways to preserve the status quo.

The argument for geoengineering received its most thorough and prominent hearing to date in the March/April 2009 issue of the journal *Foreign Affairs*. In an essay entitled "The Geoengineering Option: A Last Resort Against Global Warming?" five esteemed academics from A-list American research institutions (Stanford and Carnegie Mellon universities among them) provided a dispassionate analysis of the pros and cons of geoengineering. The article surveyed a handful of potential projects, from seeding the lower atmosphere with sea water to create a reflective layer of dense cloud to launching clusters of giant reflective discs into orbit.

The most feasible strategy, in the authors' estimation, would be "launching reflective materials into the upper stratosphere." This would be a conscious imitation of the eruption of Mount Pinatubo in 1991, which created a plume of sulphur dioxide particles large enough to temporarily reduce the entire planet's mean temperature by about 1 degree Fahrenheit. This would apparently be no great challenge from an engineering point of view, using either sulfur dioxide itself or "self-levitating and self-orienting designer particles engineered to migrate to the Polar Regions and remain in place for long periods." The particles, in either case, could be deployed by "high-flying aircraft, naval guns or giant balloons." The only real question was whether or not this would be a useful strategy. "Fiddling with the climate to fix the climate strikes most people as a strikingly bad idea," the authors conceded. But it's only prudent, they argued, to find out just how bad, thus to demonstrate that geoengineering is "a true option of last resort."

Alas, time has not been kind to the option of first resort: a coordinated global initiative to reduce greenhouse gas emissions. The pursuit of such an agreement began at the Earth Summit in Rio in 1992, took formal shape as the Kyoto Protocol in 1997, and derailed pretty much completely at the COP15 climate summit in Copenhagen in December 2009. From a certain angle, this must surely have seemed inevitable, even welcome in its way. After all, the decade or so lived under the Kyoto Protocol had seen nothing but record growth in global greenhouse gas emissions, at the same time providing a big, easy target that served as a sort of rallying point for the defenders of the status quo. From the point of view of many governments and their business allies, Kyoto was an outside influence with no real authority attempting to micromanage their environmental and energy policies—a big, hairy, toothless beast, mostly harmless but easy to demonize. Best, perhaps, to let the failed process die, so that the best minds in the climate action game could focus their energies on something with hope of actually creating lasting change.

In truth, there are much better tools for action on the climate crisis. Had the delegates simply stepped out the conference centre doors and explored the city of Copenhagen, for example, they'd have found a vast treasure trove of greenhouse-gas-reducing tools, easily implemented at the national or subnational level. (I'll examine many of these in Chapter Five.) Indeed the would-be champions of climate action are guilty of many of the same blind spots and bad habits as the defenders of business as usual. They are unwilling to consider structural changes to their own processes, which were better calibrated for acute environmental problems with precisely defined parameters — the use of ozone-depleting chemicals, for example, which was effectively contained by a UN-sponsored global ban. To eliminate greenhouse gas emissions, however, is to change the world's primary fuel sources, which is to fundamentally reconfigure the entire global economy and the priorities of pretty much every society on earth. It changes *everything*. To approach it with a solution that requires a consensus on core issues of energy, industry, production and consumption on a scale with no precedent in the history of human civilization is to consign that solution to derailment before it has even begun. It's a bit like the geoengineering question, actually — an extraordinary flurry of ambitious visioning and innovative thinking, all aimed at building a tool too big to be swung.

Go looking instead for breakthroughs in real, transformative climate action — legislative coups, cleantech booms, radically altered energy regimes — and you'll find they were launched at a scale far less than global. You'll also generally find their architects either indifferent to or openly dismissive of the Kyoto-Copenhagen circus. Terry Tamminen, for example, ran California's Environmental Protection Agency as it embraced the most ambitious greenhouse-gas-reductions commitments of any American state, after which he was deputized by then governor Arnold Schwarzenegger to "Johnny Appleseed" his approach to state and provincial governments across North America. And what does Tamminen think about the Copenhagen Climate Conference of 2009? He's relieved, actually, that President Obama attended, and that he essentially rejected the whole process.

"The one thing that Obama did that did the world a favour in Copenhagen was without saying it, he was trying to be as polite as he could, but the reality is he did say, the emperor has no clothes," Tamminen told me a few weeks after the conference. "A process where 192 nations all have to agree on something, and where Somalia gets the same vote as China, is not a process by which you can really expect to make progress commensurate with the urgency of this threat."

Urgency is very much the operative word here. The UN climate process to date has tried to be commensurate with the *scale* of the problem—a global treaty for a global crisis—but that very scale essentially guarantees a slow, imprecise response. A more urgent approach would be to simply pick up the tools at hand, begin building the solutions, and pull more people and larger jurisdictions into the project as you go along.

This, in essence, is the story of how Germany came to be far and away the most radical actor on climate and energy issues of any major industrial nation. An innovative new law (the feed-in tariff, the full details of which I'll explain in Chapter Three) was tested at town council scale, then "Johann-Apfelseeded" in larger and larger municipalities, and eventually enacted at the national level. And the national law's co-author and most vocal champion, the left-wing parliamentarian Hermann Scheer, was as strident and withering a critic of the Kyoto-Copenhagen process as you could find anywhere. (Scheer passed away in October 2010, at the age of 66.)

I met with Scheer a few months before the Copenhagen conference, and he assured me then it would come to nothing. He likened it to an international drug control effort—call it "the Cali Protocol," he sardonically suggested, after the Colombian city notorious as a drug-trafficking hub—in which the best minds in drug control, public health and harm reduction get together, legalize drug trafficking, then ask the traffickers to reduce their sales by 10 percent over the next ten years. Or, if that's too much to ask, perhaps they could buy the right to sell more drugs from those traffickers who've reduced their sales by even more than 10 percent.

This, Scheer argued, was the "market solution" that was fought for so passionately in Copenhagen: a global cap-and-trade system in which the worst traffickers—conventional energy companies—were permitted to control the pace and parameters of change. It makes sense, of course, if you're in the oil or coal business. As Scheer liked to point out, those are the only ones who stand to lose from the jump to renewable energy:

> The problem of this whole Kyoto Protocol negotiation process is that they estimate steps to overcome these emissions by a shift to renewable energies—this is estimated to be an economic burden. And based on this premise, they come automatically to the burden-sharing bazaar. Automatically. And this at a global level, with countries which have very, very different economic developments and very, very different energy consumptions. If you would recognize that this is not an economic burden, but this creates a lot of new benefits, including economic benefits, nobody would need the treaty.

Instead, they would do as Germany has done. They would simply assemble the proper tools and leap directly onto the right track.

THE RIGHT TRACK

In search of the right tools for the job, let's return one last time to Paul Hawken's mission statement: *Civilization needs a new operating system, you are the programmers, and we need it within a few decades.*

The operating system Hawken refers to goes by a range of names already: *green, carbon neutral, environmentally conscious, eco-friendly, emissions-free.* None of these, though, encompasses all three dimensions of the chasm that looms before us—climate, energy and economics—and none articulates a full system response to the Total System FAIL that has brought us to this treacherous ledge. The term that comes closest to describing that new operating system is *sustainability*, and it's the term I'll use from here on out.

Sustainability is already a widely used label for much of what The Leap entails. This ubiquity is both a boon (in that it has already been acknowledged almost universally as a good and desirable thing) and also a bit of a curse, in that so many incomplete definitions and ineffective approaches have been attached to it. As for succinct one-line definitions, my current favourite comes from the futurist Bruce Sterling. "Sustainable practices," he writes, "navigate successfully through time and space, while others crack up and vanish."

Sustainability is the new operating system for society. It is the new bottom line, the basis on which all else depends. If a thing is not sustainable—whether it be a manufactured good or a business unit, a farm or a hospital, a state government or a multinational corporation, a community or a megacity, a vehicle or the road it's on—it will not survive the twenty-first century. And in order to *thrive* in this altered and unstable climate, where energy is scarce and the economics are changing rapidly, that operating system needs some slick software. The rest of this book is a sort of field guide to the best sustainability software on the market today.

There is a wide range of such software already available in the global marketplace of ideas. There are energy policies, urban design techniques, new accounting methods for calculating economic worth, sleek new engines and stunningly fast tracks. All these new systems share certain vital characteristics. They favour the use of renewable resources over nonrenewable ones—not just in terms of energy use and not just as exceptions to long-established rules. They replace rigid and mostly static hierarchies with loose, highly adaptable webs. And for the most part they represent a move from big and centralized systems and networks to smaller and much more dispersed ones.

Probably the best analogy for this shift comes from the digital world from which Hawken drew his metaphor: the jump from analog to digital telecommunications. The replacement of Ma Bell's hierarchical network of static, wall-mounted telephone boxes and unidirectional television signals with the widely dispersed, omnidirectional, limitlessly interconnected web of the internet—this is the sort of transformation ushered in by the move to sustainability as an operating system.

Let's look, as a case in point, at one particularly clever piece of sustainability software—a design strategy for human habitat known as *resilience*. Resilience functions in sustainable society like the shocks on a car or the ballast in a boat or the stabilizers on a train car. Resilience anticipates bumps in the path, counts on rough weather and bracing crosswinds, and it plans for sudden alterations in course. As a scientific concept, resilience emerged from the ecological research of a Canadian-born academic named Buzz Holling at the University of Florida, which has since been expanded by a global research network called the Resilience Alliance. "Ecosystem resilience"—this is the Resilience Alliance website's definition—"is the capacity of an ecosystem to tolerate disturbance without collapsing into a qualitatively different state that is controlled by a different set of processes. A resilient ecosystem can withstand shocks and rebuild itself when necessary."

Resilience Alliance researchers often refer to their field of study as "social-ecological resilience," suggesting that people are as essential to the process as any other species in the ecosystem. This is a complete break with the old notion of Nature as a thing that exists only in the absence of humanity and the environment as a system separate from human systems. Indeed real resilience is created in the complex, unpredictable interplay *between* human and other natural systems. As leading resilience researcher Brian Walker of Australia's Commonwealth Scientific and Industrial Research Organization (CSIRO) puts it, "Ecological systems are inextricably linked with the social systems of people—in effect, all life exists within a social-ecological system."

These systems, Walker notes, are never static, and the resilience of such a system actually decreases as it becomes more efficient. He calls this the "paradox of optimization." Think of a mature forest, where massive trees have locked up much of the available energy in the system, decreasing biodiversity and making the whole forest more vulnerable to fire and pests. Or think of a single-use residential development on the distant exurban fringe of a city, lying vacant now in the wake of the economic meltdown.

Resilience, then, embraces change as the natural state of being on earth. It values adaptation over stasis, diffuse systems over centralized ones, loosely interconnected webs over strict hierarchies. It favours diversity (both biological and social) and redundancy, and it works best with a range of interchangeable, modular components. It places paramount value on natural capital (the trees in the forest, the oil in the ground) and social capital (the hearts and minds and passionate actions of the public). It responds best with tight feedback loops, where, for example, the squandering of that capital has immediate, negative consequences. It encourages learning new tricks and following local rules and customs.

Above all, resilience is comfortable with loss, because it recognizes that there remains much to be gained from epochal, transformative change. Resilience, like any effective piece of sustainability software, anticipates big changes, understanding them to be not only inevitable but also rich in opportunity. And so it goes for The Leap itself: it sizes up our traverse over the chasm before us not as a daunting challenge to be feared and avoided but as a broad jump toward a better place, an ambitious move toward our brightest possible future.

< TWO >

THE MECHANICS OF THE LEAP

"NOW ALL CONSPIRE IN ONE GRAND CAUSE"

ON THE FOURTH OF JULY, 1817, in a birch forest near the village of Rome in central New York state, a small crowd of engineers, minor dignitaries and well-wishers held a modest groundbreaking ceremony. There, along the muddy banks of a backwoods creek, the village president led a team of oxen as they plowed a short furrow in the earth, commencing construction of what was then called the "Western Canal."

The event was considered so insignificant that only a single newspaper in the whole state, the *Utica Gazette*, paid it any notice, and that came eleven days after the fact. Even the canal's chief proponent, DeWitt Clinton, the newly elected governor of New York, was absent, instead attending his own inaugural festivities in faraway New York City. Eight years and 363 miles (584 kilometres) later, the new canal would link the Lake Erie port of Buffalo to the Hudson River at Albany, ultimately connecting New York City's bustling harbour to the Great Lakes and the resource-rich interior of the American continent. In time, the canal would come to be known as the Erie, and generations of American schoolchildren would be taught that the United States owed its place at the front ranks of the modern industrial world to the Erie Canal's foresighted construction.

The digging of the Erie Canal was easily the most ambitious engineering project of its day, and more than that it was the prototypical Great Leap Sideways—a single improbable jump across an uncharted and perilous wilderness, landing in a transformed world of unparalleled prosperity. And despite the wide range of circumstances under which such leaps are launched, there are key processes common to all of them. I've distilled these into four Laws of Leap Mechanics, four key principles that determine the trajectory of a jump and govern its success or failure at crossing the chasm. All four can be found between the lines in the colourful story of the Erie Canal. Let's outline these four principles from this vantage point before moving on to their relevance to the sustainability project.

The Erie Canal's inauspicious ceremonial launch notwithstanding, its architects had grandiose plans from the very start. The idea of a navigable waterway linking the east coast of the US with the vastness beyond the Appalachian Mountains had been a topic of grand musings and vague schemes as far back as 1776, when George Washington launched a doomed effort to build such a canal across Virginia. In the early 1790s, the idea of building the link instead across the sparsely populated expanse of upstate New York took hold, and for the next twenty years it inspired studies, speeches and one ill-conceived, abortive construction project. Finally, in 1810, the Erie Canal plan found its ultimate champion in DeWitt Clinton, then the most powerful figure in New York state politics.

Clinton, who was mayor of New York City at the time, embraced the canal project as his own and advocated on its behalf even after his political fortunes flagged. In 1816, Clinton presented a stirring address to the state legislature extolling the benefits of the canal. It would, he asserted, "convey more riches on its waters than any other canal in the world" and turn the city of New York into "the great depot and warehouse of the western world." It would open up the American interior to what was then called "improvement"—the cornerstone of nineteenth-century progress—and create a market for the manufactures of New York's fledgling industrial sector. It would unite the fractious United States and secure the continent against further European encroachment.

"It remains for a free state to create a new era in history," Clinton concluded, "and to erect a work more stupendous, more magnificent, and more beneficial than has hitherto been achieved by the human race." The canal plan brought new momentum to Clinton's political career. He was elected governor in 1817 and immediately set to work on fulfilling his vision.

Clinton's vision was far from universally shared. In 1809, with no canal longer than a couple of miles extant anywhere in America, and war with Britain on the horizon, Thomas Jefferson famously dismissed the Erie project as "little short of madness." His successor, James Madison, was no more convinced, and the federal government ultimately contributed no funds whatsoever to the project. Clinton's opponents in the state legislature dismissed the plan as the deluded work of "a madman or a fool," and his powerful enemies at Tammany Hall in New York City composed a mocking ode to "Clinton's ditch," distributed by handbill: "How absurd! But why should you grin? / It will do to bury its mad author in." Beyond this, New York City merchants convinced themselves the canal would do little or nothing for their businesses while adding substantially to their tax burdens, farmers and small factory owners feared the canal would leech business away from the rest of the state, and many other citizens expressed disbelief in the engineering fundamentals of the project.

The skepticism was, in many respects, eminently reasonable. The proposed canal would be more than three times the length of the longest one ever built, which ran through densely populated southern France, as opposed to the swampy wilderness of western New York. And it would be designed and constructed by a team composed exclusively of novices. On the day ground was broken in upstate New York, there was no civil engineering school nor even a single professionally trained civil engineer anywhere in America. The work would be done by local contractors with no canal-building experience, sometimes under the guidance of "engineers" who'd been farmers or judges just a few months before. The official estimate for the total cost of the canal was $4.85 million—a staggering sum for the early 1800s, more than ten times the cost of any previous American canal project—and Clinton himself admitted the price tag could climb as high as $12 million and take fifteen years to complete.

The Erie Canal was ridiculously ambitious, crazily risky both politically and practically, and an economic liability without equal in its time. It should have been a cautionary tale. It was, instead, an immediate and enormous success, an object of wonder, a transformative force of revolutionary scale. A Great Leap Sideways, in other words—the industrial-age archetype of The Leap.

Even while still under construction, the canal's impact had begun to surprise backers and detractors alike. By 1824, a year before completion, interest payments on the project's debt were being fully covered by toll revenue from traffic on the finished portions of the canal, and the cost of shipping wheat by canal was just one-tenth of what it had been by road. The nationwide financial panic of 1819 and ensuing economic decline had greatly reduced construction costs, and Erie Canal bonds emerged from the recession as a safe investment bet. The total price tag, $7.896

million, was paid back in full from toll receipts by 1837, after which the canal generated $41 million in profit until user fees were eliminated entirely in 1881. At the base level of profit, the Erie Canal was an unqualified success.

The canal's true value, though, was its incalculable influence on the nation as a whole. It carried the bulk of immigrants and merchandise into the American Midwest and transported the grain and livestock produced there to New York and the markets of Europe beyond. From 1825 to 1850, the United States underwent one of the most intense periods of growth experienced by any nation anywhere ever. New York City grew by a factor of four, Rochester became the world's largest producer of flour, and Chicago emerged from a pestilent swamp to become the largest granary and lumberyard on earth. Canal historian Peter L. Bernstein: "This narrow ribbon of ditch, less than 375 miles long, provided the spark, the flashpoint, and the inspiration for a burst of progress in America that would eventually coin the buzzwords of the early twenty-first century: economic growth, urbanization, national unity, networking, and technological innovation."

In place of passing notice in the Utica paper and the jeers of Tammany Hall, the canal's completion in 1825 was celebrated in New York's streets with a raucous festival that one canal historian has called "Woodstock for the dawning 'Age of Acquisition.'" There was also a stirring "Ode on the Completion of the Erie Canal" by a Utica minister: "Now all conspire in one grand cause, / And swell the notes of just applause."

Those lines could serve, actually, as a fitting benediction for any Leap.

TECHNICAL SPECS: THE FOUR LAWS OF LEAP MECHANICS

Written in the jagged arc the Erie Canal traced across the map of nineteenth-century New York is the first draft of the four core principles of The Leap, the essential tools and techniques for providing sufficient propulsion and lift to *any* Leap. Let's call them the Four Laws of Leap Mechanics. Here they are:

1) A chasm can only be crossed in a single Leap
2) The sustainable horizon is only visible from the sustainable track (or, You can't see there from here)
3) A *quantum leap* cannot be measured with a yardstick
4) A Leap is powered not by a disruptive technology but by a disruptive technique.

Let's take a brief look at each in turn, through the crooked lens of the Erie Canal.

"Don't be afraid to take a big step if one is indicated; you can't cross a chasm in two small jumps." So goes a famous axiom attributed to David Lloyd George, prime minister of Britain in the early 1900s. Its corollary—A *chasm can only be crossed in a single leap*— is the First Law of Leap Mechanics, and it was critical to the Erie Canal's extraordinary success.

Prior to the Erie, the few canals that had been built in America were modest affairs for local use. Even those with loftier ambitions remained regional in scope; they had no real transformational effect on the greater economy and thus failed to justify their expense. (Such was the fate of both George Washington's Potomac canal across Virginia and an Erie precursor built along a stretch of the Mohawk River in upstate New York.) The Erie's visionaries, however, recognized early on that their canal was a national project. Its intent was not just to improve transport across one region or state but to unite them all in what DeWitt Clinton called a "bond of union." For flour mills to flourish in Rochester, they would need a steady supply of Midwestern grain, and both would have to rely on the port of New York to reach international markets. Even the cotton fields of the South would benefit from the trade boom, joining grain shipments in New York to feed the mills and markets of Europe. The whole chain would be a sum much greater than its parts and exponentially more valuable than any single length of the canal. To build the Erie Canal piecemeal, by increments, would very likely have doomed it to failure, as each link in the chain would have been unable, on its own, to generate the kind of transformative power that ultimately justified the entire project. What's more, time was of the essence — the resource-hungry colonial powers of Spain, France and Britain already had designs on the American interior. The job had to be done in a single leap of colossal scale.

A few years before ground was broken on the Erie Canal, the grandiloquent Gouverneur Morris, a Founding Father and ardent backer of the project, composed a report on its potential for his compatriots, girding them for the nasty political squabbles to come. Their opponents, he warned, would surely underestimate and misconstrue the potential benefits of the canal and greatly exaggerate the costs and risks. "There can be no doubt," Morris wrote, "that those microcosmic minds which, habitually occupied in the consideration of what is little, are incapable of discerning what is great."

This is the essence of the Second Law of Leap Mechanics: *The sustainable horizon is only visible from the sustainable track.* The scale of a Leap of Erie Canal magnitude is so large and its transformative impact so profound that the enormous benefits to be reaped upon completion are rarely visible from this side of the chasm. The blinders of business as usual—an amalgam of apprehension, risk aversion and plain lack of perspective—block our ability to see the new horizon and discern the riches waiting on the other side. In other words, *you can't see there from here.*

Probably no single example illustrates this mechanical law as well as the simple fact of America's Second City, Chicago, wrought almost exclusively by the Erie's transformative force.

On the summer day the Erie Canal's construction began in 1817, Chicago was a reeking marsh—*Chicagua,* "place of the skunkweed"—of little interest to the Native Americans who inhabited the region. Even four years after the canal's completion, Chicago was nothing more than a fort and way station. It was finally incorporated as a town in 1833, with a population of 350; that year, 20,000 immigrants boarded ships at the western terminus of the Erie Canal in Buffalo and sailed the Great Lakes to Chicago. Most of them passed quickly through the muddy townsite en route to the prime farmland of the Mississippi Valley, but before long some of those westbound migrants instead decided to try their luck in the emerging boomtown. By 1837, Chicago had a population of more than 4,000, and ground had been broken on a canal to link the newborn city's port to the Illinois River 96 miles (155 kilometres) away. Upon its completion in 1848, the new canal formed the final link in an unbroken chain of navigable water from the Mississippi River to the harbour of New York. And Chicago was transformed overnight from a half-built backwater into the nexus of the continent's most important transportation network.

Chicago grew by a factor of ten from 1850 to 1870, becoming the world's largest shipping centre for grain and timber and America's premier railroad hub. The mechanical reaper and

Pullman car were invented in Chicago in those years, and so was the mail-order catalogue. The city's meatpacking "disassembly" lines would inspire Henry Ford to dream up his assembly line, and the dismal conditions on their killing floors instigated many of the key reforms governing modern food safety. Much of the socioeconomic apparatus of modern American business—from the skyscraper to the retail empire to organized labour—was born in Chicago, and all of it arose as a mostly unforeseen and unintended consequence of a Leap launched in New York's state legislature.

The Third Law of Leap Mechanics—*A quantum leap cannot be measured with a yardstick*—is closely related to the second, revolving again around matters of scale and focus. Though the term *quantum leap* has come to imply simply a *very large* leap, it more precisely refers to a change of unfathomable speed and intensity (not distance). In a quantum leap, an electron jumps instantaneously from one spot to another in the nucleus without passing through any of the places in between, the amount of energy it contains changing in the process. Or, metaphorically speaking, a single shift in an organization's (or a nation's) standard operations realigns the entire system under which it operates. The change is, in any case, rapid and fundamental, and it can no more be measured with the tools employed in the pre-Leap phase than a yardstick could be used to measure the electron's trip across the nucleus. In essence, there is no trajectory to be tracked and quantified. There is only before and after; the data attesting to the success of The Leap once it has been completed was impossible to obtain beforehand.

The metrics of the Erie Canal's success are a case study in benefits beyond measure. What, after all, was the total return on investment in the birth of the city of Chicago? The development of the Midwest? What was the bottom-line sum of total revenue accumulated by the emergence of the United States as a great power—eventually the greatest power—in global economic affairs? The best illustration of the Third Law, though, occurred at a more mundane and microcosmic scale—that of the small merchant's furrowed brow as he warily eyed *his* bottom line in a New York City counting house in 1817.

Few individuals would gain more from the Erie's largesse than New York City's merchants, and no other city would be so enhanced by its position on the new trade route. Nevertheless, many of the city's merchants vehemently opposed the state government's decision to fund the construction of the Erie Canal. From their pre-Leap vantage point, the Erie was seen strictly as a liability, an impossibly expensive public work measured mainly as a projected increase in their taxes. The benefits to be accrued through large-scale shipping from upstate New York—let alone from cities in the Midwest that didn't exist yet—were beyond their ability to measure.

In those days, it was routine to pay five or six times the face value of goods simply to move them from the Hudson River to the sparsely inhabited hinterland just a couple of hundred miles away. The idea that merchandise would soon be shipped in bulk more than a thousand miles farther inland, and that grain from those same places would flow steadily to the port of New York for generations, giving rise to a whole city just to mill it en route and all but erasing the agricultural business from a significant swath of Europe—all of this was simply impossible to calculate in 1817. So was the way in which the Erie Canal secured New York's primacy in the commerce and culture of the nation (and the world). Before the construction of the canal, the port of New York handled 38 percent of America's imports; by the late 1830s, 62 percent of all imports passed through the city. In 1835, 62 percent of Midwestern commodities were shipped down the Mississippi River to New Orleans and just 24 percent went to New York; less than twenty years later, New York's share was 62 percent.

Five hundred new merchant houses opened in New York City in just the first few months after the opening of the canal. One of the pillars of the banking apparatus that would transform many of New York's merchants into globe-conquering financial titans arose directly out of the brisk trade in Erie Canal stock. The list of such unforeseen benefits is almost endless. Nevertheless, the city's merchants assayed this potential bounty and assessed it as an intolerably steep tax hike. The quantum leap to come simply could not be measured by the yardsticks on hand.

Given the extraordinary array of forces working *against* a decision to make a Great Leap, it can begin to seem impossible that one ever occurs. The reason they do is explained in large measure by the Fourth Law: *A Leap is powered not by a disruptive technology but by a disruptive technique.* That disruptive technique is, in essence, a fundamental shift in point of view that provides some of the proper measurement tools and the right perspective to see the bountiful horizon at the end of the new track. This cognitive leap transforms economic burdens to be avoided into unbridled opportunities to be seized, and it makes the impossible seem inevitable.

In the case of the Erie Canal, the disruptive technique was a kind of rational faith in the American democratic experiment that came to be known as Progress. In the first decades of American independence, the patriotic spirit of the Revolutionary War effort turned into a belief in the self-reinforcing common good of "improvement" or "progress." Prosperity and growth—physical as well as economic—were understood to be the engines of a great nation. And the United States was believed to be in possession of a unique endowment of the raw materials for such improvement—so much so that many decided the bounty must have been heaven sent. To nineteenth-century Americans, progress meant, as historian Carol Sheriff puts it, "that men and women were taking an active role in realizing a divinely sanctioned movement toward the perfectibility of the natural and human worlds." A canal was not just a piece of infrastructure but a tool to make God's plan for humanity manifest on American soil. As DeWitt Clinton told the New York legislature in 1815, "The overflowing blessings from this great fountain of public good and national abundance, will be as extensive as our country and as durable as time."

The progress doctrine was just as important to the canal's construction on a practical level. It was faith in America's unique potential for progress that guided the decision to allow amateurs and novices to design and build the canal, and those amateurs and novices were in turn guided by unwavering resolve in their own inborn skills and gumption—a sort of practical progressive faith that came to be known, over the course of the canal's construction, as "Yankee ingenuity."

Canal contractors, most of them hired simply because they lived on the route, designed "tree fellers" and "stump pullers" on the work site to clear the way for the canal. At one spot on the route, a cutting blade was affixed to a wrought-iron plow to carve quickly through smaller roots in the excavation process; the contraption was then duplicated the length of the dig. And the "Deep Cut" in the canal's final section—basically a trench 3 miles long and 30 feet deep, carved and blasted out of solid Niagara Escarpment bedrock—inspired the invention of a crane and horse-operated boom apparatus to move all the crumbled stone.

The scale of the excavation was not far from what Panama Canal crews would struggle to accomplish using gas-powered engines almost a century later.

Because their progressive vision was unwavering, the builders of the Erie Canal never entertained the idea of quitting the job. No problem was beyond solving, no obstacle too large. These sound like corporate clichés to modern ears, but along the Erie Canal they were carved clean and new from ancient stone.

The only essential fuel needed to launch a Leap is the vision to see the better horizon—whether a progressive horizon in the America of 1817 or the sustainable horizon of today—and to embrace the shift in perspective needed to reach it. The Leap is, first and foremost, a *cognitive leap*. Without it, there will never be proper tools to move all the stone that blocks our path, and after it there can be no rock too large to stop our progress.

This, then, is the prototypical Leap of the Erie Canal. Let's turn now to the Leaps of today to explain the mechanical laws in modern terms.

A CHASM CAN ONLY BE CROSSED IN A SINGLE LEAP

In nature and in most human systems, change is an incremental thing, a slow shift across multiple generations. Evolution, as Charles Darwin first explained, is an accumulation of countless imperceptible changes stretching far beyond the scope of a single lifetime. This has provided justification for the slow-but-steady approach to change ever since.

More recent evidence, however—not just from the fields of biology and physics, but also from the study of human language, modern business management and the process of scientific discovery—reveal that Great Leaps are intrinsic to the survival of *any* system, and they often govern the time periods crucial to the long-term success or failure of the system as a whole. The sustainability of the system, in other words, is disproportionately dependent on its ability to make a Great Leap at a crucial moment.

The terminology for this evolutionary leap varies from field to field, but the process being described is remarkably similar. Biologists now speak of a *punctuated equilibrium*, wherein long phases of gradual and imperceptible evolutionary change give way to rapid transformation under extreme environmental stress. A recent groundbreaking study of the evolution of human languages by Mark Pagel of the University of Reading, meanwhile, refers to this process as a *punctuational burst*, and notes that it occurs in the same fashion whether the subject is a living, leaf-bearing, photosynthesizing tree or the tangled family tree of a human language. In either case, a significant portion of the evolutionary process occurs in a single, sudden alteration, inspired by dramatic changes in circumstance. On average, more than a fifth of all the evolving done across the millennia by a given species of tree happens in these punctuational bursts.

A number of studies in recent years have observed an even more dramatic phenomenon at work in the nature of climate change. "All the evidence"—so concludes a recent paper on the process that ended the last ice age—"indicates that most long-term climate change occurs in sudden jumps rather than incremental changes." Ice ages begin and end with shocking abruptness once a certain critical point (what resilience researchers call a *threshold*) is passed. Leading coral reef scientist Charlie Veron has identified a similar threshold and "sudden jump" at work in the mass extinctions and dramatic rebirths that have seen all the world's coral reefs vanish and reappear five times in the earth's history. The geologic record, Veron explains, reveals not a "gradual evolutionary development" but a "start-stop response" governing the life and death of coral reefs.

In molecular physics, there is a crucial process known as a *phase transition*—the mechanism by which, for example, solids become liquids and materials switch from magnetic to non-magnetic. The English physicist and author Philip Ball offers this description of the phase transition in *Critical Mass*, his 2004 study of abrupt change: "The phase transition happens when some global influence which acts upon the particles reaches a certain threshold value. One moment the particles are behaving 'normally,' as if nothing were amiss; then without warning . . . they switch to some entirely different mode of behaviour." These phase transitions generally occur between states of equilibrium—think of a still pool of water trapped in a canal lock, and then the gate suddenly opening to allow the water to pour into the lock below, where it finds another placid equilibrium.

Non-equilibrium systems, however, also maintain steady states—imagine the smooth flow of a river, which is never in equilibrium but remains broadly predictable—and these steady states undergo phase transitions as well. For such a system, the critical moment is called the *bifurcation point*. As Ball explains, fluctuations are constant within many natural systems. Even the temperature of a substance, for example, is actually a sort of average of the temperatures of individual atoms as they vary constantly up and down with each passing moment. Physicists refer to this generically as "noise" in the larger system, and most of the time it has no impact on the state of the system as a whole. The system remains in a steady state, in other words, despite all the routine noise. A bifurcation point, however, occurs when the system has entered a period of crisis. At that moment, the system is, as Ball puts it, "poised on a razor's edge," and the noisy fluctuating atoms (not the steady-state parts of the system) become the masters of the system as a whole; at such moments, a single fluctuating atom can seal its fate one way or another. The final drops of rain that fall into a river before it floods its banks, for example, are the "noisy" drops inducing the bifurcation point in the entire system.

The existence of these instantaneous phase transitions in dynamic, non-equilibrium systems has particularly important repercussions for *human* systems. Far beyond the Petri dish, Ball explains, the precise statistical process of such a phase transition governs the flow of vehicles on a highway before and after a traffic jam forms and the behaviour of a crowd of people (or a crowd of stock traders) before and after the onset of a panic.

This bifurcation point is pretty much exactly what Andy Grove, founder of computer chip giant Intel, describes in business terms as a "strategic inflection point" in the business cycle. Grove: "A strategic inflection point is a time in the life of a business when its fundamentals are about to change. That change can mean an opportunity to rise to new heights. But it may just as likely signal the beginning of the end." A sudden change might occur in the technological basis of a given market or the values and priorities of its customers—the emergence of free online classified advertising, say, or a widespread jump in consumer preference for more fuel-efficient vehicles—and the businesses that prosper will be the ones that recognize the inflection point's arrival and fundamentally alter their business strategies to fit the new reality.

The *strategic inflection point* and *phase transition* and *punctuational burst* all describe the same essential phenomenon—a Leap from one structural basis to another. What was once business as usual is now obsolescence; what was once a river flowing smoothly past is now a devastating flood bursting its banks; what was once a place locked permanently in thick ice is now a temperate climate with predictable seasons; what was once an arduous journey over-land is now a quick, routine trip down a canal. Our most broadly used catch-all phrase for such a phenomenon is *paradigm shift*.

The term *paradigm shift* traces its origins back to Thomas Kuhn's seminal 1962 study of the history of science, *The Structure of Scientific Revolutions*. In describing the way one set of scientific norms supplants another, Kuhn refuted the idea that science pro-gressed only through the slow, steady, incremental accumulation of new facts—the idea that scientific discovery is inherently and invariably evolutionary. *Most* scientific progress, Kuhn explained, proceeds this way; he called this *normal science*. Periodically, how-ever, a new breakthrough is made or a theory proposed that is both "sufficiently unprecedented to attract an enduring group of adher-ents away from competing modes of scientific activity" and "suffi-ciently open-ended to leave all sorts of problems" to be solved. Kuhn called these dramatic changes in the basis of scientific inquiry *paradigms*, describing them as "desertions" of normal science that serve as "the pivots about which scientific revolutions turn."

Kuhn never actually used the phrase *paradigm shift*, but this became the common term for such fundamental transitions. Like *quantum leap*, *paradigm shift* has become an overused, almost meaningless buzz phrase, used to refer to almost any kind of change. But I'd like to restore it to its original meaning, because it precisely describes the transformational mechanics of a Leap.

In times of general agreement on the basics, Kuhn explained, normal science focuses on solving puzzles and clarifying fuzzy details within the existing paradigm. Anomalies are ignored, incongruent results set aside. The emergence of a new paradigm, however, induces a state of crisis. The process, he notes, directly parallels regime change in a political revolution. "The choice between . . . competing paradigms proves to be a choice between incompatible modes of community life," resulting in an interim phase, a sort of bifurcation point during which neither paradigm is in full control. What's more, the competing world views are so wholly incompatible that the data and logic of neither one is sufficient on its own to force the compliance of the other one. It is only through "the techniques of persuasive argumentation" that the revolution is won—and even then, there are some adherents to the old paradigm who never shift. The objective truth of the observable world never changes, of course, but our perception of it—our understanding of how and why it is the way it is—alters fundamentally. The paradigm shift, in other words, is ultimately as much cultural as scientific.

The same is true of Great Leaps, and this is a key reason why they can only be completed in a single bound. They are first and foremost *cognitive* leaps. They are as much about winning hearts as convincing minds, and in most cases they are launched with many minds still unconvinced and hearts unwon. The crisis obliging The Leap is real, proximate, enormous and intensifying. The core adherents to the old paradigm—the failing track—are deeply entrenched, deep-pocketed and wholly convinced of the rightness of their course. The transition phase is a battleground of ideas and values as much as economics and statistics. And even when The Leap achieves unprecedented success, it often remains contested and distrusted in some circles. This indeed is a core lesson to be drawn from the single greatest leap toward sustainability yet launched—The Leap in energy policy made by Germany at national scale over the last ten years.

In 2000, after several years of sporadic, incremental change by half-measures and test runs, the German government passed a wholesale revision of its energy policy. It was a deceptively simple piece of legislation known as a "feed-in tariff," which obliged grid operators (the companies that transmit electricity from power plants to customers) to buy power from renewable sources at rates far above the standard rate for electricity. Disguised as an effort to introduce a little green power to the German grid, the feed-in tariff has fundamentally changed the way the entire nation approaches the energy and climate crises and laid the foundations for the second industrial revolution.

Germany now produces almost 20 percent of its electricity from renewables (up from 6 percent ten years ago), and it is on track to generate at least 35 percent of its power from renewable sources (wind, solar, biomass and some small-scale hydro) by 2020. Germany has exceeded its Kyoto targets for greenhouse-gas-emissions reductions. The feed-in tariff has created more than a quarter of a million German jobs in just a decade and given rise to a $50-billion renewable energy business in Germany alone.

Germany is not particularly windy or sunny, and it isn't blessed with an abundance of open space or coastline, but it is now the global production and research hub for solar power and both on- and offshore wind energy production. By 2020, cleantech will likely be a bigger business than automobiles in the land of Volkswagen and BMW. Cleantech jobs have tamed the chronic unemployment crisis in the former East Germany, and the feed-in tariff has also inspired subsequent leaps in building design, energy efficiency and urban planning across the country. Hundreds of thousands of German households now sell power back to the grid at a premium, in certain ambitious cases transforming their homes into net power producers. And the feed-in tariff has done all this without any direct taxation, by imposing a surcharge of about 3 percent on every kilowatt-hour of energy consumed in the country—an added cost passed on to German energy users that amounts to less than

€4 per month on the average household electricity bill.

"It's a cup of coffee per month for saving the climate, for creating jobs and all these other things which have happened"—this is how German solar energy executive David Wortmann put it to me. (Wortmann was on the parliamentary staff of one of the feed-in tariff's authors and now oversees German operations for the thin-film solar company First Solar.) And yet the feed-in tariff has endured consistent and strident opposition throughout its decade of success—not just from political opponents of the government that enacted it and entrenched interests in the conventional energy industry, but even from proponents of renewable energy outside Germany who continue to subscribe to the basic tenets of the old paradigm. As recently as 2006, for example, I often heard predictions of nationwide economic disaster for Germany when I asked American renewable energy advocates for their opinion on feed-in tariffs. Mistaking the feed-in tariff for a simple substitution of one kind of power plant for another—an incremental change, not a structural one—the tariff's critics profoundly underestimated its transformative power, its ability to reimagine the *economics* of power generation as well as the physics. Wortmann:

> I think the whole reason for this mental block is that we really have a paradigm shift going on. It's not only about producing this solar panel. It's about constructing houses which in the first place get down the energy demand, and then very smartly integrate these new kinds of technology. So you have a whole infrastructure change going on. We are at the middle of a revolution—a revolution instead of an evolution, because we are not replacing a gas power station with, I don't know, large windmill stations, and that's it. It's about changing the whole infrastructure.

A cross-cultural comparison with Britain's approach to renewable energy provides a particularly striking example of the difference in effectiveness between an incremental strategy and a full-blown Leap. An antecedent of what became the feed-in tariff was passed in Germany in the early 1990s; around the same time, the British government introduced "Renewables Obligation Certificates" (ROCs). Both policies were substantially expanded around 2000, and both had the same stated goals: to provide strong incentives for the production of renewable power and to encourage the development of a domestic manufacturing industry in renewable energy technologies.

The British approach was deemed to be much more "market-friendly," because it did not directly control the price of a kilowatt-hour of electricity. Instead, it obliged grid operators to buy a fixed percentage of their power from renewable sources. If they fell short, they could buy ROCs from the operators of renewable energy plants. The idea was that the ROCs, which were priced according to demand on the open market just like any wholesale commodity, would become so precious that they would inspire a gold rush toward the manufacture and installation of green power. The opposite happened—the price of ROCs collapsed, and Britain's fledgling renewable energy industry languished. In 2010, the policy was finally scrapped in favour of a steep feed-in tariff, with a particular emphasis on wind power. A substantial share of the billions of pounds in new wind energy installation contracts issued in its wake were snatched up by German wind companies, which had thrived for a decade under the feed-in tariff and now boasted better technology, deeper expertise, and economies of scale over their British competitors.

Similar cautionary tales have emerged in every jurisdiction that has taken a less decisive approach than the German feed-in model.

In the US, for example, the preferred strategy has been a mix of state-level Renewable Portfolio Standards (RPSs), which set a target percentage of the state grid to be converted to renewable sources by a fixed date, and federal tax incentives and grants that require annual renewal in Washington. The latter have proved particularly problematic for large-scale manufacturers, who far prefer a stable market and investment climate—the feed-in tariff provides this stability by guaranteeing its rates for twenty years from the time a new renewable power plant is installed. Even as US states race to meet their portfolio standards, often as not they're relying on imported equipment from Germany or from other countries (such as Spain, Denmark and China) that have already enacted feed-in tariffs or similar long-term incentives. In the midst of the emerging energy crisis, the German approach has boldly forced the system in a single direction toward a new, renewably powered equilibrium. The less certain policies, like sandbags piled against a rising river, have merely extended the period of crisis and prevented the status quo flow from reaching its inevitable bifurcation point.

The German feed-in tariff is, in short, the quintessential Great Leap Sideways. It is a gamechanger, a paradigm shifter, revolutionary in impact and global in scale. Germany's 2004 boost in the price paid for solar power, for example, transformed the global solar industry almost overnight from struggling cottage industry into mature manufacturing business. (This ambitious amplification of solar's feed-in rate inspired the most hysterical predictions of Germany's economic doom.) Wherever the solar business finds itself in a generation, it will forever owe its emergence to that decisive German Leap, as surely as America's industrial base traces its origins to the digging of the Erie Canal.

That sense of panic induced by Germany's bold solar rates is intrinsic to The Leap as a process. The necessity of a single jump across the chasm instills a dizzying sensation of free fall. This is evident even in Leaps of far smaller scale than Germany's. Consider the case of Newton, Iowa, a small manufacturing town coerced into a Leap of its own back in 2004.

For most of the twentieth century, Newton was essentially a company town, and that company was Maytag. Fred L. Maytag built his very first hand-cranked washing machine in Newton in 1907 and headquartered his appliance empire there. But in 2004, Whirlpool announced it was purchasing Maytag and shuttering the last of its Newton operations. The appliance manufacturing business had been bleeding jobs to cheaper labour markets for years, but the Whirlpool purchase was still a catastrophe. When the deal was finalized in 2006, 2,000 jobs vanished overnight from a town of 16,000, and Newton's very identity was in crisis. Generations of Newton's children had grown up playing in Maytag Park, swimming in Maytag Pool, performing on the stage at the Maytag Amphitheater. What was left for them now besides the name?

Around the same time, the state of Iowa began to experience the first rumblings of a serious boom in wind power. Local officials in Newton—particularly a youthful new mayor named Chaz Allen—spotted an opportunity, a new direction for the town. Municipalities across the state had begun introducing enticements to attract turbine manufacturers, but few had the waiting workforce and physical infrastructure that Newton did. Wind turbines, though, were an unknown commodity. People would always need washing machines, but who knew how long this green power thing would stick around?

In retrospect it came to look like a no-brainer—more than 800 new jobs created in the wind industry, including 175 making structural towers right in the old Maytag factory—but at the decisive moment, that crucial bifurcation point, it felt even to its backers like a leap into the abyss. "We pushed the plane off the cliff and then started working on the motors," Allen told me. "I joke about that, but that's kind of how we felt—okay, we'll build the motor on the way down. We were pretty aggressive." On Earth Day 2009, when President Obama laid out his plan for America's clean energy future, he made the announcement from the old Maytag factory in Newton. Just three years after the town's Leap, it was the very model of America's new industrial base.

Nothing inspires a Leap quite like the sight of a successful one nearby. So it has gone, for example, in Denver, Colorado, where a single suburban government's Leap has given rise to a citywide paradigm shift in urban design. That first Leap occurred in Lakewood, Colorado, which began wrestling in the late 1990s with what has become a common feature of older suburbs: a dying shopping mall. In Lakewood's case, a grand old retail palace called Villa Italia, the largest mall anyone had seen west of Chicago upon its completion in the mid-1960s, had fallen into decline. Its vacancy rate was 30 percent and its parking lot had become a crime magnet. The standard approach to a dying shopping mall was to extend the status quo another generation by redesigning the old building, putting in some skylights and an expansive new play area, and offering sweetheart deals to trendy retailers to set up shop. (This, in fact, was exactly the approach taken across town at the Aurora Mall.)

Lakewood's mayor instead made a Great Leap in the direction of the "mixed use" strategy favoured by proponents of the design philosophy known as New Urbanism. The mall was razed to the ground, the parking lot carved up into a tidy grid of city streets, offices and downtown-style loft apartments built above stores along handsome promenades with wide sidewalks. There was a new central plaza, a farmers' market, even an art gallery. A proper city centre was finally built for a city that never really had one. Where once was found the American West's first megamall, its first sub-urban downtown now stood.

Less than a decade after the old Villa Italia met the wrecking ball, the model New Urbanist neighbourhood of Belmar is already thriving. Condo prices verged on downtown levels right out of the gate, selling for up to 60 percent more per square foot than single-family homes in the surrounding neighbourhood, and the art gallery now co-sponsors exhibitions with elite European museums. And more than this, Lakewood's approach has become the new para-digm for suburban redevelopment in Denver. At last count, seven of thirteen vintage shopping malls in the area were undergoing mixed-use retrofits in the Belmar style, inspired either by Belmar itself or by another New Urbanist project launched around the same time on the site of the abandoned Stapleton International Airport.

This suburban design boom has been accompanied by a renewed commitment to mixed-use urban design in Denver's long-neglected downtown core, where Belmar's primary developer has started work on a massive project adjacent to the main train station. The Denver area has also embarked on the most expan-sive rapid transit construction project in the country, with light rail lines snaking out to the new suburban downtowns on all sides. In just a decade, Denver has reinvented itself wholesale through an interlocking chain of Leaps. Long a poster child for sprawl, once ranking as high as number three nationwide in traffic con-gestion, the city is now a national model for sustainable urban redevelopment. (It is also no longer in the congestion Top Ten.)

Denver's suburban renaissance illustrates another key aspect of The Leap: by trying to jump one chasm, you sometimes sail over several. A sharper example of this phenomenon has emerged in the business world in recent years with the "greening" of the chemical product giant Clorox. A brand name once synonymous with chlorine bleach, one of the most dangerous chemicals in our homes, Clorox has become a model for real sustainability at the supermarket.

Clorox's Leap began around 2006 with a twofold shift in perspective. First, the company realized that the market for "green" household products—spray cleaners, detergents, moisturizers and soaps that were biodegradable and free of petrochemicals and other toxins—was on the verge of a boom, and they wanted a share of it. The second and more transformative aspect was that they knew there was no way to retrofit Clorox's existing products to instigate that expansion. Neither of these realizations pointed to a sure thing. As with wind turbines in Iowa, green consumerism might be a passing trend, and the Clorox brand in any case might've proven too heavily bleached to win the trust of green consumers. In a conscious effort to alleviate the latter concern, Clorox bought an established green brand—the hugely successful Burt's Bees line of beeswax personal care products—and began developing its own cleaning-product line, GreenWorks, from scratch.

GreenWorks represented a single Leap substantial enough that the Sierra Club—one of America's oldest and most influential environmental groups—awarded it the first seal of approval it had ever granted to a consumer brand. And more importantly, GreenWorks was both a big enough and timely enough Leap that it radically expanded the market for green consumer products all by itself. Not only did the product line ring up $40 million in sales in its first year, but it did so, for the most part, not by stealing customers from established brands like Seventh Generation that produced only green products (which they sold mostly in specialty stores), but by carving out a new space and a new customer base in the mainstream supermarket. In many grocery stores, GreenWorks was the *only* green brand in the cleaning aisle that first year. This is, however, no longer the case — in fact, as of July 2010, it is no longer the case *by law* in sixteen US states. Those states have passed bans on dishwashing detergents containing environmentally damaging phosphates, forcing the entire industry to make the same jump Clorox made by choice. It's a veritable certainty that this is just the first obligatory leap of many for the world's packaged-goods giants. And so, as its competitors scramble to retool their products to fit new legal frameworks, Clorox will in many cases find itself already sitting alone on the shelf. This is the chasm Clorox crossed without even knowing it.

As stomach churning as the inevitable sense of free fall might be, The Leap works best as a single jump. This is very often a matter of necessity, but it is a question of practical efficiency and strategic advantage even when there might be other ways across the chasm. And the single leap crosses a distance far greater than the breadth of the chasm itself. It bestows unforeseen benefits and advantages — a prime spot on a supermarket shelf, for example, or the lead role in the second industrial revolution.

YOU CAN'T SEE THERE FROM HERE

One of the most widespread sustainability campaigns to date has been mounted in hotel rooms around the world. It's also among the most inconsequential: a voluntary program consisting of small signs placed next to sinks or mounted on bathroom mirrors, urging guests to help reduce the hotel's water and energy use by reusing their towels. Often this incidental act is couched in terms of conserving precious resources or even saving the whole planet. Outsized as those claims are, they might turn out to contain a kernel of truth—the towel-reuse campaign has indeed led the way toward much broader salvation. It's not about the towels, though; it's about the signs. Maybe the most essential factor in a Great Leap Sideways is the collective will to jump, and those innocuous towel signs have taught a vital lesson in how to build that will.

A few years ago, Robert Cialdini, then a marketing professor at Arizona State University, launched a study of the effectiveness of hotel towel signage (co-authored with Vladas Griskevicius and Noah Goldstein). Cialdini and his colleagues discovered that by adding just a few words to a sign's message, explaining that the majority of previous guests at that particular hotel reused their towels, participation increased by 26 percent. A subsequent sign was more specific, informing guests that the majority of people who'd stayed in that very room had reused their towels; this increased participation by 33 percent over the usual "save the planet" signage. Communicating a social norm to which guests could conform turned out to be dramatically more effective than persuasive argument, reams of energy and emissions statistics, or emotional appeals to the fate of the biosphere. Cialdini and his colleagues anticipated the *irrationality* of human behaviour and shaped their message to channel it into the desired action. Out of the trivial stuff of towel reuse, they discovered a powerful new tool to propel The Leap.

I'll return shortly to the surprising motivating force of irrationality; first, though, let's talk about its opposite. There are few modern myths more pervasive than the one about the "rational actor." Not only is it the baseline assumption upon which our entire economic system is built, but it's a key tenet of the Enlightenment philosophy that gave birth to the modern age. Reason, it's presumed, is the primary driver of human action and the engine of the market economy. Consumers make perfectly rational choices about what to buy (and what not to). In order to decide what to make for them and what to charge, producers respond like clockwork to supply and demand data. And as free-willed individuals, we're all sure we know what's best for ourselves. We maximize our happiness and minimize our pain. We enhance our status and defend our self-interest. We get the facts, discard the fictions and act decisively. We are reasonable people and rational actors. We know what we want.

Like hell we do.

The sustainable horizon—so goes The Leap's second law—*is only visible from the sustainable track*. Not only are we unable to get a clear view of our brightest possible future, we're terrible at identifying it as such when we can see it. More often than not, we are clueless about our best interests and hopeless at finding our way to them even when we do manage to identify them correctly. Whether it's in the pursuit of happiness or the quest for sustainability, the axiom holds: *You can't see there from here*.

Pointing out the inherent irrationality of humanity is, of course, as simple as picking up a newspaper or, let's be honest, looking in the mirror. But the full implications of that irrationality—and, moreover, the consequences of basing the systems that govern our collective action on the patently false notion that we are "rational actors"—have only just begun to be explored. But this ongoing investigation has already provided the essential tools that launch The Leap. These tools remove the supply obstacles ahead of us and the will to change and the clarity of vision to choose the right track.

The attack on the rational actor myth began with the pioneering work of the psychologist Daniel Kahneman. (Kahneman's status in his field is such that it belittles his import to attach a specialty or institutional affiliation to his name; he is the only psychologist ever awarded the Nobel Prize in economics and is referred to with some frequency as the most influential psychologist on the planet.) Starting in the 1970s with his research partner Amos Tversky, Kahneman has dismantled the foundations of conventional economic theory brick by brick, beginning with the concept of the rational actor.

Kahneman's first major breakthrough was the identification of what he calls "Bernoulli's error." Actors in the marketplace—so went the seminal argument of eighteenth-century mathematician Daniel Bernoulli—endeavour to maximize their wealth. They weigh choices objectively by the effect each option will have on their bottom line and pursue the most efficient means of obtaining the greatest sum. This is the "utility of wealth," and it is a pillar of the global market economy, propping up the belief that competitive enterprises in an unfettered marketplace will efficiently serve the needs of consumers.

Bernoulli's error, in Kahneman's analysis, was to equate utility of wealth with utility of *gains*. To Bernoulli, a dollar earned (or saved or spent or won in a contest) meant the same to you whether you had 10 bucks or 10 million to your name. Kahneman, on the contrary, knew that *relative* gains—and, more importantly, our inborn, often irrational fear of potential losses—were much stronger motivators than rational calculations of objective wealth. "Where you are turns out to be a fundamentally important parameter"—this is how Kahneman has phrased it.

One of Kahneman and Tversky's most famous experiments tested people's willingness to drive out of their way for a bargain. Offer a $7 discount on a $25 pen, and the majority of respondents are eager to drive fifteen minutes extra to save the cash. Offer a $7 discount on a $455 suit, however—in Bernoulli's terms, a proposition identical in its utility of wealth—and the vast majority *won't* go out of their way. Relative savings matter; where you are, as Kahneman puts it, in terms of the proportion of your total expense that 7 bucks saves you, is in fact the decisive figure in the whole equation. And it is entirely absent from utility theory, and thus from conventional economics in general.

The paradigm-shifting aspect of Kahneman's work was that he brought the messy, self-contradictory, emotion-driven, wildly irrational stuff of human psychology to bear on economics. (His Nobel citation specifically praises him for "having integrated insights from psychological research into economic science, especially concerning human judgment and decision-making under uncertainty.")

"It turns out," Kahneman told an audience of elite business leaders at a 2007 seminar, "that people's beliefs about what will make them happier are mostly wrong, and they are wrong very predictably." Kahneman's research has demonstrated not only that the baseline assumptions of our economic system are incorrect, but that the broader social apparatus we've erected to guide our collective decision-making can be reshaped into a more efficient system that anticipates our irrationalities and guides them more accurately in the direction of our best interests.

In the wake of Kahneman's corrections to utility theory, an academic niche emerged and then blossomed into a whole new field of economic theory. That field is known as "behavioural economics," and it represents a profound shift in our understanding of how we make decisions and operate collectively as economies. This is in the end the only *essential* Leap—the cognitive shift we must make in order to comprehend the necessity and benefit of all others. Because we can't see there from here, behavioural economics presents itself as a sort of beam of light through the fog of our irrationalities and misconceptions, leading us safely and efficiently to the sustainable side of the chasm.

In academic essays, scientific studies in the laboratory and in the field, and in the pages of a growing stack of general interest books with titles like *Sway* and *Nudge* and *Switch*, newly converted behavioural economists—their ranks filled by psychologists, neuroscientists and management theorists as well as exclusive practitioners of the dismal science—have revolutionized our understanding of the basic mechanics of the economy. Their first order of business has been to dispel forever the myth of the rational actor. Richard Thaler, a University of Chicago business professor hailed by many (including Kahneman) as "the father of behavioural economics," calls this mythic figure *Homo economicus*. In his book *Nudge* (co-authored with Cass R. Sunstein), Thaler defines this infallible humanoid as someone who can "think like Albert Einstein, store as much memory as IBM's Big Blue, and exercise the will power of Mahatma Gandhi." Thaler contrasts this superman starkly with the infinitely fallible *Homo sapiens* of flesh-and-blood everyday life, whose misguided, wonky, bias-ridden, emotion-twisted decisions actually drive our economy.

The many consistent biases governing human decision-making form the core of the behavioural-economic critique of classical economics. Many of these derive from the cognitive dissonance between our rational, conscious thoughts and our emotional, reflexive mind—what Thaler calls our "Reflective Systems" (which mull carefully and consciously over facts before making choices) and our "Automatic Systems" (which are driven by reflex and emotion and are highly susceptible to systemic errors and biases).

In *The Political Mind*, linguist George Lakoff characterizes the Reflective side as the embodiment of the "Old Enlightenment" conception of reason—the idea that people and the institutions that represent them will choose to act in their best interest once presented with the right set of facts and logical arguments. This is a misconception still widely held today in many social-enterprise circles, such as environmental activism, that would like to inspire broad changes in human behaviour. Pile the catastrophic data high enough—the fifteen-million-year high in atmospheric carbon dioxide levels, the two trillion tonnes of melted sea ice, the steeply declining EROEI ratio for unconventional oil sources, the towering bars on the graph representing toxic assets and defaulted loans—and people will see the light of reason. They'll change. They'll *get it*. This is a notion as mythic as the rational actor himself, and as clear an indication as any of just how fully we have botched the job of shaping our choices and pursuing our best interests.

Behavioural economics has much to say about the reasons why we've done such a lousy job. The short answer is that the human mind is plagued with cognitive biases, which collectively form a thick fog of misapprehension between our conscious minds and every decision we've ever made (or, if you prefer, between the hard math of economic theory and the chaos of economic reality).

We are deluded by *optimism bias*—the vast majority of us, for example, rank our ability to drive a car or make a fortune as above average, even though it is of course mathematically impossible for 90 percent of a group to be above average. An "illusion of control" perverts our assessment of our ability to make favourable outcomes happen.

As a result of what Thaler calls *availability bias*, we're easily convinced some rare occurrence—a robbery, a terrorist attack, a cash windfall—is more likely to happen because such an event has just conspicuously transpired up the block or in the news, making a case in point readily available to our irrational minds.

Similarly, *representativeness bias* tells us erroneously that something we've just seen happen more than once is governed by skill and not by chance. Thaler's case in point is the "hot hand" myth in basketball—the idea that a player who has sunk several shots in a row has a better chance of sinking another, which numerous studies have disproven.

Studies have also shown, repeatedly and across cultural divides, that we are hugely susceptible to social pressure even when we claim it has no effect on us, and we are naturally inclined to conform with the behaviours and opinions of others, even when we know they are wrong. Indeed recent research has found that *cultural cognition*—our tendency to align our perspectives with the cultural groups with which we most closely identify—is more important than age or education or professed political affiliation in determining what we believe to be true, even about independently verifiable scientific facts. And finally our *affective forecasting*—our ability, that is, to determine whether our choices will lead to outcomes that improve our well-being—is simply abysmal.

Probably the biggest obstacle in the way of a successful Leap (and an efficient economy) is the *status quo bias* that derives from our aversion to loss. We are much more deeply invested in where we are than in where we might be able to go. This was the discovery that launched the whole field of behavioural economics—Kahneman's realization that utility theory made no distinction between a dollar gained and a dollar lost. *People*, on the other hand, make enormous distinctions between the two. For example, he and his fellow researchers uncovered a powerful force they called the *endowment effect*, which strongly biases us in favour of clinging to what we have—to the status quo.

There's a particularly clear illustration of the endowment effect in an experiment conducted by behavioural economist Dan Ariely and recounted in his best-selling book *Predictably Irrational*. Ariely teaches at basketball-mad Duke University, where a lottery is held each year to determine which students will get tickets to see the men's basketball playoffs. Students camp out in front of the ticket office for days in advance of the lottery, even though being first in line only guarantees them a ticket in the lottery, not admission to a playoff game. One year, Ariely talked to more than a hundred lottery participants after the draw had been completed, asking the winners what price they would sell their tickets for and asking the losers what price they would pay. On average, the losers were willing to pay about $170 for a ticket; the winners wanted $2,400. "Not a single person was willing to sell a ticket at a price that someone else was willing to pay," Ariely writes. The reason for this irreconcilable gap is that as we contemplate a change, "we focus on what we may lose, rather than what we may gain." In other words, we almost always overvalue the things we already have, and we assume they will seem as valuable to everyone else as they feel to us. This makes us hugely resistant to making a change—whether it's the sale of a ticket or the switch to a new energy source—no matter how much better what we stand to gain may be compared to what we might lose.

One of the critical details in Ariely's experiment is the huge range in *value* assigned to the ticket. How could $2,400 and $170 possibly seem like reasonable prices for the exact same thing? Ariely explains this by way of a concept he calls *arbitrary coherence*. In a wide range of situations, he found that people used wholly arbitrary base prices as "anchors" and then projected a false coherence on the whole market from that anchor. In one experiment, Ariely discovered that he could persuade his subjects to anchor their auction bids on a range of random luxury goods of unknown value simply by getting them to write down the last two digits of their Social

Security numbers. On average, those with higher numbers wound up willing to bid significantly more than those with lower numbers. "Our first decisions," Ariely concluded, "resonate over a long sequence of decisions. First impressions are important, whether they involve remembering that our first DVD player cost much more than such players cost today . . . or remembering that gas was once a dollar a gallon, which makes every trip to the gas station a painful experience. In all these cases the random, and not so random, anchors that we encountered along the way and were swayed by remain with us long after the initial decision itself."

The arbitrary coherence of pricing, the endowment effect on value, the very fact of emotion and bias in economic decision-making—all of this combines to eviscerate the mythic rational actor and undermine the basis of classical economics. This represents a huge obstacle facing the shift to sustainability—maybe the greatest one—because coaxing mainstream economists over to the behavioural side is essential to the Great Leap. Daniel Kahneman explains why:

> Many people think of economics as the discipline that deals with such things as housing prices, recessions, trade and unemployment. This view of economics is far too narrow. Economists and others who apply the ideas of economics deal with most aspects of life . . . Economists are also the gatekeepers who control the flow of facts and ideas from the worlds of social science and technology to the world of policy. The findings of educators, epidemiologists and sociologists as well as the inventions of scientists and engineers are almost always filtered through an economic analysis before they are allowed to influence the decisions of policy makers.

In essence, economists are the arbiters of what is feasible, the hidden authors of those messages like the ones about hotel room towels that explain what people like us are capable of doing. Convincing just a few influential economists of the feasibility of a Leap, then, could be as valuable to its successful launch as a grassroots campaign with adherents in the millions.

The obstacles obscuring our ability to see the sustainable *there* from our unsustainable *here* extend far beyond the spreadsheets of conventional economists. There is, for example, an endlessly chattering class of "experts" on public policy, the economy, climate and energy issues who have been vested with a collective voice of authority despite showing no ability to outperform blind guesswork in their predictions about what our future will look like. This was the upshot of *Expert Political Judgment*, a systemic, twenty-year statistical study of the accuracy of the predictions of media-sanctioned experts by the psychologist Philip E. Tetlock. Perhaps the most troubling finding of Tetlock's study was that the most prominent experts in the most specialized fields were the *least* successful at predicting future outcomes in their fields of expertise. The loudest voices in the public debate over what to do about the economy, energy scarcity, climate change, and nearly every other problem we face simply don't know what they're talking about when they talk about where we're heading or how we'll get there.

Beyond this, there are the structural biases of the system itself, the enormous forces of inertia built into the great roaring engine hauling us down this unsustainable track. Much of this stuff falls under the subcategory of "externalities"—a vast bargain bin containing everything from the actual replacement value of a nonrenewable resource like oil to the risk associated with handing out toxic loans to the billions of tons of carbon dioxide belched skyward for free each year as an untallied cost of business as usual.

In conventional accounting, the replacement cost of oil is effectively zero, in that it is assigned no value until it is extracted; but if the term means what it says, the true replacement cost of a barrel of oil (let alone eighty-six million barrels per day) might be infinity, as a stand-in for *not for all the money in the world*. And even where the real cost of such externalities can be reasonably calculated, the numbers quickly ascend to such staggering scale that to internalize them would price most of our daily lives out of the market overnight. One study factored the cost of deforestation, greenhouse gases, and employee health care into a McDonald's hamburger and estimated its full price at about $200. Or consider the staggering range of externalities associated with our reliance on the automobile for transport—the cost of damages done by carbon dioxide chugging out the tailpipe, the full price of the fuel itself, the impact on public health and the social costs of accidents and exhaust clouds and car-centred sprawl. And then consider that the estimated cost of just the *noise* all that traffic makes is around $5 billion each year in decreased property values and other such damage in the US alone. Tally up all of these externalities, and the result is a tragedy of the commons on a global scale.

There are also institutional biases contained in the problems themselves. Climate change, in particular, involves a whole host of cognitive dissonances that almost invariably add up to inaction. A task force assembled by the American Psychological Association in 2008, for example, uncovered a lengthy list of psychological barriers to significant action in response to the climate crisis. The psychologists found that the climate problem is infected with both "spatial and temporal discounting," in that the effects of any action taken now won't be felt until much later and may only be felt far away. It is also a classic case of "split incentives"—the owner of an apartment building, for example, has to cover all the costs of installing high-efficiency windows, while the renters reap much if not all of the benefit. The consequences of climate change are unpredictable in their timing and uncertain in their scale, scope and location. And in any case they are most likely to occur in the distant future, without obvious analogies in the present or recent past; they amount to a fuzzy knot of potential problems barely visible on the far horizon. The *costs* of bold action, meanwhile, are immediate and definite—often as close and tangible as next month's power bill. Then there is peer pressure, misinformation, mounting distrust in authorities and institutions generally, even "simple habit"—all of it combining to create a steady and powerful collective pressure against changing our ways.

So then. We pretty much pluck the value of things out of thin air, and then we cling to those arbitrarily precious things as if our lives depend on it. We can't see our own blind spots, and we're easily manipulated by our peers and by the persuasive propaganda of the myriad defenders of the status quo, who we are naturally inclined to conform with anyway. We know nothing of the real cost of things and we've externalized the most significant items on the bill. We are terrible at predicting what will make us happy and improve our future well-being under the best of circumstances, and we face a cluster of problems characterized by long time horizons, massive uncertainties as to scale and scope, significant short-term costs and unknown long-term benefits, and few precedents.

We are, in effect, stumbling blind on the edge of a cliff of unknown width and depth, utterly incapable of seeing what's on the other side or assessing its use to us even if we could see it.

And in any case, we have barely a clue how to build a bridge across or even what such a bridge might look like. The price tag seems too high and we are suspicious of the builders, the engineers, even the *building materials*. We are inclined by habit, circumstance and genetic disposition to stay where we are. These are the dimensions of the obstacles in our path.

We can't *see* there from here? Hell, we barely know what we mean by *here* and *there*. And the best tools we've found to leap over the whole confused mess are the heretical notions of a few rogue economic theorists and the lab trickery of a handful of unconventional psychologists? Could that possibly be enough?

The answer, just maybe, is yes. The main lesson of behavioural economics is that this heap of obstacles *can* be surmounted—using preposterously simple tools, it turns out—as long as you take all those biases and misconceptions into account. The trick is simply to see the obstacles clearly and design the system to anticipate them and channel them in the direction of the desired outcome. Every highway in North America provides a case study in this process—not only in the careful engineering and elaborate signage of the road itself but also in the way everything from underfunded public transit and poorly designed bike lanes to property-tax codes and municipal zoning regimes have strongly encouraged the use of the private automobile. Richard Thaler and Cass Sunstein call this design process "choice architecture."

A particularly high-profile example of the effectiveness of choice architecture was Barack Obama's presidential campaign, the messaging for which was quietly guided behind the scenes by a team that included Thaler and Sunstein, as well as Daniel Kahneman and Dan Ariely. Their timely advice on how to frame and deliver messages helped Obama navigate a political minefield that had derailed the campaigns of previous Democratic candidates.

Another member of Obama's messaging team was Robert Cialdini, who has expanded greatly on his work with hotel towel signage, bringing the principles of behavioural economics closer to the consumer mainstream than any of his colleagues. Cialdini's pioneering work in the subtle art of mass persuasion has produced such surprising results that he has found himself a new career in cleantech consulting. As chief scientist for a company called Opower, he has essentially become a choice architect for the consumer energy business, assisting dozens of utility companies with their communications, all with the simple but elusive aim of encouraging customers to use less energy. Opower's preferred tool is so trivial—so juvenile, really—that it sounds at first like a joke. What is this revolutionary tool? A smiley face.

Here's how Cialdini and his Opower colleagues discovered the surprising power of a cartoon smile. In a series of studies and billing experiments, they examined a variety of ways to reward customers for reducing their energy use. In an early field test in San Diego, California, Cialdini simply hung information cards with a range of messages from customers' doorknobs. Some urged customers to cut their consumption for the sake of the environment or the well-being of future generations, while others explained in clear, rational terms how much money could be saved. These households did no better at saving energy than those that received no message at all. "Information and exhortation was the same as nothing," Cialdini later told a reporter. "Changing people's knowledge, changing people's attitudes, changing people's beliefs are all on the surface of changing their behaviour. So let's cut to the chase: Let's change their behaviour."

The only sign that had a significant impact was one stating that the majority of the recipient's neighbours were participating. Cialdini again: "If your neighbors are doing it, it means it's feasible. It's practicable. You can do it—people like you. It was very important that we say 'people in your neighbourhood.' If we said 'the majority of Americans,' that wasn't effective. If we said 'the majority of Californians,' that was more effective. If we said 'the majority of San Diegans,' that was more effective. But the most effective was 'the majority of your neighbours.' That's how you decide what's possible for you: what people in your circumstance are able to do."

In his work with Opower, Cialdini instructed his utility company clients to add a small packet of data to the power bills, a tidy bar graph indicating the average consumption for the neighbourhood and a comparative stat for the household receiving the bill. This tactic inspired considerable energy savings in homes that were using more power than the average. But it backfired with households that were beating the average; the knowledge that they were using less than the norm led them to actually increase their use, as if they'd been given licence to be a little more wasteful. On later bills, households performing better than the norm had smiley faces printed next to their consumption figure. This turned out to be the key to across-the-board success. At more than thirty utility companies, Opower's smiley-face bill has reduced energy consumption by 1.5 to 3.5 percent. It has done so consistently, at a cost of almost nothing. It doesn't sound like much, but in the conservation game this is a substantial shift in consumer behaviour, and more than that it provides an effective template, a new way of thinking through the process of change. When it comes time to ask everyone to jump, this is the way the call to action must be phrased.

It may turn out that we won't see the sustainable horizon with real clarity until we've arrived there. And in any case it turns out the best way to get everyone on board for the trip from here to there is not to paint a vivid picture of the wonders to be found there or of the horrors that await those who stay here. The truly vital piece of information is a sort of self-fulfilling prophecy. We are all going to make The Leap because we hear that everyone is doing it.

A QUANTUM LEAP CANNOT BE MEASURED WITH A YARDSTICK

Measurement tools have built-in biases as surely as human beings do. Our arsenal of socioeconomic yardsticks was designed to measure particular things on specific scales. The statistics they yield often have enormous blind spots, and they ignore anything they can't measure, often turning the most vital details into de facto externalities. The examples of these miscalculations are the stuff of the worst daily news, from the colossal miscalculation of risk that saw rating agencies award their highest certifications to bundles of toxic loans just before they erased trillions of dollars from the global economy to the most basic measure of economic health—GDP—which among other things adjudged the 1989 Exxon Valdez oil spill to be a net benefit to the Alaskan economy.

Let's stick with GDP, because it is probably the most important measurement we collect as societies—it is the bottom line in every nation's internal accounting, the short answer to the everyday question of how the economy is doing—and because its externalities are so enormous and potentially catastrophic. In response to climate change and other ecological crises, economists have begun to calculate the staggering scope of the accounting errors built into GDP measurement. One of the most ambitious of these is The Economics of Ecosystems and Biodiversity project (TEEB), a joint UN and European Union initiative. TEEB engaged Deutsche Bank economist Pavan Sukhdev and a team of specialists in a three-year study of the total value of "ecosystem services" such as clean water, flood protection and carbon sequestration provided by the earth's natural systems. Sukhdev found that environmental degradation by the world's three thousand largest corporations alone destroyed more than $2 trillion in natural capital annually. The TEEB team also discovered that the return on an investment in natural capital dwarfs even the most spectacular stock market performers. A mere $45 billion invested in the conservation of key ecosystems worldwide, for example, could generate as much as $5 trillion worth of annual ecosystem services. And the world economy could deduct $3.7 trillion from the price of reducing greenhouse gas emissions over the next twenty years simply by cutting deforestation in half over the same period.

The final TEEB report overflowed with hard data intended to make the full value of natural capital visible through conventional economic lenses. The free labour of the planet's insects, for example, provides an estimated $200 billion in pollination services each year. The city of New York saved $6 billion in wastewater treatment costs by paying landowners upriver to better manage their runoff; preserved swampland outside Kangala, Uganda, provides a similar service. Toronto's greenbelt provides a range of ecosystem services valued at CAD$2.6 billion annually. "TEEB's approach," Sukhdev explained, "can reset the economic compass and herald a new era in which the value of nature's services is made visible and becomes an explicit part of policy and business decision-making."

Another crucial metric that falls outside the purview of GDP and other conventional economic yardsticks is *social capital*. The term refers to a vital but elusive social force, an admixture of trust, reciprocity, co-operation and information exchange that forms the glue of civil society. Wherever researchers have found social capital in abundance, they've also found lower crime rates, better public health, less official corruption, and more efficient capital and labour markets. As the British government's Office of National Statistics puts it, people living in places rich in social capital tend to be "housed, healthy, hired and happy."

Social capital has, however, proven extremely difficult to quantify, leading to a tragic underestimation of its value. "Social capital"—so began a 1999 lecture on the subject by the influential political theorist Francis Fukuyama—"is important to the efficient functioning of modern economies, and is the *sine qua non* of stable liberal democracy." Alas, as Fukuyama noted, "producing anything like a believable census of a society's stock of social capital is nearly impossible." And since governments and businesses are loathe to prioritize that which they can't precisely measure, the era of ballooning GDP after the Second World War has been accompanied by a precipitous decline in social capital supplies in much of the world.

Because attending a meeting of the local community association or having the neighbours over for dinner doesn't directly contribute to GDP, it has been discounted by the same blunt accounting that sees no value in trees left standing or oil left underground. And the habitual oversight of social capital points at one of the most damaging effects of GDP as a measurement: its total blindness to the essential but intangible details of healthy, sustainable human life. GDP can measure average incomes and material standards of living, but it says very little about well-being and quality of life.

For these and many other reasons, a cottage industry has emerged in recent years to formulate alternative measurements of national well-being. One of the most widely cited is the UN's Human Development Index (HDI), which emphasizes quality-of-life variables such as life expectancy, public health expenditures and gender equality alongside GDP; one of the quirkiest is the "Gross National Happiness" stat invented by the tiny Buddhist kingdom of Bhutan. Probably the most ambitious, though, is the French government's Commission on the Measurement of Economic Performance and Social Progress, which charged Nobel-laureate economists Joseph Stiglitz and Amartya Sen and a team of other experts with finding a better shorthand for the overall health of France than the raw measurement of all the commercial activity taking place inside its borders.

The Stiglitz-Sen team reported back to the French government in September 2009 with a somewhat disappointing short answer: Well-being is simply too complex to be accurately tracked by a single measurement. *The New York Times* called the report "a treatise on the inadequacy of GDP growth as an indication of overall economic health." The report itself used the metaphor of trying to operate a car with only one gauge on its dashboard, recommending instead at least seven new "indicators" of overall performance to be added to GDP, from health and education statistics to connectedness, equity and sustainability. Stiglitz and Sen also recommended the introduction of a "depletion charge" to compensate for the externalized costs as natural resources are brought into production and added to GDP. "What you measure affects what you do," Stiglitz told reporters upon the report's publication. "If you don't measure the right thing, you don't do the right thing."

Though commissioned by President Nicolas Sarkozy himself and thoroughly reviewed by top officials at both the Organization for Economic Co-operation and Development (OECD) and the European Union, the Stiglitz-Sen report probably won't lead to the obsolescence of GDP in France or anywhere else any time soon; there are simply too many gears in the global economy's clockwork timed to its rhythms for any single jurisdiction to change the pace without throwing off the whole mechanism. It's highly unlikely, in other words, that the proper instruments will be in place ahead of time to accurately measure the scope and impact of The Leap. To try and measure its costs and benefits solely using conventional economic metrics like GDP would in any case be something like trying to test a canal's efficiency on horseback. You would get a result, but it wouldn't be accurate and it would likely indicate failure.

Consider Europe's experience with renewable energy, routinely dismissed until just a few years ago as a niche alternative power source verging on irrelevancy and still often discussed in the distant future tense. In 2009, more renewable energy came online in Europe than power from new coal, natural gas and nuclear facilities *combined*. Wind and solar power in particular have so thoroughly surpassed their predicted near-term limits that there should by rights be no credibility left to the forecasts of conventional energy planners and economists. And all this without even getting into the truly revolutionary impact renewables have on the way we measure energy (which I'll return to a little later).

Let's start with the forecasting failure. As in all things renewable, Germany has been the source of some of the most startling results. One of the earliest expert claims about Germany's renewable energy potential emerged from the German Nuclear Forum in the wake of the passage of the first modest feed-in tariff for wind energy in 1990. Renewable energy, the study insisted, would never produce more than 1 percent of Germany's power. Today, it contributes a 17 percent share, and it is on track to overtake nuclear itself as a power source in Germany within a few years.

Another study, this one a government-mandated forecast published in 1998, made a prediction for the size of the renewable sector's contribution to the German grid in 2000—just two years after the study's publication—that underestimated the reality by a factor of three. The same study's estimate for the total size of German solar installations by 2020, meanwhile, was exceeded in 2008 *by a factor of ten.* Twelve years ahead of forecast, Germany had ten times as much solar power as the study anticipated— which is to say solar capacity has grown at least 220 percent faster than predicted. Just before Angela Merkel's election as German chancellor in 2005, she dismissed plans for a 20 percent share from renewables by 2020 as "unrealistic." She soon unveiled plans to build twenty-six new coal plants to make up the forecasted shortfall as nuclear plants came offline. The vast majority of these plants are now on hold, have had their intended power source switched to natural gas or biomass, or have been scrapped entirely, and her own environment ministry has embraced a 35 percent target for renewables by 2020.

The forecasters tell similar fairy tales of dwarfish growth beyond Germany's borders. Consider the 2002 *World Energy Outlook,* published by the IEA (that most trusted name in conventional energy number-crunching). Its estimate of total installed wind energy capacity for the European Union in 2020 (57,000 megawatts, or MW) was surpassed in 2008; the actual installed capacity across the EU at the end of 2009 (74,767 MW) beat the *World Energy Outlook* prediction for 2030 (71,000 MW). To underscore: Europe is *twenty-one years* ahead of schedule on its wind energy production. Even the renewable energy industry itself has been prone to underestimating its potential. A 2004 report by the European Photovoltaic Industry Association, for example, cited 3,000 MW of installed solar power across Europe as a realistic estimate for 2010, with 5,000 MW as a best case. Germany cleared the best-case target for the whole continent all by itself in 2008.

There is, in short, an enormous status quo bias in the energy industry that permeates through to the estimation of the merits of new players in the game. This is perhaps to be expected, since energy is the world's largest industry and one of its most vital — its status quo is weighed down with more baggage than any other. But its most important end product is nevertheless intangible and wholly fungible — a stream of electricity will light up the same bulbs and power the same appliances regardless of its source. Its customers, in other words, have no particular investment in *how* electricity is made, only that it is readily available. The current players thus have huge and uniquely vulnerable vested interests in the conventional structure of the industry, which rests on generations of habit, subsidy and bias, beginning with a sort of unintentional original sin. To wit: since the introduction of the electricity meter shortly after the invention of the electricity grid itself, the primary interest of the energy producer has been in the *volume* of electricity sold, not the efficiency of the energy system as a whole.

From this foundation, the conventional energy business has developed its own logic and hierarchy, its own authorities and institutions, a range of presumptions, habits and cultural norms that amount to something like a world view. All of it works under the assumption that, like an expanding GDP, an increase in energy consumption is a universal good. And all of this is ultimately distilled and titrated into a single measurement of value: price per kilowatt-hour. The bottom line on the average consumer's energy bill.

Renewable energy is not simply the substitution of one power source for another—it introduces a wholly new paradigm to the energy business and provides a case study in the sometimes incompatible scales of competing measurement systems. Until the subsidies and biases of conventional energy are removed from the equation—or renewable energy's biases factored in—the value of renewables will never be accurately measured in price per kilowatt-hour.

The lead author of Germany's revolutionary renewable energy act, Hermann Scheer (whom we met in Chapter One), has provided an eloquent summation of the nature of this fundamental shift in the energy game. Here's how Scheer put it:

> The transition to renewable energy is a switch from imported energy to indigenous energies, from commercial fuels to non-commercial fuels, from large power plants to small and medium production facilities and to new conversion technologies—and not just the avoidance of emissions and nuclear waste. The totality of expenses for renewable energies—except for biofuels—results from technology costs. This is a transition from fuel business to technology business, from energy dependence to energy autonomy. I call this the techno-logic of energy sources.

The import of this new techno-logic cannot be overstated. The shift "from commercial to non-commercial fuels" alone rewrites the economics of energy production from top to bottom. Think of all the embedded and externalized costs of the supply chain leading, for example, from the mines of West Virginia to a coal-fired power plant feeding electricity to New York City's grid. The overwhelming majority of the cost—and the value—in the chain is in the process of commercializing a deeply buried and geographically proscribed fuel source. Coal companies make all their money mining, refining and delivering the fuel, and power companies make most of theirs by burning it and transmitting the electricity thus generated. From mine shaft to wall outlet, the entire value proposition is in maximizing the amount of power the consumer uses.

What's more, almost all of the externalized costs derive from this commercialization process, and they are staggering in their size. What, after all, would be an appropriate dollar figure for the replacement cost of the top 800 feet of an Appalachian mountain? What would be adequate compensation for rendering the fish in every one of the Great Lakes unfit for human consumption by blowing so much mercury out the smokestacks of coal-fired power plants? The per capita value of the loss for the estimated 13,000 people who die prematurely due to coal plant emissions every year in the United States alone? Think of all the subsidies, deferred costs, externalized risks and other biases built into a system in order to make coal-fired electricity a cheap fuel, the one with the lowest price per kilowatt-hour in many jurisdictions. This is the techno-logic of conventional energy production. This is the current energy paradigm.

Now compare this supply and value chain to the one for a renewable power source. The fuel is free, limitless, abundant and pollution-free—a legitimate cost-free externality. Once the wind turbine is erected or the solar panel mounted, the ongoing cost of operation is limited almost exclusively to routine maintenance and repair for the life of the machine. This already describes a different kind of business—one focused not on extraction and refining but on manufacturing and installation. There are virtually no externalized costs, the system rewards efficiency, and there is the net benefit of reducing fossil fuel dependence and greenhouse gas emissions in a single gesture. Renewable power can be produced much closer to the place it is used—on the same site in many cases—and its impact on the immediate environment in which it is situated is virtually nil (notwithstanding the trumped-up charges of North America's anti-wind lobby, which as I noted in Chapter One is funded in large measure by the conventional energy business itself). Because the vast majority of the cost of the whole system is embedded in the design, manufacture and installation of the physical plant, and because that cost is absorbed mostly by the manufacturer and passed on to the consumer, renewable energy remains, under the techno-logic and measurement schemes of the old paradigm, a relatively expensive fuel.

This is why the German feed-in tariff is such a revolutionary piece of legislation. It recalibrates the measuring tool on the only scale that ultimately matters: price per kilowatt-hour. Instead of attempting to factor in the externalized costs of conventional fuels—for example through a carbon tax or emissions-trading scheme—it instead factors the benefits of renewables into the electricity price. It's a simple and easily copied piece of legislation because it doesn't need to fuss with existing energy policies and subsidies and requires no elaborate emissions-measuring and trading regime or credit-swapping system. It simply translates the quantum leap Hermann Scheer described into a price point at which the system's existing logic will begin to favour it. If solar power, for example, is priced at several times as much as Germany's coal-derived electricity, then all of the externalized costs and historic subsidies are properly counterbalanced, and a solar panel becomes the better investment.

Still, for all its ingenious simplicity, the feed-in tariff's pricing scheme is not a complete measurement of renewable energy's impact, and it can't account for all of the quirks of the new paradigm by itself. Probably the single biggest drawback to most renewable energy sources, for example, is that they are intermittent, their generation levels varying with the intensity of the daylight or the force of the wind at any given moment, and there is not yet a cost-effective storage solution for industrial-scale power. Fortunately, grappling with this problem points us toward an even greater potential embedded in renewable energy's techno-logic: the smart grid.

There are few core energy technologies performing essential functions in homes and offices today that are as old as the electrical grid. For more than a century, nearly all the electricity production on earth has been conducted under a single structural model—the hub-and-spoke configuration of large, centralized power plants linked by high-voltage power lines to cities and towns across a wide geographic expanse. This model made perfect sense under the techno-logic of conventional energy. The Industrial Revolution's key fuel sources were found for the most part in rich caches far from population centres—coal mines, oil fields, natural gas reservoirs. The infrastructure for refining, transporting and combusting the fuel was expensive and technologically complex; minimizing the number of hubs on the grid was thus logistically and economically advantageous. Power plants were built at the mine's mouth or near the refinery or at a central repository, to which continent-wide pipes or global supply chains could be tidily tethered. Hydro and nuclear power, governed by the same techno-logic of big centralized production facilities (though not cursed with such outsized carbon footprints), fit neatly into the same model.

The conventional energy industry is a conservative one, and grid operators and big utilities especially so. As Kurt Yeager of the Galvin Electricity Initiative (a think tank founded by former Motorola CEO Bob Galvin in 2004 for the purpose of reconfiguring the American electricity grid) put it, "The electricity sector is dominated by monopolies that are traditionally resistant to innovation and consumer empowerment." Naturally, then, that sector has tended to view the biases of renewable energy on a difficulty scale ranging from massively inconvenient and far too costly to simply insurmountable. Renewable energy fits only awkwardly into the hub-and-spoke grid. Yes, there are scattered pockets particularly rich in fuel—windswept plains and coasts, hot and sunny deserts—but they tend to be remote from population centres and existing transmission lines, and they remain intermittently productive in any case.

The measuring tools of conventional energy count in large units, regulated by switches that can be turned on and off as needed. Even if there are huge inefficiencies—coal plants generate power at about 28 percent efficiency on average, for example, and approximately 45 percent of US power plants serve as "excess capacity," waiting on standby to be brought online in moments of maximum demand—these are *known* inefficiencies. They're factored in and accounted for. Renewables, with their frontloaded cost structures, their intermittent electricity flows and their small and dispersed generating capacities, are an expensive hassle—far more trouble than the single-digit percentages they currently contribute to most electrical grids can justify.

Look from a less blinkered point of view, however, and the most intractable problems with renewable energy become the locus of greatest opportunity. This is the lesson being learned in the country where wind power contributes the largest share to the national grid anywhere in the world—Denmark. For a generation now, the Danes have been world leaders in wind energy production and turbine manufacturing. The wind industry employs more than 20,000 people in Denmark—a substantial figure in a country of five and a half million—and wind turbines generate more than 20 percent of its electricity. Doubling down on its early success, the Danish government recently committed the country to expanding wind capacity to 50 percent of its grid by 2025.

As Danish energy officials began making plans for this expansion, they quickly encountered several of the biggest knocks against renewables—particularly the problems of intermittency and storage. At present, Denmark "balances" its wind energy load by borrowing energy from its hydropowered neighbours, Sweden and Norway, when the wind isn't blowing, and by selling excess wind power in the other direction when it is. But this is an expensive and complicated process that couldn't reasonably be expanded to the scale of a grid drawing the majority of its power from the wind, and the grid itself would need an expensive upgrade in any case. In a country with no other domestic energy sources and such substantial investment and employment in the wind sector, abandoning the 50 percent goal was not an option. Instead, the response to these challenges was to simply hunt harder for a solution.

A consortium of academics and industry experts was assembled to tackle the problem, but the intermittency issue seemed intractable—until the Danes discovered a new sort of yardstick. There was another ambitious national program just getting underway, a plan to expand the number of electric vehicles (EVs) on the road from basically zero to as many as 500,000 by 2025. Danes pay a steep 200 percent luxury tax on new automobiles, but this tax will be waived for electric cars. So what would happen if the grid developers were to assume that goal was met—to assume, that is, that hundreds of thousands of EV's was deployed across the country? Cars scattered as far and wide as wind turbines, parked overnight (when the wind blows strongest) in garages and breezeways, and parked again during the day (when electricity demand peaks) in the lots of offices and factories and malls? What if you measured balancing capacity not in the number of grid connections to Swedish hydroelectric plants but in the number of electric-car batteries parked across the country? Feed the wind power to plugged-in car batteries overnight, feed it back to the grid by day. The Danes would have a durable solution to their grid problem, and the car owner would profit at both ends—buying cheap, abundant electricity for the car when demand was at its lowest and selling excess stored power at a premium when demand peaked.

This value proposition became the backbone of Project EDISON (short for Electric vehicles in a Distributed and Integrated market using Sustainable energy and Open Networks)—Denmark's trailblazing experiment in smart-grid development. The timing proved fruitful: the Danes hatched their plan in 2008, just as the smart grid was becoming one of the hottest buzzwords in all of high-tech. Now, *smart grid* refers to an electrical grid integrated with two-way electricity meters fitted with digital communications tools to enable a vast range of new management and pricing features. Which is a dry way of saying the smart grid gets entrepreneurial minds racing and investment capital flowing at a speed and scale heretofore reserved for world-beating internet companies. Project EDISON's industry partners soon included German industrial titan Siemens and US computing giant IBM, and tiny Denmark emerged as the test bed for the state of the art in an industry that attracted more venture capital investment worldwide in 2009 than any other sector outside biotech and could be worth almost $200 billion by 2015 (up from $69 billion in 2009). Faced with a messy conundrum posed by renewable energy's new paradigm, the Danes swapped their old yardstick for a new one and found themselves sizing up the dimensions on a new headquarters for the smart grid's Silicon Valley.

Not that this emerging smart-grid boom has been limited to Denmark. Indeed Project EDISON's enticing value proposition—the compound sum reached by combining renewable power with digital communications (with or without electric cars)—has found enthusiastic support and major financial backing in Silicon Valley itself and far beyond. In addition to old-guard electricity companies such as Siemens and GE, the smart grid's promise has attracted the companies that built the internet's backbone (Cisco, Sun Microsystems) and its most important applications (Google, Microsoft), plus a host of smaller software firms and the Chinese government. John Chambers, CEO of digital network giant Cisco, called smart grids a business opportunity "several times as big as the internet," while a California utility executive predicted, "We'll see more change on the electric grid in the next twenty years than we saw in the last hundred."

The enthusiasm is understandable: electricity production is a multi-trillion-dollar operation, and for most of its history it has been the sole domain of a handful of slumbering giants. Approximately 75 percent of US utility companies, for example, are private monopolies whose success is wholly tethered to increasing energy demand. Electricity prices, meanwhile, are often flat, distorted "blended" rates—averages that combine absolute peaks (when highly inefficient and expensive excess-capacity plants are brought online) with deepest lulls (when demand sometimes drops well below supply). This has left a staggering abundance of low-hanging fruit—in the US, just a 5 percent cut in peak electricity demand could eliminate the need for 625 new power plants over the next 20 years. A pilot project conducted by Connecticut Light & Power in 3,000 homes saw its customers reduce their peak energy use by more than 16 percent using a combination of smart-grid applications and time-of-use energy pricing.

As for *how* such enormous change could occur, the answer is ultimately not in any particular technological breakthrough but in its application—not in what energy is used for but in how it is counted. The killer app is a new measuring tool, a *smart meter* calibrated for the other side of a quantum leap in energy accounting, where the goal is no longer to maximize the volume of energy produced but instead to maximize the *efficiency* of production.

Employing a host of internet communications tools, smart meters work together with time-of-use pricing and wireless appliances to maximize efficiencies across the whole system. Energy is bought (and, as renewables expand to household and commercial rooftops, sold) based on actual demand; a washing machine is told to wait awhile for the price to drop before starting its wash cycle; an air conditioner or furnace shuts itself off as prices climb; and the electric car in the garage or parking lot responds in kind, replenishing itself when the price is cheap, with the option of selling off spare power when the price is highest. As is the case with many Leaps, the benefits of the smart grid are *compound* benefits, mutually reinforcing. The smart grid yields unexpected bounties far larger than could have possibly been measured with conventional energy's production-driven yardsticks.

Recall Joseph Stiglitz's caveat about conventional measures of economic success: *What you measure affects what you do.* In the case of energy, our traditional yardstick has determined the entire industry's fundamental alignment toward the relentless production and use of more. But measuring tools affect what we do in more subtle ways that can also prove to be serious impediments to a Leap. Urban planning, for example, provides a stark illustration of how much bias is built into the simple decision of what to measure and what not to.

In cities around the world, there are few problems more intractable than traffic. And such is the scope of the problem that there are few problems more meticulously studied, analyzed, measured. At most city halls, though, such measurement has long been limited almost exclusively to motor vehicles. *Traffic* refers by default to the volume of motor vehicles on a given roadway, and it is measured by counting cars and parking spots and the length and duration of motorized commutes and highway traffic jams.

But in 1962, in Copenhagen, Denmark, the main downtown shopping street was closed forever to motor vehicles, and a young researcher from the local architecture school named Jan Gehl began to count other things. He counted people strolling and window-shopping, people sitting on the rims of fountains and in the seats at Copenhagen's precious few outdoor cafés. He counted people on bicycles. Working all by himself at first, Gehl developed the modern city's first database of non-motorized traffic. In the decades that followed, his statistics would inspire an urban planning revolution that has come to span the globe.

Gehl's revolution began in Copenhagen itself, where pedestrianization of the main drag had been enormously unpopular when first proposed and cursed as the death of downtown shopping by local merchants. By sharing his data with city officials, Gehl was instrumental in persuading them of the value of the initial closure and the wisdom of closing further streets to automotive traffic, expanding the city's network of bike lanes, and encouraging the proliferation of outdoor café seating. Year to year and decade to decade, Copenhagen's planners could track their success, tweak the system and improve its efficiency.

Copenhagen now boasts possibly the world's best pedestrian and bicycle infrastructure, which has been seamlessly integrated with its public transit and road systems—just a few of the factors that have made it one of the most livable and sustainable cities on the planet. And thanks to Gehl and his simple set of data-gathering tools, it has become an easily imitated global model for urban redesign. All this simply by creating a new measuring tool—one that clearly quantifies the value of a Great Leap in sustainable urban design so it makes immediate sense to planning and transportation departments in cities the world over.

From London, England, to Melbourne, Australia, Jan Gehl's number-crunching technique has been widely disseminated in recent years, leading to welcome and dramatic change. Downtown Melbourne provides a particularly strong example of the impact of Gehl's "Copenhagenization" process. Once dismissed as "an empty, soulless city centre," Melbourne's inner city has become a densely populated, round-the-clock hub and the envy of cities across Australia.

A more recent case study, just underway, demonstrates how broadly Copenhagen's approach to measurement can be applied, because it deals with such a singular city: New York. With the aid of Gehl's consulting firm, New York's Department of Transportation and its dynamic commissioner, Janette Sadik-Khan, assembled an unprecedented array of statistics about New York's street life, from accident and vacancy rates along congested thoroughfares to the surprising paucity of street cafés on Broadway. The data sold New York's technocratic mayor, Michael Bloomberg, on the idea of a broad Copenhagenization plan—a Leap from gridlock to street-level sustainability. Within two years of Gehl's first surveys, Sadik-Khan's team had added 200 miles (about 320 kilometres) of new bike lanes and dozens of new public squares and plazas, and they've redesigned the whole length of several major thoroughfares to better accommodate pedestrians and bikes as well as cars.

An even more dramatic transformation in the transportation game has taken place on the legendary plain in Spain. It is a story of fast trains and their lasting impact far beyond the station, and it begins with a bold and risky Leap made in the early 1990s by Spain's president, Felipe González Márquez. González came to office after several generations of decline and infrastructural decay under the brutal Franco dictatorship, inheriting a nation whose woes included a rail network that was a continental laughingstock. The Spanish system was antiquated and legendarily inefficient, and it included strangely gauged trains requiring pointless mid-journey transfers.

With the Barcelona Olympics and the Seville World's Fair in the offing and a generous flow of European Union money coming in, ambitious infrastructure was suddenly all the rage in Spain, so González decided to look beyond incremental upgrades. He decided not to settle for a slightly less pathetic system; instead, he committed Spain to building Europe's most advanced high-speed train network, and he began with a link between the capital, Madrid, and his hometown of Seville. It was an unpopular move, especially among González's opponents in Spain's hyper-partisan political arena, who saw the choice of Seville as an outsized handout to González's constituency. The most obvious and practical test route for this crazily ambitious scheme was the much more densely populated corridor between the two largest cities, Madrid and Barcelona, not from Madrid to Seville across the windswept Castilian plain traversed in fiction by the hapless Don Quixote. Like Cervantes's doomed hero, González looked like he had lost his way—and his political legacy—tilting at windmills in La Mancha.

A generation later, González looks like one of the world's great transportation visionaries. High-speed rail is fast emerging as *the* great global infrastructure play of the early twenty-first century, and Spain is now blessed with possibly the world's best model— the Alta Velocidad Española (AVE) network. By 2020, 90 percent of Spaniards will reside within fifty kilometres of a high-speed rail station, and the country will be as well positioned as any in Europe for the transportation needs of an unstable climate and scarce fossil fuels. Within a year of the launch of the Madrid–Barcelona AVE line in 2009, air traffic along the route fell 46 percent.

What's more, Spain discovered the compound effect of a Great Leap. It began with the careful measurement of passenger traffic along that first AVE route from Madrid to Seville, which uncovered a wholly unexpected result—trains that were leaving Madrid full were arriving in Seville half-empty. The entire focus of high-speed rail had been improving transportation between the big cities, so this appeared at first to be a problem. Passengers were inexplicably getting off at one of the first stops outside the Madrid metropolitan area Ciudad Real, a mostly forgotten city on the Castilian plain, 200 kilometres south of the capital.

Ciudad Real had been several hours from Madrid by slow train or highway, but now it was less than an hour's pleasant train journey at 300 kilometres per hour. With little in the way of encouragement, a growing number of people had taken to using the train to commute to and from Madrid. Spanish rail officials quickly realized their problem was actually an enormous opportunity, and so as the network expanded, a second category of service was introduced, a regional network called Avant, a more affordable half-step below the AVE in terms of speed (260 kilometres per hour max) and amenities, aimed at commuters.

Ciudad Real soon found itself welcoming new housing developments. Its colleges and hospitals were able to attract a higher calibre of staff, since top-notch doctors and professors could now live in Madrid and commute out to the smaller city. José María de Ureña Francés, head of the planning department at the University of Castilla–La Mancha (UCLM), is one of those professors, commuting daily to his Ciudad Real office by Avant train. "Before, the economy was very close and very local," he told me. "Now in a sense Ciudad Real is becoming part of the metropolis of Madrid. And that happens a lot within one hour of commuting."

Communities along every subsequent AVE line have witnessed the same compound effect. Segovia, an ancient clifftop jewel of a town over a high mountain range from Madrid, has been transformed from sleepy tourist burgh to commuter hub. The old industrial cities of Valladolid and Lleida along the Barcelona–Madrid line have finally been connected to the modern economy, and the second-tier manufacturing city of Zaragoza now steals conference traffic from the larger centres at both ends. The high-speed trains have transformed much more than the way Spaniards travel from one place to another. They've redrawn the map, pulling the nation together and enlarging the canvas of its collective imagination as surely as the Erie Canal once did in nineteenth-century America. In both cases, the full impact of the new transportation system could not be properly measured until after it was built.

In a similar vein, there is probably no Leap as freighted with potential—nor as difficult to measure at present—as the Great Leapfrog underway in the two most populous nations on earth, India and China. Here are Asia's two largest economies, rapidly expanding, industrializing faster than any other places in history— leapfrogging directly from a nineteenth-century industrial base to a twenty-first-century one, and throwing off wildly contradictory statistical messages like so many multicoloured fireworks in the process.

India is home to the first Leadership in Energy and Environmental Design (LEED) platinum office building ever erected outside the United States—the absolute state of the art in sustainable construction—but greenhouse gas emissions across the nation skyrocketed 58 percent in the four years after its completion. Indian cities endure rolling blackouts from a woefully overtaxed and mostly fossil-powered grid, while Suzlon Energy, born in one of those cities (Pune) ships wind turbines to new installations in the American heartland. India's industrial agriculture system teeters on the edge of collapse, while microcredit in the countryside finances a hugely successful solar-powered rural electrification program and the central government hatches one of the world's most ambitious solar energy build-outs.

China's data is even more self-contradictory. Over the course of 2009, China vaulted to the global lead in almost all the major cleantech industries. It's the world leader in the manufacture of solar panels and wind turbines, and upstart Chinese companies are vying with American and Japanese automakers for pole position in the electric car race. Just a couple of years earlier, China also became the world's number one emitter of greenhouse gases, and the equivalent of three smog-belching coal plants is being brought onto the Chinese grid every week; at one point in 2010 a twelve-day traffic jam consisting predominantly of trucks laden with coal blocked the highway into Beijing.

There is little doubt China and India will continue to be ecological nightmares for the next ten years, likely even longer. All the frantic cleantech activity at the periphery, however, hints that they may be positioning themselves for a leapfrog of unprecedented scale. Rather than spend a century or more expanding national grids, building conventional infrastructure, and mastering business-as-usual manufacturing, they could be preparing for a jump to the front ranks of the twenty-first century's sustainable global economy. In India, for example, which has never had a fully functional national electricity grid and where more than one-third of all households (and half of all rural homes) have never had electric power, the appeal of decentralized, locally produced renewable energy is much more immediate than it is in the fully gridded West. There are fewer vested interests, and there is less bias already built into energy prices. Indian telecommunications has just completed such a leapfrog: in a nation of more than a billion people served by just forty million conventional land-line telephone accounts, a nation in which the overwhelming majority of phone calls were placed at neighbourhood call booths as recently as the year 2000, more than 500 million mobile phones now operate. For many of the young Indians working in the country's nascent information economy, the phone calls they handle at call centres will be the only ones they ever negotiate on land lines. Indian telecommunications essentially skipped the twentieth century. In a generation, similar things may be said about its energy systems.

It's too soon to tell, of course, whether this emerging potential will be realized. But a key lesson of Leap Mechanics teaches us that existing yardsticks—for example, the ones that currently size up India and China as huge and fast-growing parts of the problem—have rarely proven accurate. We will only know how Asia's Leapfrog measures up once it has landed.

A LEAP IS POWERED NOT BY A DISRUPTIVE TECHNOLOGY BUT BY A DISRUPTIVE TECHNIQUE

In November 2009, the government of India unveiled an audacious plan to vault to the front ranks of the global solar industry. Freighted with the grandiose title the Jawaharlal Nehru National Solar Mission, India's new policy set as its goal the expansion of installed solar power to 22,000 MW by 2022. This represents a mammoth leap from its current capacity of just 10 MW today—which, though it provides significant impact at household scale in the rural communities where much of India's solar power has been installed thus far, is a statistical irrelevancy in a nation India's size. (It's also less total generating capacity than your typical municipal utility's solar farm in Germany.) "The objective of the National Solar Mission," the official plan declared, "is to establish India as a global leader in solar energy."

In the near term, the plan committed nearly a billion dollars in government money to developing 1,300 MW of solar power in less than five years—the lion's share of it to be drawn from large-scale solar plants. The most important piece of the plan's first-phase budget, however, might turn out to be the 10 percent of the investment dedicated to more of those small-scale rural solar installations in the mountainous far north. And it is solar panels on Indian village rooftops, in any case, that best illustrate the fourth principle of Leap Mechanics: *A leap is powered not by a disruptive technology but by a disruptive technique.*

I'll come back to the village roofs of India in a moment, but first let me be clear what I mean by a "disruptive technique." The phrase is a riff on the idea of *disruptive technology*, which was a common buzz word in the first heady days of the internet boom in the 1990s. It refers to the way certain kinds of technological innovation—graphical user interfaces, for example, those easy-to-use website–browsing applications like Microsoft's Internet Explorer—reordered every system they came into contact with. To cite again just one random example of its disruptive impact, the Web browser and its clickable, searchable, free-of-charge, instant-access approach to media content reinvented classified advertising as a free online service (under such banners as Craigslist and Kijiji), reducing a critical pillar of the financial foundation of the modern newspaper to rubble. Such is the Tasmanian Devil nature of a disruptive technology.

A Great Leap Sideways, on the other hand, is not about any given technology but about its application. It begins with a disruptive *technique*, a change in perspective and priorities that creates a new understanding of value and necessity and leads to new ways of solving problems and organizing systems. The core technologies that propel Leaps are often far from the bleeding edge. Solar photovoltaic (PV) panels are 50 years old, and the first wind-generated electricity came online in Denmark a century ago; the pedestrianized downtown is as old as civilization itself.

Technological innovation and its implementation may determine *how* a Leap is made, but first we must recognize an urgent need and find the will to fulfill it. "It took us five thousand years to put wheels on our luggage"—so goes a one-liner the sustainable design guru William McDonough frequently uses in his lectures to highlight the shifting nature of necessity.

Which brings us back to rural India, to some of the poorest places on earth. Somewhere in the neighbourhood of half a billion Indians live in homes without any electricity at all, most of them in small villages. One of the chief missions of the entire half-century enterprise of international development and humanitarian aid has been to bring basic modern necessities to such places—to deliver medicine and farming tools and electric light to the world's darkest corners—and yet the project has thus far failed 500 million Indians (and a billion more people around the world). It was in the story of a remarkable endeavour to finally deliver to rural India on development's promise that I first encountered the phrase *disruptive technique*.

The tale was told by Phil LaRocco, a gregarious New Yorker who'd spent the first two acts of his career managing his hometown's airports and working for conventional charitable foundations. In the third act, he launched a development project of his own—a reimagining of the conventional NGO as a kind of incubator for start-up energy companies. He called it E+Co, and it was founded on a pair of unconventional assumptions. First: except in emergencies, international development should be driven not by charitable public works but by private entrepreneurship, aimed at a public good but kick-started by private investment. Second: renewable energy, far from being a luxury for the world's urban elite, would find its best application among the world's rural poor. E+Co established itself with the sole purpose of soliciting investments from the wealthy to fund private businesses to install renewable power plants in impoverished villages around the world. "We think of ourselves," LaRocco told me, "not so much as a disruptive technology but as a disruptive technique."

One of E+Co's greatest successes to date is the Solar Electric Light Company of India (SELCO), which has set up more than 100,000 solar PV systems on village rooftops across rural India and provided a powerful demonstration of the impact of LaRocco's disruptive technique. From its birth in 1995, SELCO adhered to some contrapuntal ideas of its own—particularly a drive to dispel the myths that new technologies could not be afforded and used by poor people and that social ventures could not also be successful commercial enterprises. SELCO is a private, for-profit enterprise, and its customers, though they live on less than $100 per month on average, own their solar systems, buying them with microcredit financing SELCO helps them obtain from rural banks. As India contemplates its National Solar Mission, it would do well to consider the lessons SELCO has learned in the country's villages.

For more than forty years, as India followed the conventional route toward industrialization, the residents of Bommalapura, a tiny village of thirty-two households in the southern Indian state of Karnataka, looked on helplessly as modernity raced past. A major transmission line was strung just 11 kilometres up the road, and the city of Bangalore, a couple of hours down the highway, became a global hub for digital technology. But still not a single electric light pierced the night in Bommalapura—until SELCO arrived. The villagers obtained their loans in groups from a regional bank, and now all thirty-two homes have solar-powered lights. At night, they no longer need to choke on kerosene fumes so their kids can learn to read. For inspiration, those kids can look to the high school in nearby Mysore, where in 2010 a young woman educated by SELCO's lights took top marks in the whole state on her college entrance exams.

India's National Solar Mission is a plan top-heavy with big central power projects—the sort of scale that has failed the people of Bommalapura and hundreds of millions of others for generations. The country's conventional energy bureaucrats have mostly neglected to recognize the bias embedded in renewable energy—its unique ability to thrive at small scale across a decentralized and dispersed network. They have focused entirely on the fact of renewable energy technology and the technical challenges of its implementation, and not at all on the power of disruptive techniques to drive their Leap. SELCO's rural program has been held up by officials in the Indian government and beyond as a model of enlightened development for its ability to make an everyday business of what once seemed impossible—the leapfrogging of rural villages from pre-industrial darkness to renewably powered light. There is no reason to think it can't be expanded to national scale. The technique, after all, is far more important than the technology.

Government policy can itself be a disruptive technique, and it can inspire Leaps in perspective far beyond the halls of the legislature. I've already mentioned the extraordinarily disruptive force of Germany's feed-in tariff, which has turned the energy and climate crises into the wellspring of the second industrial revolution. But even less ambitious policies can create such disruptions, as oil-rich Norway has learned in the twenty years since it passed the industrial world's first direct tax on carbon dioxide emissions.

New taxes are political risks to begin with; a tax on a byproduct of the very engine of business as usual is seen as political suicide. So in most jurisdictions, the prospect of a "carbon tax" has been viewed roughly the way Superman looks at kryptonite. The Norwegian government, however, was led in the late 1980s and early 1990s by a most disruptive prime minister. In fact, her name is the short form for the UN report that first popularized the term "sustainable development." Gro Harlem Brundtland was the lead author of the 1987 report *Our Common Future*, a massively influential document often referred to as the Brundtland Report that provided the catalyst for the Rio Earth Summit and the Kyoto Protocol and more or less invented the idea of climate policy. In 1992, under Brundtland's leadership, the Norwegian government passed a piece of legislation that would be a near-impossible sell in most other oil-producing nations even today: a carbon tax specifically targeting the country's enormous oil and gas industry in the North Sea.

Oil prices were low in the early 1990s, and Norway's fossil fuel industry was already anxiety-ridden; the consensus viewpoint was that the new carbon tax would be a disaster. Instead, it proved to be a disruptive technique remarkably effective at inspiring innovation. The carbon tax said nothing about technology; it merely obliged oil companies to shift their perspective, to place a bottom-line cost on carbon dioxide emissions. Only *after* this obligatory shift in the industry's perspective did the great wave of North Sea technological change occur—particularly for Statoil, Norway's homegrown oil company.

In the 20 years since Norway passed its carbon tax, other oil companies—most famously BP in its "Beyond Petroleum" initiatives—have toyed with new energy technologies, but only Statoil leads entire sectors of the cleantech business. Statoil pioneered carbon capture and storage technology on a North Sea natural gas rig and is a lead partner in a Scandinavia-wide "hydrogen highway" initiative for emissions-free vehicles. The company also established what it calls "the first self-contained hydrogen society in the world" on the tiny Norwegian island of Utsira, pairing renewable energy with hydrogen fuel cells to develop a self-sufficient energy system at microcosmic scale. Perhaps its most substantial effort to date, however, is its trailblazing R&D work in offshore wind energy.

Here's the transformative power of a disruptive technique in a snapshot: In the wake of the carbon tax, Statoil looked at the mobile offshore drilling platforms it had been using for years to extract oil from deep beneath the North Sea, and for the first time it saw wind turbines. Floating wind turbines, moored to the ocean floor by the exact same apparatus that secures its deepwater drilling rigs. They could be installed much farther offshore than ever before, far out of sight over the horizon. With very little in the way of technological innovation, Statoil had exponentially increased the amount of offshore wind available for harvesting, incidentally also discovering a way to dodge the meddlesome opposition to wind turbines as eyesores on the landscape.

The company dubbed this new system Hywind. In 2009, Statoil installed its first floating turbine in the North Sea. Its performance, in the company's own estimation, was successful "beyond expectations," and it is embarking on its first commercial installation off the coast of Scotland (to be up and running by 2015). And in the meantime, Statoil has become a major player in offshore wind development generally. In January 2010 the Forewind consortium—a partnership between Statoil and three European renewable energy companies—signed a contract with the British government to develop as much as 9,000 MW of wind power off the east coast of England, in the same waters in which Statoil had conducted fossil-fuel drilling for decades. In less than twenty years, an oil company had been transformed into one of the world's major wind developers. Such is the ripple effect of a disruptive technique.

A disruptive technique can do more than merely alter a perception; it can entirely invert it. A city synonymous with crime, corruption and disorder, for example, can become a byword for sustainable development, its poorest slums reborn as models of urban renewal. Such is the case with not just one city in Colombia but the two largest: Bogotá and Medellín.

Rewind to the early 1990s, and both cities were ringed by shantytowns full of refugees from brutal military conflict in the countryside, riven by violent crime, drug trafficking and corruption—all but ungovernable. In 1991, Medellín saw an average of 381 homicides per 100,000 residents, earning it the dubious title of "most dangerous city in the world." The city's very name was inextricably linked with drug kingpin Pablo Escobar, who wielded more power on Medellín's streets than any government official. Meanwhile in Bogotá, the poor navigated nearly as violent a city on a transit system owned and operated in warring pieces by competing criminal syndicates. Taming the epidemic of violence seemed generations away; to suggest that either city would soon be any kind of model for the rest of the developing world was almost beyond imagining.

Now fast-forward to 2010. Bogotá's homicide rate has dropped 70 percent from its 1990s peak; Medellín's has plummeted more than 90 percent below its 1991 worst-in-the-world high, and it now sees fewer murders than Washington, D.C. Bogotá's TransMilenio bus rapid transit (BRT) system—a wholly public marvel that carries half a million commuters a day and helped reduce traffic congestion by 40 percent citywide—is a global model emulated from Peru to India. The city has more than 300 kilometres of new bike paths, and the weekly pedestrian festival on its main thoroughfare inspired New York's "Summer Streets" pedestrianization of Park Avenue. Medellín, for its part, has a vastly improved transit system, including an expansive cable-car network linking its poorest slums to the rest of the city. This Metrocable network's stations have become hubs of new commercial development. Those same poor neighbourhoods are studded with five "library-parks"—models of public placemaking crowned with world-class architecture. All of this and much more, most of it put in place in just the last ten years, has transformed two of the world's most notorious urban hellholes into case studies in low-cost sustainable development.

And the engine of this miraculous transformation? A disruptive technique strikingly similar to the one that brought solar-powered light to rural India. In both cities, visionary mayors—Bogotá's Enrique Peñalosa, in power from 1998 to 2001, and Medellín's Sergio Fajardo, who served from 2004 to 2007—took office with clear mandates for change and the same disruptive technique: an unwavering reform agenda based on the idea that cities, even impoverished and crime-plagued ones, were first and foremost places for people and public spaces, not motor vehicles and private enterprise.

Here's Peñalosa on how the technique worked in Bogotá: "I have never known a city where the people hated their city so much as Bogotá. People thought it was the most horrible city—even fourth-generation immigrants, they continued to say that they were from the origin they came from, because they did not want to say they were from Bogotá. It was a city that really was without hope, without self-esteem. And what is really amazing is it really changed beyond all my expectations. And how did it change? Really because we started making a city a little more for people and not so much for cars. It sounds very simplistic, it's almost dumb. But the fact is that we are really trying to learn a different way of life."

In Bogotá, the people learned this lesson simply by being provided with the public space in which to experience something beyond grim survival. The TransMilenio BRT system established exclusive corridors along the city's main arteries for buses, even inviting the corrupt, inefficient old private bus companies to join the network in order to avoid conflict. Public transit became, almost overnight, the most efficient way of getting around the city—faster even than a gangster's luxury car. Sidewalks across the city had long been perpetually clogged with parked cars, so Peñalosa banned sidewalk parking and strictly enforced the ban; local merchants were so incensed they nearly had the mayor impeached, but he stuck to his agenda, and in time they discovered that functional sidewalks were actually good for their businesses. Under Peñalosa, Bogotá's government established or redesigned more than a thousand parks and built dozens of new schools and libraries, boosting public school enrolment by 34 percent in the three years of his tenure. The city's poorest districts were strung together with a 17-kilometre public promenade, a car-free space called the Alameda El Porvenir that was intended merely for transportation but soon became a beloved ersatz park.

Peñalosa has pointed to the 300-plus kilometres of new bike paths as the strongest example of his disruptive perspective. "When we have a protected bicycle way, this is important because it protects cyclists. But it is also very important because it's a symbol, because it shows that a citizen on a $30 bicycle is equally important to one in a $30,000 car. This is a very powerful symbol for democracy."

Sergio Fajardo was driven by a similar sense of the power of symbols. In his reimagining of Medellín, his government's first major initiative was to build library-parks in the city's barrios—expansive green spaces with magnificent public buildings at their centre. High-quality school buildings soon followed. This is how Fajardo responded to his critics' assertion that fancy architecture was a waste of precious civic funds:

> People who say that a beautiful building doesn't improve education don't understand something critical. We have to build Medellín's most beautiful buildings in the places where there has never been a real state. The first step toward quality education is the dignity of the space. When the poorest kid in Medellín arrives in the best classroom in the city, there is a powerful message of social inclusion.

That kid has a newfound self-esteem, and he learns math more easily. If you give the most humble neighborhoods beautiful libraries, you make those communities proud of the libraries. That is powerful. We are saying that that library or school, with its spectacular architecture, is the most important building in the neighbourhood. And it is sending the rest of society a very clear message of social transformation, but of social transformation without rage. This is our revolution. The most powerful people see us focusing on the most humble, and they are supporting us—that is an important achievement.

In the extraordinary, unexpected Leaps made by Colombia's two largest cities, you can find not just a disruptive technique but all four of the Laws of Leap Mechanics at work.

A *chasm can only be crossed in a single Leap*—this first law was implicit in the first decisions made by Peñalosa and Fajardo. "The essence of the conflict today really is cars and people," Peñalosa observed, looking back half a decade after he stepped down as mayor. "That is the essence of the whole discussion. We can have a city that is very friendly to cars or a city that is very friendly to people. We cannot have both." A single Leap, then, from one hierarchy to the other, and on the other side a city that works for all its citizens, not just the minority of Bogotá's residents who own motor vehicles.

The Second Law of Leap Mechanics states that *the sustainable horizon is only visible from the sustainable track* (or, *you can't see there from here*)—again, this was a critical lesson learned on the streets of Bogotá and Medellín. In Bogotá, the idea of civic pride was far beyond the visible horizon of a self-loathing populace; in Medellín, the last thing anyone expected to see was an architectural landmark in the middle of a slum. The immediate agenda spoke of crime rates and traffic snarls. When Peñalosa arrived in the mayor's office, he was presented with an expensive study by Japanese experts, recommending that $5 billion be spent on seven new elevated highways. Mass transit was considered far beyond the budget of the impoverished city. The simple, cheap concept of exclusive bus lanes was nowhere on the planning horizon. Who knew, until it was up and running at one-thirtieth of the cost per mile for a subway system and lower operational costs than the bus system it supplanted, that a transit network capable of carrying 1.6 million passengers per day was so near at hand?

Existing measures of success were just as blind to the potential of Colombia's beleaguered metropolises. *A quantum leap cannot be measured with a yardstick*—so goes the Third Law of Leap Mechanics, and so it went on the streets of Bogotá and Medellín. How, after all, did Sergio Fajardo determine where to site his library-parks? By per-capita income? No—he used the UN's Human Development Index to decide which neighbourhoods were most in need of a monumental dose of dignity. And why did the merchant class of Bogotá and their car-driving customers attempt, very nearly with success, to have Peñalosa impeached? Because they simply could not imagine a functional civic economy without the freedom to park their cars anywhere they wanted. Only when Peñalosa's administration took into account the vast majority of Bogotá's citizens who had no cars but still had lives to lead and purchases to make did the Great Leap's logic become apparent.

"As a fish needs to swim, we need to walk. Not to survive, but to be happy." Peñalosa again—an oft-quoted maxim he learned street by street in Bogotá. A slogan to summarize the disruptive technique that drives a Great Leap, as simple as a proverb or Zen koan.

Out of such simplicity, much more complex and powerful transformation can arise. The Great Leap's narrative arcs trace paths of inspiration and liberation, reimagination and renewal. They leave contrails that point as one to our brightest possible future.

With our understanding of the mechanics now in hand, let's move on to these more detailed stories of the Great Leap in action.

< THREE >

THE LEAP IN THE NATION

THE GOOD LIFE, TWENTY-FIRST CENTURY EDITION
(TRANSLATED FROM THE ORIGINAL GERMAN)

THE MODERN INDUSTRIAL nation-state is often an unwieldy thing. Its priorities are difficult to measure, let alone to change, and in most cases its political culture is riven with fissures and fractures carved so deeply they seem as ageless and immovable as the national geography. The nation-state is a hulking rudderless barge carrying too much cargo in choppy seas, all but impossible to steer with any precision. To manoeuvre such a clumsy vessel into the proper position and correctly calculate the trajectory of its Leap, to get all its engines firing at once in the same general direction and land the thing safely on the far side—wildly improbable. To take a modern industrial society from the unsustainable track to the sustainable one in a single, unequivocal policy gesture—preposterous.

For all these reasons and more, the most impressive Great Leap Sideways yet taken is one I've already noted, the one Germany made using that revolutionary energy policy known as a feed-in tariff. Understanding *how* Germany made its leap, though, and how best to follow its lead, requires an examination not just of the details of the policy but of the context—the political culture it emerged from and the way in which it has woven itself into the broader fabric of German society. In many ways, The Leap is best understood as a lesson in speaking twenty-first century German.

I'll return to the tariff itself, which was written into German law in April 2000 as the Renewable Energy Sources Act, and which is often referred to in shorthand by its German acronym EEG (short for *Erneuerbare-Energien-Gesetz*). I'll examine as well the extraordinarily shrewd backroom negotiations that got it passed, and the staggering impact it has had on the German industrial economy and the very landscape of the country.

Let's start, though, with the inspirational end result—the exact spot all of us would surely most want to land, were we to fantasize about our brightest possible future. I would like to begin, that is, in a house at the end of the sustainable track, a home sweet sustainable home where humankind's fundamental relationship with energy has been summarily reversed after a million years of consistent flow in only one direction.

Meet Harald Müller and Barbara Braun, middle-aged, middle-class German homeowners. They live on the fringe of the city of Freiburg in the southwest of Germany, in a cozy community at the base of a steep Black Forest hillside. Harald is an engineer and Barbara was a teacher until they started their family; now her primary occupation is raising their two girls. Harald's got a lot of that famous German engineer's practicality to him, and Barbara likes to poke affectionate fun at his earnest home improvement efforts. They've got a little sign in their kitchen that reads: *Ihr seid die Hoffnung Gesicht*. Which means: *You are the face of hope.* Their Freiburg townhouse, which they purchased as it was being built in 2001, is the first home they've ever owned, and they reckon it may well be the only one. Small wonder: it's one of the first dwellings of any kind, anywhere, ever, that produces more energy than it uses.

I couldn't help but be a little skeptical about this last point, given that as long as human beings have lived in houses — really since we first captured fire — we've had a one-way relationship with energy. We've found fuel — we've gathered wood or animal dung, cut peat, dug up coal or added fluorine to uranium ore to enrich it into a fissile isotope — and then we've consumed it to cook our food, light and heat our homes, or hurtle down the autobahn at 150 kilometres per hour. And then we've discarded what remains. I was curious, to say the least, at how the Müller-Brauns of Freiburg had spun this relationship into a loop. Really, I wanted hard evidence they'd actually even done it. So I asked to see their power bills.

They were immediately forthcoming, if just a bit bemused about it all. They know on some level their house is an energy-generating wonder, but they don't quite *feel* it. They are, after all, just a couple in a townhouse, living the same life they have for almost a decade now.

They laid the bills out on their handsome wooden dining table, next to a plate of cookies. The figures were unambiguous. In 2008, the Müller-Braun household used 1,329 kilowatt-hours (kwh) of electricity and 1,757 kwh of heat energy — 3,086 kwh in total. The bank of solar panels that tiles the south-facing slope of their townhouse's roof, meanwhile, produced 7,457 kwh of power, more than double what they'd consumed.

The economics were even more impressive. They'd paid a total of €731.50 for the energy they'd used, and they'd earned €3,750.29 for the electricity produced by the solar panels on their roof — a net revenue of €3,018.79 (about $4,500). They conceded they were still a couple of years away from paying off the full cost of the solar system, but by 2012 or so, that money will be pure profit.

A number of factors contributed to the good energy fortunes of the Müller-Brauns. The light pouring onto their dining table, for example, demonstrated their townhouse's meticulous "passive solar" design. The structure's south wall is comprised of almost nothing but triple-glazed, vacuum-insulated glass, coated on the inside with an infrared seal to trap heat. The insulation is state-of-the-art, the doors and windows flawlessly sealed, interior walls coated with some next-generation "phase changing" material to trap and release heat as needed. The home's every detail had been chosen with efficiency in mind.

Harald and Barbara's townhouse was one of fifty such units in a development called the *Solarsiedlung* ("Solar Settlement"). The community was designed by a pioneering German architect named Rolf Disch to demonstrate the mass-market viability of his "surplus-energy" housing concept. (Disch's motto: *Every building a solar power station!*)

"I didn't want to buy an old-fashioned house," Harald explained, "because I just want to have something which is ade-quate for the next century." This was just grandiose enough to earn a chuckle from Barbara. "Not centuries," he conceded, "but dec-ades. Because energy prices rise in the future, and so we want to have something where you don't have to spend too much money to afford the heating and the energy."

The Müller-Brauns had been living in their power-plant house for almost ten years. They had the usual homeowners' quib-bles with this or that detail—Harald replaced the ventilation system himself because the house wasn't letting enough moisture escape for their liking—but mostly it was a house like any other. And the remarkable thing, the key detail that made it all possible, wasn't the phase-changing paint or triple-glazed glass. It wasn't that their household energy use was less than a third of the German average or that their solar-tiled roof happened to be tucked into one of the sunnier corners of Germany.

No, the truly remarkable thing, the final answer to the question of *how* this had all come to pass, was the feed-in tariff, Germany's EEG—the paradigm-shifting incentive enacted in 2000 and then substantially amplified in 2004. Like Jeremiah Thompson's promise to set sail *full or not full*, it was the long-term, unconditional guarantee the whole system needed in order to thrive. The Müller-Brauns, like hundreds of thousands of German homeowners, sell their solar-generated electricity back to the grid operator at more than four times the price they pay for power. (In return they, like all other German electricity users, pay an extra euro cent or so for each kilowatt-hour they use.) The selling rate declines over the life of the solar panels, and it is guaranteed for twenty years.

This is how a feed-in tariff works: it turns an everyday townhouse into an engine that generates five grand a year in profit. It turns homes into power plants. This is what made Rolf Disch's surplus-energy idea commercially viable at neighbourhood scale, what made it an affordable option for his clients, what has made Germany the global pacesetter—by a wide margin—in the global cleantech business.

SNAPSHOTS FROM THE SECOND INDUSTRIAL REVOLUTION

On a global scale, as I mentioned in the previous chapter, Germany is not particularly sunny and not all that windy. It has only a modest amount of coastline and not much in the way of empty space—in fact, it's one of the most densely populated countries in Europe. And it entered the twenty-first century dragging along the debt, social decay and obsolete industrial base of a failed state of sixteen million people—the defunct German Democratic Republic (the former East Germany, or GDR). A composite picture of Germany on New Year's Day 2000 might well have looked, to many eyes, like a chronic care patient's troubling X-ray.

The EEG, as I mentioned, became law in April 2000. The German economy—indeed, the very German landscape—is all but unrecognizable ten years later.

In the first decade of the feed-in tariff, Germany vaulted to the forefront of the $500-billion global renewable energy industry, with more than $50 billion in annual revenue and 300,000-plus jobs in the sector.

Germany's share of the global solar PV market is about 42 percent, and it generated revenues of more than $13 billion in 2009. There are more than 700,000 individual solar installations across Germany. More than 90 percent of these are small systems on the rooftops of residential and commercial buildings, but the remaining share includes five of the fifteen largest PV plants on the planet. New solar installations in 2010 alone amounted to more than 7.4 gigawatts (GW) of generating capacity, roughly the size of eight nuclear reactors. All told, German solar panels have a capacity of about 12 GW.

Germany is number three (behind the US and China) in terms of total installed wind energy capacity, but it remains the world's leading exporter of wind turbines and equipment. Domestically, a significant chunk of Germany's wind industry has moved from land to water—the plan is to build as many as eighty offshore wind parks (capable of generating up to 25 GW of electricity in total) in the North and Baltic seas by 2030. This new offshore wind industry has already reinvigorated the German port cities of Bremerhaven, Cuxhaven and Rostock. Their waters are

filled with the traffic of new installation vessels and tugboats hauling turbine parts, and new warehouses on the docks have been
configured for a staggeringly scaled business in the manufacture
of turbine hardware. At Bremerhaven, for example, a company
called Weserwind now produces tripod bases for giant 5-MW turbines, each of them 150 feet tall and weighing about as much as
three hundred pickup trucks, in something as close to mass production as equipment that large can come. This is Henry Ford
production at Seven Wonders scale.

It goes on and on like this.

International cleantech firms arrive and expand almost weekly,
even in the midst of worldwide economic calamity. Arizona-based
First Solar, for example, inaugurated a $230-million, 53-MW solar
farm in eastern Germany in the fall of 2009, rehabilitating an
abandoned, bomb-strewn military base in the process. The farm's
560,000 panels, manufactured at First Solar's enormous new
German manufacturing plant, are fully recyclable. Another East
German solar plant covers a decommissioned coal mine, another
still has brought new development to an old airfield that last
thrived in the age of the zeppelin.

The passive solar design principles that have made Freiburg's
surplus-energy houses such marvels of efficiency are now enshrined
in nationwide "passive house" building standards; one city,
Marburg, has also made rooftop solar water heating mandatory on
all new buildings.

New housing developments in the industrial wastes of the
GDR welcome the families of solar industry employees, and the
port at Bremerhaven is basking in its first employment boom since
the 1980s. Municipal utilities from the Baltic to the Alps are jumping into the power production business, embracing a welcome
new revenue stream.

There is, in short, virtually no corner of the country and few patches of the socioeconomic fabric untouched by Germany's Leap.

Owing to the nature of the feed-in tariff, the cost of Germany's enormous Leap is recorded almost entirely in the price of a kilowatt-hour of electricity. The final tally, as I noted last chapter, is about €3 per month on the average German homeowner's bill, or roughly €40 per year. Fifty bucks or so, then, in North American terms, for an overwhelming head start in the great industrial race of the twenty-first century.

And as much as any of these stats and snippets, there's something intangible, a big-picture kind of pride in all that the feed-in tariff has wrought. A sense amongst Germans that the Leap their country has taken had to happen somewhere, that some major industrial nation had to stop flirting and hedging and head faking and just jump already. And a sort of delighted wonder that it was Germany, having spent much of the second half of the twentieth century haunted by the ghastly legacy of totalitarian madness, that jumped first.

Here's how Tobias Homann, a solar expert at Germany Trade & Invest, the federal government's economic development arm, put it to me: "The German electricity consumer pays a higher price for this energy revolution than others do. And so people, I think, will thank Germany in the future for its role. But Germany also wins a lot from this."

Such, then, is the reward for a well-timed, perfectly orchestrated Leap. Let's take a look at how it came to pass.

GERMANY'S GREAT COGNITIVE LEAP

For Hermann Scheer—who, as I've noted, was a chief architect of the federal feed-in tariff—the path to The Leap began with a heated debate over the hot-button energy issue of a previous generation. In German activist circles in the mid-1980s, no issue was deemed more vital than the elimination of nuclear power plants from the national electricity regime.

"The main focus of the environmental movement, or of the anti-nuclear movement, was energy saving, energy efficiency, energy sufficiency," Scheer told me. "These three targets. And then the big question I put on the table was: What is the non-fossil alternative to nuclear energy?" Scheer's activist colleagues had no clear answer. He dedicated his career thereafter to finding one. "It was necessary to find a new energy paradigm—and to bring it into policies, to develop a central political strategy for that."

Scheer took to writing papers and policy proposals—one, the Solar Development Initiative (SDI), playfully echoed the acronym of Ronald Reagan's overwrought "Star Wars" Strategic Defense Initiative from the 1980s—but the work proceeded slowly. His first chance to accelerate the development of renewable energy came with the West German government's final legislative act prior to unification with the GDR in 1990: a weak surcharge on wind power, an incidental afterthought in the eyes of everyone but Scheer.

By this point, the looming menace of climate change had begun to overshadow worries about the dangers of nuclear power, and Scheer understood far ahead of his colleagues—ahead of pretty much the entirety of the global environmental movement, in fact—that the climate problem was a wholly different kind of challenge. It was far greater in scale and universal in its impact, and it would thus require a policy leap of commensurate scale. While much of the conversation in Germany and beyond focused on emissions reductions and punitive pollution policies, Scheer saw immediately that the issue's real fulcrum was not the clouds of smoke but the fuel being burned to generate them. Climate policy, as it began to emerge, would inevitably be energy policy by proxy, and the battle could only be won by supplanting the world's richest and most powerful industrial sector: the conventional energy business.

Scheer's great cognitive leap contained two more critical observations that remain unrecognized in the vast majority of the world's legislatures and parliaments. The first of these, as I explained in Chapter Two, is that the switch from nonrenewable to renewable fuel sources will by necessity reconfigure the global energy economy and build a whole new socioeconomic foundation in the nations where it is widely deployed. Renewables come with their own "techno-logic," in Scheer's phrase, beginning from the simple fact that the fuel sources themselves are free.

Scheer's second essential observation was that the leap from nonrenewable to renewable energy is best understood not as an economic burden but as the biggest and most transformative business opportunity since the dawn of the industrial age — "the second industrial revolution," as Scheer often called it. For this reason, he was a vocal critic of the UN-led emissions-target approach to climate change, which frames the climate change as a burden to be shared. Scheer argued that if the economic benefits were properly recognized, there would be no need to sign an international treaty; the cleantech industry would do its profit-making work just as well without one. When the Kyoto Protocol finally came before the German parliament for ratification in the mid-1990s, Scheer was the only member of any party to vote against it. "The Kyoto Protocol," he told me, "is not a real locomotive. It is a barrier."

Here, in sum, was Scheer's great cognitive Leap: the recognition that addressing climate change was fundamentally a question of energy; that switching to renewable fuel would precipitate a full-scale structural change of the global energy economy; that making this switch was an opportunity to replace scarce and expensive primary resources with new technology; and that it would not be accomplished by burden-sharing among conventional energy companies and bureaucracies but by replacing them with a whole new energy regime. This conceptual innovation, more than the feed-in tariff itself, is the primary engine of the social and industrial transformation now well underway in Germany.

There would come, in time, great infrastructure projects of Erie Canal scale (the colossal offshore-wind construction projects in German harbours, for example) and the innovations of a new class of industrialists reaping Vanderbilt-sized rewards (in recent years, the German stock market's TecDAX index of technology companies has become so crowded with solar companies that it's sometimes jokingly referred to as the "SolarDAX"). Before all this, though, there was Hermann Scheer, the Jeremiah Thompson of the Bundestag, setting the market conditions so that all of it could thrive—building a springboard large and sturdy enough for a nation of eighty million to leap from.

Luckily for Scheer, a grassroots campaign was already underway in a number of small cities, assembling the key components of that springboard.

THE STRATEGIC LEAP

In 1990—around the same time Hermann Scheer embarked upon his cognitive leap—the man who would become his chief parliamentary ally was elected to the municipal council in a small Bavarian town called Hammelburg. His name was Hans-Josef Fell, and he'd been awakened to the worldchanging potential of solar power at a conference the previous year. By 1993 he'd convinced the Hammelburg council to pass "cost-covering compensations" to encourage residents to put solar panels on their roofs. Similar legislation was adopted in two other German cities that year, and by the mid-1990s these newfangled feed-in tariffs had attracted the interest of municipal governments across Germany.

In Berlin, meanwhile, Scheer carried on the trench work of building cross-party political alliances and pushing for small-scale renewable energy experiments. (For example, the German government mandated a small subsidy for household-scale solar panels in a "1,000 Rooftops" initiative, which ran from 1991 to 1994.) Much more crucial, however, was the work Scheer and his growing cadre of allies undertook to lay the legal framework for the feed-in tariff. Scheer anticipated—correctly, as it turned out—that opponents of a feed-in tariff would challenge it in the European Court of Justice, arguing that it was an anti-competitive breach of European Union trade rules. So Scheer recruited legal scholars and helped establish a new journal to develop a cache of sound argumentation differentiating feed-in tariffs from (forbidden) direct subsidies.

In the federal elections of 1998, a once-in-a-political-lifetime opportunity emerged. Germany's soaring post-reunification unemployment rate sunk the ruling centre-right coalition, and an alliance of Scheer's Social Democrats and Alliance '90/The Greens (Germany's awkwardly monikered Green party) came to power, forming the "Red-Green Coalition." One of the new Green parliamentarians was Hans-Josef Fell. While Scheer piloted a "100,000 Solar Roofs" initiative through the Bundestag to get the cleantech industry geared up, Fell set to work drafting a federal feed-in tariff.

Fell had eight years of experience with municipal-scale feed-in tariffs to draw on, and he knew exactly how he wanted the new policy to be constructed. From the outset, he dismissed arguments in favour of "free market" orthodoxy, which in the case of renewable energy recommended cumbersome systems of quotas and tendering processes. (These would be tried and found wanting from the UK to the province of Ontario, both of which have switched to feed-in tariffs.) Not only was the sanctity of the free market far less important than the public good of climate protection, Fell would later write, but there wasn't an existing free market in energy to protect—it was rather "a monopolistic industry dominated by a few power groups with identical interests." Only when the feed-in tariff opened up the German energy market to new actors—smaller ones, especially—could old-fashioned marketplace competition decide the winners in this new industrial sector.

Beyond this, Fell recognized that the new policy had to provide a secure environment for large-scale investment and a market large enough to encourage economies of scale. Feed-in rates would be set high enough to ensure profitability and they would vary by energy source. The rate for solar, for example, was set substantially higher than the one for the more mature wind industry. The rates would also be guaranteed for twenty years. Red tape would be kept to a minimum. There would be no protracted approval processes, no awkward caps or Byzantine specifications on the size and placement of new power plants—simply a set price for power from each source. And since the price was to be paid not by the federal government itself but by electricity grid operators, the additional costs would be passed on to their customers. This "ratepayer model" was initially adapted to satisfy European Union trade agreements, but it turned out, as Fell later noted, to be a "decisive factor" in the new law's success. Because it required no taxpayer money whatsoever, the feed-in tariff would be free from the year-to-year budgetary whims of successive governments.

The distance between a good idea and its on-the-ground

reality is often maddeningly wide—especially in government, especially when the idea in question is a fundamental realignment of a nation's biggest industry, to be implemented by one of its most unwieldy bureaucratic arms. After considerable internal debate and negotiation, Scheer and Fell had sold the feed-in tariff concept to both governing parties. But could it possibly make it through the bureaucracy of the energy industry intact?

Here, Scheer's tactical prowess, sharpened by eighteen years in parliament, was instrumental. Before tabling their version of the law, the parliamentarians gave the ministry a tight deadline to produce a draft of its own, and even a second deadline when it failed to meet the first. The energy bureaucrats, they assumed, would be wholly incapable of reimagining their whole portfolio in a few short months. After the second deadline passed with no workable draft forthcoming, Scheer and his allies had the political capital to demand passage of the draft they'd produced. It became law—concise, crystal-clear law—in April 2000, just eighteen months after the Red-Green Coalition had come to power.

All of which is to say: Scheer and his allies understood the mechanics of The Leap intuitively, and they played the German bureaucracy with the virtuoso skill of behavioural economists to make it happen. They knew the law had to be thorough and decisive—a single leap across the chasm—but they didn't mind if it came disguised as simply a practical alternative to a bureaucratic bungle at the margins of the bigger German energy picture. What's more, they knew the entrenched bureaucracy wouldn't be able to properly map out The Leap's trajectory, let alone measure its impact. They couldn't possibly see there from here. There were several disruptive techniques at work, not least of which was the decision to anticipate the energy bureaucracy's inertia and use it as a tool to force their own draft through.

THE FOLLY OF FORECASTING

Like the Erie Canal's restructuring of American industry, the feed-in tariff inspired a rash of predictions portending doom as its architects set about reconfiguring the energy grid for the second industrial revolution. Critics deemed the rates for renewables to be far too high—rooftop solar, for example, was now selling electricity to grid operators at four or five times the price of conventional energy, threatening to smother German ratepayers in outsized electricity bills. And the targets were deemed much too ambitious for such unproven, small-scale technologies. When the government announced plans shortly after the passage of the feed-in tariff to phase out Germany's seventeen nuclear plants, critics bellowed that the coming shortfall could only be avoided by building an arsenal of coal-fired power plants.

The forecasts of catastrophe grew only more emphatic when the German government revisited tariff rates in 2003 and 2004. The law had always called for a reconsideration of the rates for each power source every four years, but solar rates were tweaked ahead of time. The 100,000 Roofs program, introduced before the law, had just ended, and the fledgling German solar industry was in grave danger of grinding to a standstill. So the feed-in price for solar power was given a significant boost, leading even some renewable energy experts—particularly those in North America— to argue that the German government had gone too far.

When I mentioned Germany's feed-in tariff to John Anderson, a solar energy analyst at Colorado's Rocky Mountain Institute, at a meeting back in 2006, for example, he quoted the going rate for German solar power and said, "I could put monkeys in cages and make power for that and make money. Good lord!" Then he settled down a bit and told me, "A certain amount of that kind of thing your economy can stand. But it can't become a very big part of your economy or your economy goes down the toilet." And then, almost in the next breath, he wondered if there might be something he was overlooking—something indeed very similar to the Laws of Leap Mechanics, particularly the ones that say yardsticks can't measure quantum leaps and that the sustainable horizon can't be seen from the unsustainable track.

"Okay, now look,"—this is how Anderson put it—"if in 1980 you'd come into my office, I'd have said I was pretty happy with telecom. Had a box on the desk in the office, had a box on the wall at home. Telecom's great. Love it. If you told me that for thirty bucks I could buy one of these things"—here he held up his mobile phone—"call anywhere in the world from anywhere, I mean I would've laughed at you. *Then* if you'd told me the highest, best economic use of that was for my thirteen-year-old daughter to stand in one end of the mall and talk to her friend at the other end of the mall while they're shopping? I mean, I'd have had you committed. That's *clearly* insane, right? Nobody would do that with something so valuable. That's absurd. That's the kind of paradigm shift that I think electric utilities are facing."

Anderson's final hunch was, in the event, the more accurate one. Far from crippling the German economy, the feed-in tariff shifted it instantly into the new paradigm Hermann Scheer had been aiming for. The new cleantech industry, already roaring along during the first four-year cycle of the feed-in tariff, truly started to fly down the track after solar was given its big boost in 2004 and offshore wind was similarly amplified in 2008 (the latter mandated by Angela Merkel's conservative government, even though her party had opposed the feed-in tariff when they were in opposition). The German solar business, for example, expanded so rapidly in 2004 it precipitated a global shortage in the silicon ingots required to manufacture solar cells.

It should be noted that Scheer fought against setting targets for renewables from the very first draft of the feed-in tariff. Why put an artificial brake on this sleek new locomotive? Why ask it to slow down just when it's hitting cruising speed? It was one of the rare arguments Scheer lost—in 2000, the German government set a goal of producing 12 percent of its electricity from renewable sources by 2010. But at Scheer's insistence, a single word was added to the official statement of the target: *mindestens*. "At least."

By the end of 2010, fully 17 percent of Germany's electricity was coming from renewables. That year alone, Germany brought more new solar generating capacity onto its grid than existed on the whole planet in 2005. The German solar industry reached the European Photovoltaic Industry Association's most optimistic 2010 target for all of Europe's solar capacity in 2008, and then added five nuclear power plants' worth of solar on top of that in just the first eight months of 2010—adding new generating capacity with a speed that beats nukes, touted for their ability to "scale" faster than renewables, by a factor of at least ten. The new national target for renewable electricity is 35 percent by 2020. *At least* 35 percent, that is.

One of the most common and sweeping expert pronouncements I've encountered on the subject of renewable energy's natural limit goes like this: *You couldn't possibly run a major industrial economy on renewable energy alone.* Impressive as Germany's transformation may be—so goes this conventional line of reasoning—it will never be total. Wind turbines and solar panels feed the grid intermittently, at the whim of the everchanging weather. The transmission grid itself isn't configured to move around such a substantial amount of renewable energy. In time, the starry-eyed dreamers of the cleantech world will have to come back to earth and see nuclear energy (and/or "clean coal") as their only emissions-free salvation. The tone of this argument is often emphatic, its conclusion presented as unassailable truth: There will *never* be a large modern nation powered exclusively by renewables. These experts clearly underestimate the tenacity and skill of German engineers.

In 2007 three major German cleantech firms—a wind turbine maker, a producer of solar panels, and a biogas-plant developer—joined researchers at the University of Kassel to conduct an experiment dubbed *Kombikraftwerk* ("Combined Power Plant"). The Kombikraftwerk project linked together thirty-six renewable energy installations across the country—wind farms, solar arrays, biogas-fuelled power plants and small hydroelectric facilities—and ran a national grid at 1/10,000th scale. This was not a simulation or a model. The project's operating system combined the actual real-world power flows from these scattered power plants, and used them to power a grid around the clock. The hydro and biomass backed up abundant but intermittent solar and wind, and the whole system was as reliable as any modern grid. As Solar World CEO Frank H. Asbeck explained, "The Combined Power Plant shows in miniature what is also possible on a large scale: 100 percent electricity provision using renewable energy sources." It is still early days for the German cleantech boom, the research and next-generation development only just begun, but I'd be willing to predict that this is not the last myth its new industry will dispel.

Predictions of impossibly high energy prices and full-scale economic collapse have proven no more accurate. The strongest drag on the German economy, ten years into the reign of the feed-in tariff, is a downturn in exports across the board as a result of the global financial meltdown. Compared to the economic fallout from the delusions of free-market fundamentalists, the $50-a-year surcharge on a German homeowner's energy bill seems like a wise investment indeed. Most of us rack up more charges than that every month on our mobile phones. Fifty bucks for a quarter of a million new jobs and $50 billion in annual revenues. Fifty bucks for a national grid that gets 17 percent of its power from renewables and climbing, and greenhouse gas emissions down 22 percent and still falling. Fifty bucks for a vanguard position in the second industrial revolution. Fifty bucks for a ticket to ride the right kind of train, pulled by a fast clean engine down sturdy new tracks, headed—the smart money would not bet against German engineering—for the world's first wholly clean-powered economy.

That's not to say there aren't some dark horses and promising long shots in this race. One of Germany's chief exports in recent years, after all, is the feed-in tariff itself.

THE FEED-IN TARIFF GOES VIRAL

In the two decades since the Rio Summit put climate change on the global policy agenda, a wide range of strategies have been deployed to reduce greenhouse gas emissions and encourage the move to renewable sources of energy. There have been rebate programs and tax breaks, direct subsidies and baroque credit-trading schemes, a UN-brokered accord mandating across-the-board emissions cuts worldwide that was widely endorsed and sporadically ratified but rarely implemented in full. Carbon trading markets have emerged to provide financial incentives for industrial polluters to reduce their emissions by whatever means they can find, and a handful of governments have introduced direct taxation—carbon taxes—on the emissions themselves.

None of these, though, has spread from one jurisdiction to another with the speed and promiscuous ease of the feed-in tariff, particularly once the German renewable sector hit its full stride after 2004.

At last count, versions of the law have been introduced in more than sixty jurisdictions worldwide, with many more pending. It has spread across vast swaths of Europe, from Ireland to Finland to Switzerland to Greece. Somewhat unorthodox tariffs have been passed in jurisdictions as divergent as Algeria, China and Turkey. Israel and Iran both have feed-in tariffs. One Canadian province (Ontario) and one American municipality (Gainesville, Florida) have brought the law to North America. Malaysia, Thailand and Taiwan have all recently enacted feed-in laws of their own.

Everyone wants their own piece of Germany's multibillion-euro industrial boom, of course, but there's another critical reason for the feed-in tariff's rapid spread: as energy policy goes, it's ridiculously simple and almost universally adaptable. It is indifferent to the political persuasion of its endorsers, and it works basically the same way in autocratic regimes, communally bent social democracies and neo-liberal republics. The feed-in tariff requires no fiddling with the tax code or reworking national budgets. There are no elaborate financial instruments to be priced and traded, no meticulous emissions measurements to be gathered and balanced across multiple industrial sectors. It works by the same mechanism anywhere there is a price on electricity—which is virtually everywhere—and the law itself is refreshingly straightforward. (The full text of the original German law is less than 8,000 words long.)

Italy provides probably the most striking example of the tariff's impact outside Germany. The Italian energy industry had long been one of Europe's most notable laggards, its abundant resources— one of the continent's most plentiful solar resources, in particular— squandered while its miniscule renewable energy sector toiled under a weak, ineffectual quota system for much of the past decade.

But in 2007, the Italian government extricated solar electricity from the old scheme and jolted it to life with a feed-in tariff as generous as any in Europe. Overnight, Italy vaulted to the front ranks of the global solar market. In 2009, it surpassed California in terms of installed capacity, and California's own SunEdison signed a deal in early 2010 to build Europe's largest PV plant under the abundant Italian sun. That sun, by the way, produces electricity yields 50 percent higher per panel than those installed in Germany, so Italy's solar plants are also widely expected to be the first in the world to achieve the industry's holy grail of "grid parity"—the point at which adding solar energy to the grid comes with the same price tag per installed watt as conventional sources.

The feed-in tariff's subnational experiments in North America, though less muscular than Italy's, have already reaped their own rapid successes. The province of Ontario—with a grid serving roughly one-sixth as many electricity users as Germany's does—passed its feed-in tariff, the Green Energy Act, in the summer of 2009. The act replaced an earlier version (the "Standard Offer" program, introduced in 2006) that had begun its legislative life as a direct copy of the German law before being weighed down with arbitrary caps and caveats on its way to passage. The 2009 act hewed much closer to the German model, and the contrast between versions 1.0 and 2.0 has been dramatic. In the solar sector, installed capacity grew from less than 2 MW to more than 200 MW in just the first eighteen months after the law was passed. The tariff's deeper promise—the birth of a new industrial base—came to fulfillment almost as quickly. In early 2010, the Korean electronics giant Samsung announced a CAD$6.6-billion deal to begin large-scale manufacturing of solar and wind equipment in Ontario—easily the largest direct cleantech investment of its kind to date anywhere in North America.

The case of Gainesville, Florida, is much smaller in scope, of course, but there's something almost quixotically inspiring about its quiet demonstration of the feed-in tariff's adaptability. In 2008, an assistant general manager of Gainesville Regional Utilities named Edward Regan spent ten days touring Germany with a group of other American utility executives. He was just another manager on a junket—the sort of thing not much more likely than a tourist's summer holiday to yield substantial change, let alone a city-scale Leap. Regan was struck, though, by the simplicity of the German law, its dramatic impact, the pervasive optimism it had injected into the country. He brought the law home like it was a souvenir fragment of the Berlin Wall and had it up and running in Gainesville—a collegiate city of 250,000 in central Florida— inside of five months. "It was the simplest rate design I have ever done in my life," he later told a *National Journal* reporter.

The Gainesville feed-in tariff went into effect in March 2009. By the end of the year, more than 1 MW of solar energy had been brought online, with plans in place to expand the total to 20 MW within five years—this at a time when the whole Sunshine State had only 4 MW of solar capacity. Even from just a statewide perspective, this is statistically impressive only in its insignificance— the 20-MW figure amounts to barely 0.03 percent of Florida's total generating capacity, the vast majority of which is produced by burning natural gas and coal. But the Gainesville feed-in experiment is an important asterisk in the annals of American energy policy nevertheless, simply for demonstrating with such clarity that a European-style Leap can work, quickly and exactly as originally configured, on American soil.

The feed-in tariff's most substantial impact outside Germany, meanwhile—statistically and otherwise—has been in Spain. The Spanish government passed its feed-in tariff, drafted on the

German model in direct consultation with Hermann Scheer and other German legislators, in early 2007. That year, Spain led Europe by a wide margin in new wind power installations (nearly tripling number-two Germany's total that year), and then in 2008 it led the world in new solar installations. In 2009, it was second in Europe behind Germany in both categories. Spanish wind turbine makers have emerged as global players—the largest, Gamesa, was one of the first European firms to expand into the United States, opening a major manufacturing centre in Pittsburgh in 2006—and Spain has also emerged as a major innovation hub for next-generation solar, particularly in the country's hot, sun-drenched south.

Straightforward as the feed-in tariff is, though, it can be easily misapplied, and Spain offers an object lesson in the perils of veering too far from the German template. When the Spanish government drafted its law, it made one critical digression from the German version—it decided, over Scheer's pointed advice to the contrary, to cover the difference between the standard electricity rate and the elevated feed-in rates using government revenues instead of passing the burden on to Spanish grid operators. Taxpayer money, not ratepayer fees, had to make up the additional cost of green power. This distorted the market for renewables, shifting much of the risk and management of the scale and speed of the new industry from the businesses themselves to the government's finance department. In 2008 the Spanish government was forced to reduce its tariff rates and place a cap on the number of megawatts of new renewable power that could be added each year—this just as the Spanish market was shifting into high gear.

Still, it stands as a sort of backhanded tribute to the feed-in tariff that even a deeply flawed one can vault a country into the front ranks of the global renewable energy game.

ALTERNATE LEAPING STYLES, FROM DANISH MODERNE
TO SUNNY CALIFORNIAN

There is no nation on earth that gets more of its electricity from (non-hydro) renewable energy than Denmark. As I pointed out in Chapter Two, more than 20 percent of Danish electricity is produced by wind alone, and its government intends to raise that total to 50 percent by 2025. Denmark was also the first country in the world to implement a feed-in tariff, but its pride of green-powered place is not exclusively a result of that pioneering law. Indeed by the time Denmark passed its feed-in tariff in the early 1990s, it had already made its big conceptual jump, and it lost momentum only temporarily when the feed-in tariff was phased out in favour of a mix of "bonus" tariffs, quotas and national targets for vaious renewable energy sources after 2001. In short, the German style of national Leap is not the only way across the chasm.

For Denmark, the decisive moment came during an earlier energy crisis—the one precipitated by the 1973 OPEC oil embargo. Denmark relied on oil imports for more than 90 percent of its energy in 1973—not just to fuel its vehicles but to generate electricity and feed the fires in household furnaces. The embargo was crippling; older Danes speak of whole families huddled into single rooms for most of the winter, unable to afford to heat the rest of the house.

In the years after the embargo, many of the world's major industrial nations launched their first major investments in energy efficiency and the development of renewable energy. Most, though, left these fledgling initiatives to gather dust in university labs and R&D departments when oil prices returned to pre-embargo levels in the early 1980s. But in Denmark, total dependency on foreign oil was abandoned forever.

In 1976 the Danish government undertook a wholesale rewrite of its energy policy. Self-reliance—what we now usually call energy independence—would be the baseline long-term goal. The Danish public soundly rejected nuclear power, and the flat Danish countryside contains not a single river with sufficient flow for industrial-scale hydropower. So Denmark looked instead to energy efficiency, to oil and gas from the North Sea and, with an interest that deepened through the 1980s, to renewable energy. Danish engineering firms developed efficient district heating systems, replacing whole neighbourhoods of inefficient household furnaces with a single efficient one. (More than 60 percent of Danish homes are now warmed by district heat.) They also built numerous combined-heat-and-power (CHP) plants, where waste heat from electricity generation is used to warm nearby buildings. And then in the 1990s, spurred by Denmark's pioneering feed-in tariff, the wind industry exploded, with the Danish firm Vestas, historically a maker of farm equipment, reinventing itself as the first major multinational wind turbine manufacturer (it remains the world's largest).

As the rest of the world reawakened to the need for new energy and efficiency technologies in the late 1990s, what had seemed a quirky little Scandinavian anomaly suddenly began to look like a beacon in the distance. Policy-makers and energy bureaucrats from around the world added Denmark to their itineraries, studying its district energy systems and efficiency programs and placing orders for Vestas turbines. To provide a showcase for all the attention—and to push itself to greater heights of green living—the government sponsored a contest among the dozens of small Danish islands. The winner would become the nation's first "Renewable Energy Island," completely powered by green sources, with efficiency pushed to the maximum. The ultimate goal would be to eliminate fossil fuels entirely and reduce the winning island's greenhouse gas emissions to zero. The winner of the contest was an island called Samsø, a quiet, agrarian spit of land with a population of 4,400, situated between the mainland and Zealand (the largest island, home to the capital and more than a third of the Danish population).

The transformation of Samsø is the most thorough—and the most complete—of any single jurisdiction in the industrialized world. The island of Aerø, a contest runner-up whose citizens decided to pursue their post-carbon program anyway, is a close second. In less than ten years, both islands were rendered essentially carbon-neutral and free from fossil fuels in all respects except for the vehicles on the islands and the ferries that connect them with their neighbours. In Samsø's case, an offshore wind farm was built as a sort of offset program for all the island's tailpipes; upon its completion, Samsø had effectively reduced its carbon dioxide emissions by 114 percent, transforming itself into a net carbon sink.

The array of technologies deployed across both islands—wind turbines, district heating systems fuelled variously by sun or straw or wood chips, hyper-efficient new buildings, the reuse of the waste heat from milk production to warm old-fashioned straw-roofed farmhouses—is testimony to the range of options open to a populace once it has made the conceptual jump. Outside the largest town on Aerø, brand-new solar thermal panels stand in a field mowed by a flock of sheep, providing heat for 2,300 people and reducing the cost and exhaust needed to keep the grass short. In one Samsø farmer's field, an outmoded turbine, long idle, was rebuilt to cover the energy needs after the farmhouse was converted into tourist accommodations.

The Danes have deployed their tricks and tools far beyond the confines of these showcase islands; indeed the nation exhibits the same eclectic knack for retrofit, redesign and innovation any-where you look. On the southern fringe of Copenhagen, for exam-ple, I came upon two colossally scaled wind turbines a magnitude larger than the ones found in farmers' fields in places like Samsø on a point of land next to a large industrial district. The thing was, I hadn't come to discover the state of the art in Danish wind energy but rather to gawk at the world's most efficient gas-fired power plant. There it was in the distance, framed by oscillating blades: Avedøre power plant, a sleek, grey, angular structure, resembling an Imperial Walker from the *Star Wars* movies that has lost its legs.

Avedøre is a 570-MW plant that can burn biomass as readily as natural gas; though it ran on gas at first, it is now powered pri-marily by wood chips, and by replacing three outmoded coal plants it reduced its owner's total carbon dioxide emissions by 10 percent all by itself. Even from a distance, I could plainly see the wide-bore pipe, painted bright blue, that delivers the excess heat from the plant's electricity generation to the area's homes and businesses, boosting its overall efficiency to 95 percent. When you've been looking for the right kinds of opportunities from the right perspec-tive for as long as the Danes have, innovations like this abound.

As Denmark now demonstrates nationwide, the technocratic details are means, not ends. How you change the market to favour efficiency and renewables over profligate nonrenewables is not crucial, and neither is the growth rate or profitability of any par-ticular undertaking. What's essential is making a commitment—a wholesale and unwavering commitment—to a sustainable bottom line and an end to fossil-fuel dependency. You have to decide, come what may, to leap.

Denmark's Scandinavian neighbours demonstrate two further paths to sustainability, both born of another style of national Leap:

the direct taxation of carbon dioxide emissions. Norway's carbon tax is aimed exclusively at its robust offshore oil-and-gas indus- try—domestic manufacturing and resource processing industries like aluminum and forestry were exempted to keep them from jumping to untaxed jurisdictions—and so it is in the North Sea where you find its most significant achievements.

As I pointed out in Chapter Two, the impact of Norway's carbon tax has been nearly as dramatic as any given feed-in tariff, particularly for the country's homegrown oil-and-gas company, Statoil. It is the first company ever to sequester carbon dioxide emissions from a conventional gas-drilling operation—first at an offshore natural gas drilling platform in the North Sea and then at two other gas-drilling facilities internationally. Statoil has also joined several other Norwegian energy companies on a range of next-generation R&D projects aimed at what the current prime minister refers to as the country's "moon landing" project—the total elimination of greenhouse gas emissions at a conventional gas-fired power plant. (It's too early to tell how successful these projects will be, though all have undergone delays, cost overruns or scaling down as a result of the enormous technical challenges involved.) In any case, should this carbon capture and storage technology ever become commercially viable at coal and gas plants worldwide—a proposition both the Canadian and American governments have backed with billions of dollars in R&D money—it will likely trace its roots to innovations triggered by Norway's carbon tax.

In neighbouring Sweden, a different kind of carbon tax has begun to spur innovation of its own. Swedish drivers had been paying steep emissions surcharges at the gas pump since the early 1990s, but in 2006 the Swedish government made a much broader Leap, pledging to make the whole country oil-free within a generation. The pledge included a spike in the carbon tax on gasoline, inspiring Swedish energy companies and automobile makers (especially Volvo) to transform themselves into pioneers in the use of biofuel. Swedish sales of biogas-fuelled cars were up 260 percent in 2009, and the fuel itself is now on sale at substantially lower prices than conventional gasoline from a string of gas pumps across the nation. Several municipalities, meanwhile, have converted their entire bus fleets to biofuel. In one of these—Helsingborg, a city of 95,000 on the west coast—the biogas itself comes from a conversion plant fed by the region's organic residential waste. Helsingborg's buses run on nothing but the city's trash.

For now, the United States remains without a national policy to drive the kind of changes that have become so commonplace in Europe. At the state level, though, a range of measures have begun to yield significant results. California is widely acknowledged as the American pacesetter in this field, and its former Environmental Protection Agency secretary, Terry Tamminen, now advises governors from the Pacific Northwest to the Deep South on how to make a Leap the California way.

Here's the short version of the California way: Start with a governor who understands the scope of the problem and the enormous opportunities involved in taking a leadership role in solving it—not just new economic activity but the chance to make a lasting mark on the state and build a political legacy of national or even international stature. Then simply implement a sort of two-pronged quota system—a greenhouse-gas-emissions target combined with a "renewable portfolio standard," mandating state utilities to draw a minimum percentage of their power from renewable sources.

In California's case, the source of that leadership was

Governor Arnold Schwarzenegger. Prior to his election in 2003, Schwarzenegger's only significant contribution to the global energy picture was the dubious distinction of helping convince General Motors to mass-market gargantuan Hummer SUVs. As both a European by birth and a Kennedy by marriage, however, Schwarzenegger was uniquely positioned to identify the scope of the climate problem and the opportunities presented by cleantech solutions. His government also had a robust legacy of environmental and energy efficiency leadership in California to build on. Still, the ambitious scale of its bold legislative leap in 2006 was a welcome surprise. That year, Schwarzenegger's government passed its omnibus Global Warming Solutions Act, which called for a reduction in greenhouse gas emissions to 25 percent below 1990 levels by 2020 and to 80 percent by 2050. And it made a commitment to generate 33 percent of the state's power from renewable sources by 2020 and introduced a generous subsidy for solar energy.

This legislative package inspired North America's greatest wave of cleantech development and innovation to date. Silicon Valley venture capitalists, already enamoured of the pace of innovation and growth they were seeing in the regional cleantech industry, started to pour money into it at billion-dollar scale. Digital-economy giants diversified rapidly into cleantech as well. Google, for example, blanketed its new headquarters in solar panels and established a $100-million-per-year investment fund for future-tense renewable energy technology. Bay Area start-ups like San Jose–based Nanosolar, meanwhile, took to the development of the next generation of renewable technology with a speed and entrepreneurial swagger not seen since the height of the dotcom boom.

The overnight transformation of the California solar business was particularly impressive. Announcements of power plant development deals of unprecedented size became a monthly occurrence. (In just the final few months of 2010, seven of the largest solar power plants on the planet were commissioned by Southern California Edison, promising nearly a full gigawatt of new solar energy for California by 2015.) And in the first months after the announcement of the new portfolio standard and solar subsidies back in 2006, a handful of companies—particularly SunPower and SunEdison—invaded the boardrooms of every brand-name retail giant in California. They'd amped up to industrial-scale production for the first time ever, and they were after real estate to facilitate their expansion—the broad, empty rooftops of big-box warehouse stores, that is. Great fields of empty concrete and metal, just begging to be tiled in solar panels.

By 2008 the process had more or less standardized. The solar company would lease the rooftop space for free, and in return the retailer would get its power at a rate slightly above the norm at the time of installation, guaranteed for the life of the system. In these turbulent times, the long-term guarantee proved to be worth more to many retailers than the modest near-term surcharge. At Macy's and Staples and Kohl's and Walmart stores across California, solar-panelled roofs became almost as common as sale signs—by the end of 2010, the roofs of hundreds of big-box retail outlets statewide (including eighty-eight Kohl's department store roofs alone) had become power plants.

Even in the absence of a feed-in tariff—and in the face of a federal government openly hostile to the very idea of climate action—California demonstrated how quickly and profitably a national-scale leap can be made. (As of 2006, California's economy would have been the world's eighth largest if it were counted separately, so in sheer economic terms its green-power commitment is comparable in importance to those of Spain and Italy.)

As in Germany, the cleantech industry leapt from the garage-business fringe to the industrial mainstream—literally so in the notable case of Akeena Solar, one of the state's leading installation companies.

Barry Cinnamon, Akeena's CEO, established the company in his suburban garage in 2001. At its birth, it was the kind of solar installer still common today in jurisdictions that treat the industry as an afterthought. Akeena imported solar components from wherever it could find them, cobbled them together into rooftop modules, and sold them at high cost to altruists and survivalists who made up the bulk of the solar industry's pre-Leap clients. Suppliers in the industry were often unreliable, the various parts often difficult to integrate and install. Like any immature industry, the solar business had not rationalized or standardized. It'd barely even begun to think of itself as an industry. Akeena's rapid jump from garage to warehouse, starting with the first California solar quota in 2002 and then exploding after 2006, has traced the trajectory of the whole industry.

By the end of 2007, the garage had been replaced with a dozen offices across the state and a fleet of logoed installer vans with a slogan on the side: We Make Solar Power Easy. Now if you called Akeena on a Monday for an estimate, a rep would be at your house on Tuesday to check its roof space and orientation and then hand you a tidy printed estimate. It would include the size and cost of the recommended system, its output specs, the rebates and other subsidies you qualified for by buying it, and a firm date by which it would have paid itself off. If you signed the deal, it'd be up and running by the end of the week. And the panels themselves would not be gawky grey frames with electrical boxes and wires hanging off them but a sleek black unit of Akeena's design that Cinnamon named Andalay.

Introduced in September 2007, Akeena's Andalay solar panel is possibly the first ever to be designed with the interests of the customer, not the engineer, as its highest priority—the first to take retail basics like style and appearance into consideration at all. There are no exposed wires on the Andalay unit, no unsightly gaps between modules, and the panels rest so close to the roof you could mistake them for tinted skylights. Andalay panels require 70 percent less installation hardware, so they can be mounted much faster, and they're held in place by internal ballast so they don't penetrate the roof at all. *Popular Mechanics* named the Andalay one of its ten "Most Brilliant Products" of 2009, and they became the first full-scale solar panels ever to be stocked by a major retail chain when Lowe's hardware stores added Andalays to their shelves the same year. Style, convenience, customer service—these are the sort of things that only enter into the cleantech equation at the far side of a national-scale Leap.

Still, impressive as the shift has been in places like California and Sweden, it's hard to top the feed-in tariff for full-spectrum change. Think of it this way: in California, The Leap changed the way residents thought about what a solar panel should look like. In Germany, it's changing the way people think about their entire house, the whole neighbourhood, the city and country they live in and the direction in which it is headed. It's not just a question of energy, either. You should see what the cleantech boom had done for the fortunes of the dirtiest town in Europe.

SOLAR VALLEY & THE CLEANTECH RENAISSANCE

In 2000, a group of Berlin entrepreneurs—two physicists, an engineer and a business manager—started taking meetings with local officials in the old industrial towns of the former East Germany, searching for a place to set up a small factory. As veterans of the niche-phase solar industry during its first German expansion in the mid-1990s, they were acutely aware of the chronic supply problems in the industry. Solar cells—the small silicon-wafer tiles that are mounted and wired together by the dozens to build solar panels—are, of course, vital to production, and it was maddeningly difficult to find a steady supplier of them. The Berliners had developed an efficient new cell design, and they'd decided to start a business producing just the cells—rapidly and in large quantity, as you would any industry's core technology. They'd named their new company Q-Cells and gone looking for a suitable spot to begin production. Unemployment in parts of the former GDR was pushing 30 percent, and there were generic tax breaks in place—state, federal and EU—for setting up a factory to produce *anything* there. So the Q-Cells team toured the countryside around Berlin, looking for the best offer.

Officials from a village called Thalheim, an hour south of Berlin by train, proved to be the most eager and co-operative. The mayor had taken a great personal interest in the company and stitched together a generous package of loans and other incentives. There was also some dormant local expertise in the manufacture of chemical film and other materials used in solar cell production—the area had been a chemical industry hub back in the GDR days.

In early 2001, Q-Cells gathered its workforce of nineteen in a modest wood-panelled building on the outskirts of Thalheim and began manufacturing its solar cells. The little wooden factory is still there, a tiny annex in the shadow of Q-Cells' gleaming headquarters, lost amid the sprawling complex of warehouses out of which the company's numerous high-speed production lines now operate. In 2007, Q-Cells became the world's largest producer of solar cells by volume (Suntech of China overtook it in 2009), and it now employs more than two thousand.

The gentle hollow of countryside around the Q-Cells complex has filled nearly to the horizon with subsidiaries making next-generation thin-film solar cells, suppliers producing industrial quantities of glass and silicon wafers, manufacturers of solar modules, and competitors making cells of their own. California-based Nanosolar operates the first industrial-scale production line for its revolutionary thin-film panels—which it boasts will be the fastest to produce and the least expensive in the industry—out of a retooled beer-crate factory warehouse in one nearby town; in another, the Fraunhofer Institute (Europe's biggest applied high-tech research organization) has joined a handful of companies to establish an elite "Cluster of Excellence" in solar research and charged it with reducing the volume of expensive silicon required to manufacture a solar cell by 30 percent and improving the cell's efficiency by 20 percent inside of five years.

The Elbe River crosses the rolling country between Berlin and Leipzig in a zigzagging diagonal line, forming a broad flood plain, and that's where you'll find the largest and most important solar industry hub on the planet, which local economic development officials have christened "Solar Valley." Its epicentre remains the Q-Cells complex, and the village of Thalheim is still the most wholly transformed spot on the Solar Valley map.

As the Q-Cells explosion inflated the village's tax base to implausible scale, Thalheim installed new street lights and road signs. A soccer pitch with a grandstand capable of holding half the population of the village went up, and then an expansive new children's playground was built next to that. Before the local authorities could get around to the project of paving the streets with gold, Thalheim joined a handful of neighbouring towns to form the amalgamated municipality of Bitterfeld-Wolfen and spread the boomtown largesse to its ailing neighbours. The new municipality is often simply referred to as Bitterfeld. And so today the name most closely associated with Solar Valley is one that a prominent Berlin writer had famously denounced, in the early 1980s, as "the dirtiest town in Europe." It's a superlative not even local boosters dispute—for the entire lifespan of the GDR, the twin industrial towns of Bitterfeld and Wolfen and their smaller satellites had been the centre of its chemical industry.

When I first visited Solar Valley, I traversed a broad landscape of derelict factories that had once made photographic film and pesticides and petrochemical fabric for the whole Soviet bloc. On another visit, my guide pulled over on a wooded back road to point out a body of water through the trees—a small lake, its shoreline bounded by a sandbag-like cordon of canvas sacks filled with grain. The grain was there to slowly soak up the chemical-factory effluent that had been dumped directly into an old open-pit coal mine for decades to form this "lake," beginning a detoxification process that will take a generation or more to complete. During my tour of the local-history museum, the director took special note of an artful photo filled with the silhouettes of industrial cooling towers—this, he told me jovially, was Bitterfeld's "historic image."

To get a clearer sense of where Bitterfeld had come from and where it hoped now to be going, I went with Christian Puschmann, an official from the regional economic development office, to tour its new marina. A trim new walking path snaked along the shore of the lake, and as Puschmann and I strolled he explained that this too had once been a coal mine—a broad, devastated land-scape whose excavation had swallowed up four villages in their entirety. The project of converting the dead quarry into a lake had begun in 2000, with the expectation that it would fill gradually over ten years; a flash flood in 2002 had done most of the job in just twenty-four hours. Nobody in Bitterfeld seemed entirely sure whether this was a good or a bad omen.

At the marina office, Puschmann introduced me to Andreas Beuster, a local entrepreneur who'd been involved in much of the waterfront's redevelopment. In addition to building the marina itself, Beuster had converted an old manor house into an elegant boutique hotel. He had the broad gestures and belly laugh typical of civic boosters the world over, and he recounted the reno with abundant pride. It'd been basically a ruined shell when he bought it, he explained—the East German government had housed Vietnamese "guest workers" there in work-camp squalor for years.

In the desperate first decade after reunification, flocks of the region's skilled workers fled west to find jobs and build new lives. In response, Beuster had established a "relocation" company to deliver their possessions and assist with other logistics. In Bitterfeld in the 1990s, this passed for a growth business. The passage of the feed-in tariff in 2000 inspired a literal inversion of Beuster's work. After many years moving people out of Bitterfeld, Beuster's firm took on the job of moving new Q-Cells executives into the region from across western Europe. And so as Bitterfeld transformed from the dirtiest town in Europe into the hub of Solar Valley, the former expert in exodus logistics became its busiest and most ambitious redeveloper.

In addition to the manor hotel, Beuster was an investor in a tidy new residential development of midrise waterfront condos going up on a tight grid of new streets just behind the marina. Waterfront property is sufficiently scarce in Germany that people will drive for hours to circumnavigate a Black Forest pond shoulder to shoulder with a thousand others, so the idea that Bitterfeld could attract commuters from Berlin and Leipzig to not just work but live on this new lakefront wasn't an entirely preposterous notion. In fact, new waterfront developments were intended not just to attract new residents but to help the regional economy diversify—into tourism. Puschmann pointed out a small village on the far side of Bitterfeld's new lake, where a handful of new holiday homes had gone in next to a new beach and a cushy waterfront restaurant. "Very nice view to the city and to the lake," he told me. "The best time is the sundowner."

The real measure of the success of Bitterfeld's Leap, though— and of Germany's—is not the health of this waterfront building boom, not even the health of Q-Cells or any particular solar company. The unemployment rate in the region has dropped into the low teens, but this was accomplished as much by a major refurbishment of some old chemical works as by new solar industry jobs. The true wonder of Bitterfeld is that it has learned to look to the horizon with something other than dread. Not even a generation after total national collapse, in a place that had been staring numbly down half a century of totalitarian servitude and decades of cataclysmic imperial madness before that, the feed-in tariff has bestowed upon Bitterfeld a quality that must surely have seemed lost forever: naive optimism. The sun shines on Solar Valley about as often as it does on the Alaskan panhandle. And that, it turns out, provides enough energy to power a brighter future.

< FOUR >

THE LEAP IN THE ECONOMY

SUSTAINABILITY UNDER GLASS

THERE ARE TIMES IN THE industrial history of a place—a city
or region, a state or a whole country—that come to define it. The
right people find a location blessed with the necessary resources
to meet a burgeoning need, not just raw materials but people and
capital and transport and communications, and in the collision of
these vectors a new kind of economy emerges. Packet shipping
and the construction of the Erie Canal in the first decades of the
nineteenth century established New York City's position as
America's premier international hub of transport, finance and
communications. Detroit was set on the road to Motor City legend
when Henry Ford opened the doors of his first factory in 1903.
And the innovations of a handful of computer research labs in the
early 1970s forever transformed the farmland south of San
Francisco into Silicon Valley.

For Toledo, Ohio, the pivotal moment arrived as America
emerged from the depression of 1873 into its storied Gilded Age.
Beginning with the arrival of a New England businessman named
Edward D. Libbey in 1887, Toledo transformed almost overnight
into the place described by the nickname you'll still find on a
plaque in the middle of the main square downtown: "Glass City."

Founded astride a patch of swamp at the western end of Lake Erie in 1836, Toledo was one of many infant Midwestern industrial towns born of the Erie Canal's Leap. Although it served for half a century as a key transportation hub, Toledo was still struggling to find its place in the explosive industrial economy of the Gilded Age when substantial natural gas deposits were discovered in the region in the early 1880s. Around the same time in Massachusetts, Edward Libbey inherited the faltering New England Glass Company from his father. Facing fuel shortages and labour strife, Libbey went searching for a new home for the company, just as Toledo was looking for customers for its newfound abundance of gas. In Toledo, Libbey found not only a steady fuel supply and plenty of sand and silica—the essential raw materials for glass-making—but a local elite willing to give him 4 acres, $100,000 for a new factory and fifty new houses for his workers.

Keen to establish his name on the national stage, Libbey relocated to Toledo and constructed a glittering pavilion at the epochal Columbian Exposition in Chicago in 1893. The exquisite blown-glass wonders of his exhibition were among the great sensations of the fair, establishing Toledo as the first name in American glass-making and turning Libbey's fledgling factory into a major manufacturing concern.

As America vaulted to the very front of the global economic order, Midwestern industrial cities like Toledo enjoyed unprecedented prosperity and discovered a knack for pioneering invention and on-the-fly technical skill analogous to the "Yankee ingenuity" that had built the Erie Canal. In the first years of the twentieth century, for example, Michael J. Owens, a brilliant engineer whose name would join Libbey's on the brands of several major glassmakers, invented the automatic bottlemaking machine and perfected a new technique for the quicker and cheaper manufacture of sheet glass. A generation later, Harold McMaster, who started his career at Libbey-Owens-Ford Glass in Toledo in 1940, was another key figure, his shadow cast at Edisonian length across the global glass industry for the rest of the twentieth century. During the Second World War, McMaster developed a critical system for de-icing the windshields of aircraft that is still in use to this day. He also developed a rear-vision periscope and a unique type of bent glass for the windshields of bomber aircraft. In 1948, he formed his own firm, Permaglass, which adapted the bomber windshield concept for the auto industry, whose ferocious growth and perilous decline would dictate the Toledo region's economic fortunes for the next half-century.

McMaster died in 2003 at the age of eighty-seven, with more than one hundred patents to his name. He was posthumously inducted into the National Inventors Hall of Fame for his work on tempered glass in the 1960s (machines based on his designs still produce 80 percent of the world's car windshields and half its office windows). But his most lasting contribution to the industrial economy of the twenty-first century will likely be his last handful of patents in the years before he died, which together mapped out a new way of manufacturing a whole new generation of solar PV cells. Today, at perhaps its most desperate moment, Toledo, Ohio, finds itself blessed with one of the most important hubs of next-generation solar technology on earth, the R&D engine that could provide enough power for a transformative economic Leap across the region and around the world. And all of it traces its origins to experiments Harold McMaster began in 1984.

At the time, America's industrial heartland had just begun its decline into the blighted, embittered, chronically underemployed chain of faded glory known as the Rust Belt. In certain Rust Belt cities tightly yoked to a single failed industry, there may never be a full recovery. (Detroit, for example, is seriously contemplating a renewal plan that would return a quarter of the city's land to fields and farmland, resigning itself to the likelihood that most of its ninety-thousand-plus vacant lots will never be redeveloped.) Toledo's post–war unemployment rate peaked at 15.7 percent in March of 1983 and has waxed and waned since then, climbing back into the double digits in the recession of the early 1990s and again in the wake of the financial collapse of 2008. The slightly rosier numbers in between were partially the product of a steady decline in population throughout the 1990s, as jobseekers fled Toledo by the tens of thousands. (By 2011, Toledo's population had fallen below 300,000, a level last seen in the 1930s.)

The Midwest's transformation from heartland to Rust Belt follows a distinct downward arc beginning with the energy crises of the 1970s and ending with the collapse and bailout of the American auto industry in early 2009. But few made preparations for this downfall the way Harold McMaster did. McMaster was a physicist of legendary vision and tenacity—he often told colleagues that he regretted never meeting Albert Einstein because he believed the Theory of Relativity was in desperate need of a few tweaks. The 1970s-era oil price shocks and the soaring unemployment of the early 1980s convinced McMaster that solar was the energy of the future—and the future of Toledo's glass industry. Many of the glass innovations of that era involved coating glass with a thin layer of useful chemicals—tinting to keep out the sun, a "low-E" layer to trap its heat—and McMaster was convinced a layer of conductive metal could be deposited on glass the same way to make solar PV cells. Alternatives to oil were being explored with unprecedented urgency in those years, and the big knock against PV was (and to some degree remains) its high price. This was a function of the slow speed of production and the high cost of the purified crystalline silicon wafers (nearly identical to the ones used to make computer processing chips) required to build the power-generating cell itself. But what if you could manufacture PV as quickly and easily as tinted glass? That, as McMaster recognized, would provide the catalyst for a genuine energy revolution.

McMaster settled on an uncommon metal alloy called cadmium telluride (CdTe) for his new solar cells and partnered with his longtime collaborator, Norm Nitschke, to found a pair of new companies—Glasstech Solar and then Solar Cells Inc.—to turn this "thin film" PV concept into mass-market reality. He chased down investment funding, partnered with the University of Toledo, played with prototypes, developed first one manufacturing process and then another and then another. This was blue-sky, whole-cloth stuff, brimming over with entrepreneurial zeal and the promise of a cheap, clean, universally deployable power plant.

Skip to the bottom line, and it's a Horatio Alger tale read through green-tinted glass. By early 2010, First Solar, a company built on McMaster's thin-film patents, had become the world's largest manufacturer of the most inexpensive PV panels on earth. Its largest US manufacturing facility, on the outskirts of Toledo, employs 700 people in a Rust Belt burgh desperate for signs of new economic life. In warehouses and repurposed factories across the Toledo area, former partners of McMaster's and other University of Toledo innovators have founded a handful of other burgeoning solar companies—not just thin-film competitors but makers of high-efficiency inverters and designers of large-scale solar installations, the manufacturers of glass for the panels and the steel framing to mount them on, all the ancillaries of a burgeoning industrial sector. There are more than 6,000 "green collar" jobs in the PV business in Toledo today, and the state government has designated

the region as Ohio's "Solar Energy Innovation Hub." The offices
of the Regional Growth Partnership in downtown Toledo—right
on the edge of the square with the big "Glass City" commemora-
tive plaque—double as the headquarters of the venture capital
firm that put the seed money into Nextronex, the manufacturer
of the super-efficient inverters powering the big solar installation
at Toledo's Ohio Air National Guard base, which was installed in
2008 and saved the base $140,000 on its energy bills in 2009 alone.
Out at the University of Toledo, meanwhile, students and faculty
beaver away on the *next* next generation of solar in the labs of
McMaster Hall, the Wright Center for Photovoltaics Innovation
and Commercialization, and the brand-new Scott Park Campus
of Energy and Innovation—this last situated around a quad
shaded by a gleaming array of brand-new First Solar panels.
There's someone at the county economic development office
who likes to say that Northwest Ohio could become "the Silicon
Valley of solar energy," and there's quite a lot of solid evidence
to back up that claim.

I had the case laid out most clearly for me by Norm Johnston,
a glass industry veteran turned solar entrepreneur who had worked
closely with Harold McMaster on several glass and solar projects
over the years and helped establish the Northwest Ohio Alternative
Energy Business Council (NOAE) in 2003. "In Toledo," Johnston
told me, "it didn't take till 2009 to figure out the automotive industry was gonna fail. It was already failing. The Big Three had literally run the energy dollars and health out of their automotive
supplier network. We had the city's largest bank, a couple of its
largest companies that were involved in automotive or in other
things—Owens Corning, Pilkington, a construction company, the
University of Toledo—and we said, 'This city really needs to do
something other than what it's been doing, because it's dying.'"

Out of those early NOAE meetings, a vision emerged. The crumbling industrial economy, a classic new technology cluster, the tripartite crises of economics, energy and climate—all the signs pointed in the same direction. NOAE's subsequent renewal plan placed solar front and centre and received keen early support from university officials and a local congressional representative. The state government passed a renewable portfolio standard with a modest but explicit solar requirement—roughly 900 MW of solar installed in Ohio by 2025. Johnston was even more ambitious. What if the state aimed to reach its solar goal in just seven years? There are eighty-eight counties in Ohio, many of them containing old industrial cities—like Toledo—with acres and acres of idle, heavily contaminated brownfield sites. Aren't the Germans building solar plants on sites just like that? Install just 10 MW or so in each county, and you'd reach the mark almost a decade ahead of schedule.

Here's Johnston, tracing the value chain:

Now, why is this a good business for Ohio? Here's a bunch of Ohio companies. Solar panels are nothing more than glass sandwiches. They're just like a windshield. So we've got Pilkington selling TEC glass to First Solar, 10 million square feet. They also sell to somebody over here who tempers another 10 million square feet. The tempering line was probably built by Glasstech [Harold McMaster's old company]. The buildings [for First Solar's Toledo factory] were built by a local construction company, Rudolph Libbe. The 700 people in there, 150 of them are engineers and the rest of them all are trained to put together solar panels—so they're not Hamburger Helper jobs, you need factory workers who literally got half a million dollars out of their stock options. Then they send that somewhere for installation. Well, to install that, you would need at least 250 people. Somewhere you're going to need 1.4 million miles of wire. Six million feet of framing. You could connect it to the grid, and if you can run it into homes, over 50 percent of the homes have Owens Corning insulation. How do I know that? I used to be in charge of strategic planning at Owens Corning. So try and find something else that ties up as many Northwest Ohio products and glass companies, and I don't know what it would be.

Tally it all up, and you'd have at least 4,000 Ohioans employed, learning new skills, dreaming new kinds of industrial dreams — inventing that sunnier future, some of them, in the way that Michael J. Owens and Harold McMaster had. And at the end of it you'd have nearly a gigawatt of clean energy. So, yes, Northwest Ohio *could* be the Silicon Valley of solar. This could be the start of a new economy, a Great Leap for American industry in general. But it isn't. Not yet, anyway.

First Solar's Toledo operations are at R&D scale, and they are dwarfed by its manufacturing facility in eastern Germany, which is also where you'll find the vast majority of its up-and-running solar arrays. The biggest solar plants on the company's drawing board are a pair of gigawatt-sized monsters just about to start construction in northern China. All told, about 90 percent of First Solar's 6,100-strong workforce is employed outside Ohio and more than 90 percent of its sales occur outside the US. When First Solar split off from Harold McMaster's Solar Cells Inc., it took his patents with it, so he and Norm Johnston drew up some new manufacturing plans, and Johnston's confident they'll soon be churning out thin film solar panels even less expensive than First Solar's — at a manufacturing facility in Germany's Solar Valley, under the auspices of a Q-Cells subsidiary called Calyxo. The state of Ohio has mandated a fraction of a percentage point of its grid to be converted to solar by 2025; the German solar industry added more than a full percentage point's worth to the whole country's energy mix in 2010 alone.

Pretty much every essential component of a Silicon Valley of solar energy has been assembled somewhere in the Toledo area—a university with a deep and rapidly expanding knowledge base on the subject, local companies well-versed in the technology, experienced risk-taking entrepreneurs, the tools and space to build the stuff and a skilled workforce looking for new opportunities—but the city's industrial engines remain mostly on idle. Downtown Toledo is a half-empty patchwork of abandoned pre-war brick edifices and vacant lots. There's a lovely little brand-new ballpark for the Mud Hens to play in and a convention centre with its doors chained shut half a block away. It's a ghost town after six o'clock on a weeknight. There remain, as Norm Johnston put it, "two or three too many hospitals and two or three too many country clubs." Toledo is what a Leap looks like right *before* it takes off. If it ever does.

What's held it back thus far? There are mundane things, of course: technical hurdles, policy details, political cultures at the state and federal levels in which self-preservation and re-election trump bold vision and big steps. When Harold McMaster started working on thin-film solar in the mid-1980s, he never anticipated it would be twenty years before it would be market-ready. And Ohio's outsized, semi-monopolistic utility companies, like big utilities the world over, deeply dislike the idea of small-scale, decentralized renewables and loathe big changes in general.

More than any of this, though, there is a cognitive shift that has yet to happen in Ohio—and across much of America. The essential Fourth Law of Leap Mechanics has not kicked in. That powerful disruptive technique—the mindset to recognize not only that the sustainable direction is the only way forward but that it leads to vast new opportunities—has not yet been fully embraced. Or maybe that's overstating it—maybe the problem is that America's *rhetorical* embrace of the Great Leap has not yet been broadcast to the streets and factory floors of the Rust Belt.

GREEN-COLLAR AMERICA

Let's rewind again to Earth Day 2009. In a small, struggling industrial town in Iowa at the far end of the Rust Belt from Toledo, the president of the United States delivered a speech containing a passionate commitment to an economic Leap of national scale. "On this Earth Day," Barack Obama told an audience of workers assembled in front of their factory, "it is time for us to lay a new foundation for economic growth by beginning a new era of energy exploration in America. That's why I'm here."

Obama paused to acknowledge the workers' applause and then continued:

Now, the choice we face is not between saving our environment and saving our economy. The choice we face is between prosperity and decline. We can remain the world's leading importer of oil, or we can become the world's leading exporter of clean energy. We can allow climate change to wreak unnatural havoc across the landscape, or we can create jobs working to prevent its worst effects. We can hand over the jobs of the twenty-first century to our competitors, or we can confront what countries in Europe and Asia have already recognized as both a challenge and an opportunity: the nation that leads the world in creating new energy sources will be the nation that leads the twenty-first century global economy. America can be that nation. America must be that nation. And while we seek new forms of fuel to power our homes and cars and businesses, we will rely on the same ingenuity—the same American spirit—that has always been a part of our American story.

This was as concise a description of a Great Leap Sideways as you'll find anywhere in the annals of political rhetoric—the epochal scale of the change and its vital necessity at this tumultuous moment, but also the continuity of values and goals linking one side of the chasm to the other—and Obama's choice of venue was just as precisely calibrated. As I mentioned in Chapter Two, the president delivered his Earth Day embrace of The Leap in front of a repurposed Maytag appliance factory in Newton, Iowa. It had been shuttered in October 2007, putting 1,400 Maytag employees out of work, after Whirlpool purchased the company whose founder had almost singlehandedly created Newton's industrial base. Just a month later, a company called Trinity Structural Towers announced that it would be retooling part of the old Maytag plant. The Trinity factory opened barely a year after that, after a $21-million renovation. Trinity now employed 175 workers, many of them former Maytag employees, manufacturing steel wind turbine shafts in the very space where Maytag appliances had been made for more than a century. Obama delivered his speech in front of a perfect manifestation of the transformation he was calling for.

The wind industry told similar stories for miles around.

Elsewhere in Newton, a company called TPI employed 600 work-ers in a brand-new factory making wind-turbine blades. A group of 70 former Maytag employees—essentially the entire R&D department of the old Maytag operation—had formed a new firm called Springboard Engineering, which did consulting work for the wind industry and beyond. Just up Interstate 80 in West Branch, a factory made wind-turbine generators for a Spanish wind company called Acciona. Further upstate in Cedar Rapids, Clipper Windpower of California was making turbines and over-seeing the development of wind farms. By around the time Obama showed up for his big speech, Iowa was the second biggest genera-tor of wind power by volume in the United States after Texas, and far and away the largest per capita—more than 15 percent of Iowa's electricity came from wind turbines.

None of this happened by accident. Even beyond the flawless optics of wind turbines built in a rejigged Rust Belt factory, Iowa provides probably the best American example of an economic Leap. If Toledo can be seen as a sort of German Solar Valley in waiting, then Iowa is Denmark with a Midwestern twang.

The Danes, of course, provide one of the best national-scale examples of The Leap outside of Germany itself. And like Iowa, Denmark made its jump on the strength of the winds blowing across its flat, sparsely populated, largely agrarian countryside. The Danish industrial Leap began with a generous incentive program introduced in 1979 to encourage the development of a domestic wind industry. In Iowa, the wind business started much later, with significantly less ambition out of the gate. Though the state gov-ernment passed an "alternate energy" law in 1983 mandating more than 100 MW of renewable energy to be brought online, it pro-vided little in the way of enforcement mechanisms, and utility companies were able to keep the initiative stalled well into the

1990s. In 1992, when officials from a school district in windy north-western Iowa obtained modest grants from the state and federal governments to build a wind turbine at the local elementary school, the project received only grudging support from the regional utility company. The wind industry finally found its legs in Iowa late in the decade, when the state introduced more mus-cular enforcement policies and a much more ambitious renewa-ble portfolio standard. After a two-decade false start, Iowa's Leap launched in earnest with a 2001 commitment to develop 1,000 MW of wind power in the state.

Only then did Iowans discover they were blessed with certain advantages beyond the strong breezes themselves. Not that there's any shortage of those—Iowa sits in the middle of a broad north-to-south corridor of windy plain stretching from the Canadian border to West Texas that wind industry booster T. Boone Pickens has dubbed "the Saudi Arabia of wind." There are windier parts of that corridor, but Iowa has other charms that make it particu-larly attractive not just as a site for wind farms but as a major hub of the American green-collar economy promised in Obama's speech.

I paid a visit to Barry Butler, the dean of engineering at the University of Iowa, to get a sense of the potential for the wind industry in the state. There are no other places in America's windy heartland, Butler explained, with quite the same mix of attributes that Iowa has. Its proximity to major population centres like Chicago, for example, means there is a waiting market for the electricity generated. And perhaps more importantly there is the state's long history in heavy manufacturing. Butler took down a Lego wind turbine from his bookshelf—as a proud Danish com-pany itself, Lego had branded the toy turbine with the name "Vestas." And what was Vestas, Butler pointed out, but the exact

Danish equivalent of Iowa's biggest and most famous heavy manufacturing firm—the farm-equipment maker John Deere? Maytag,
from this angle, was but a prologue.

"These turbines," Butler told me, "are just massive pieces of
equipment. And when you start looking at building this stuff, you
need the sort of people—plant managers, engineers, technicians,
factory line workers—who know what it means to be turning bolts
that are this big around." He held his hands wide in front of him
like he was holding a basketball.

Iowa also benefited from its small population base, commu-
nity-minded and closely integrated. When the state economic
development office started courting wind companies to set up shop
in Iowa, Butler told me, they could count on the co-operation of
other departments and other levels of government, universities
with sympathetic officials, colleges ready to set up new programs
to train wind technicians, that sort of thing. He described a meeting he attended where officials from a company considering a
factory site in Iowa were discussing their concerns with state
bureaucrats. The topic of shipping came up—no small issue for
the makers of enormous hunks of metal that need to be hauled
from factories to remote windswept ridges. No problem, the
bureaucrats answered. There was a single-permit process already
in place to handle exactly that. Butler: "When the guy can immediately say, 'We've got all that covered, all you need is one permit
to get through every county in the state,' that opens up the eyes
of the manufacturers."

All this awaited Newton's young mayor, Chaz Allen, when he
took office in 2004. As he contemplated new directions for Newton
in the face of Maytag's decline, he didn't have to look hard to find
a booming, dynamic new industry. But as obvious a fit as wind
power may have seemed, it was far from an effortless jump for the

town. Probably the last real innovator in Newton was Fred Maytag, who'd first set up shop in the 1890s, and most folks in Newton seemed just fine with that. Newton's a tidy little town, quintessentially middle American, a place of 4-H and Rotary and picnics in Maytag Park, of corn boils and high school football games. The biggest new game in town, not counting the wind business, is the stock-car racing out at the new motor speedway next to the Interstate. Which is where Newton's mayor asked me to meet him.

Chaz Allen is a strapping, gregarious sort with a sharp Midwestern twang and a boy's own love of fast cars. He was elected mayor at the age of thirty-four and still looks younger than that. He fits the stereotype of a cornfed Iowa boy from the cuffs of his faded jeans to the stock-car logo on his ball cap and the container of chewing tobacco on the dash of his three-quarter-ton pickup. He'd just flown home from Houston, where he'd accepted a "sustainable community" award from the US Chamber of Commerce the night before on behalf of the town of Newton "for its collaborative efforts to create a community vision and turn it into reality following the devastation of losing its longtime primary employer." Renewable energy, the Chamber's citation acknowledged, was "the centrepiece of the transformation."

Dead-obvious and slam-dunkish as Newton's shift into the wind business now looked, Allen's friends and colleagues worried it was a transient thing, a dangerous diversion from the core businesses of a traditional heartland town. Worst of all, it was a *government-backed* diversion. Allen: "It's a new field, and it was incented. We incented it. You put money into business, regardless of what kind of business, but government putting money in business, people get skeptical about that." Because Newton's sustainable horizon didn't look like Maytag appliances or John Deere tractors or Iowa corn, many locals could see only the risks involved,

. the tax breaks propping up a shiny new boondoggle. In the end, the promise of hundreds of new jobs in a town with a hemorrhaging employment base trumped the worries. They jumped.

The first company Allen courted to take over the old Maytag plant was TPI, the blade manufacturer. No amount of persuasion, though, could overcome a simple physical problem—the production line just couldn't be fitted into the space. A second round of courting, with county and state backing, set up a heavily incentivized deal for a whole new factory on the outskirts of town. A few months later, a similarly aggressive courtship brought Trinity Structural Towers to town, providing President Obama with the tidy backdrop for his Earth Day address two years after that.

In all, there are now more than 800 jobs in the wind business in Newton to patch over the 2,000 that vanished when Maytag closed its doors. There are 9,000 in cleantech statewide—including 2,300 in wind-turbine manufacturing alone—and when I visited Newton in the spring of 2010, the governor was running on a platform that promised to double that number if he was re-elected. The very fact of the contingency, however, points to the lingering, lagging difference between America's unfinished Leap and the ones taken in places like Germany and Denmark.

Barry Butler: "We missed a generation of advanced manufacturing. And one just does not simply build a factory and start producing these things from scratch. You can assemble them, but when you look at the parts that you have to put together to assemble them, some of those parts cannot be made in this country. There is machining, foundries that are needed. At least they can't be made in the quantities that are needed to meet the goals that we've set. It's going to take a good ten or fifteen years to get up to speed. And more importantly, there has to be in place the financial stability that people know that if they build a factory, and they hire people to start producing whatever part it is, whether it's the shaft or the gear box or the blades — that there's gonna be a market for that down the road."

Across America, in pieces and patches driven by fits and starts, there are young shoots of this green-collar economy trying to reach full bloom. The wind industry has established roots at several factories amid the old steelworks around Pittsburgh; the Spanish company Gamesa, in particular, employs 800 Pennsylvanians in wind-turbine manufacture. Denmark's Vestas has opened a big plant in Colorado. A next-generation solar start-up called Konarka has taken over a shuttered Polaroid film factory in suburban Boston, putting a couple of dozen former Polaroid employees back to work. Up in Michigan, Hemlock Semiconductor added 400 to its workforce in 2009 to keep pace with the booming sales to the PV market that now made up 60 percent of its business. Think, the Norwegian electric car maker, has begun construction of a plant in Elkhart, Indiana, that will not only employ 400 auto workers but make use of battery technology developed by EnerDel of nearby Indianapolis.

All of this activity happened without consistent support at all levels of government in the midst of the worst economic climate since the Great Depression. When the Obama administration's massive stimulus package stepped in with $94 billion in backing for this fledgling cleantech industry nationwide, it quickly bore rich fruit — a $118.5-million grant to EnerDel, for example, has allowed the company to ramp up production from 1,200 batteries per year to 60,000, expanding its workforce from 150 to 1,400 in the process.

This is some of the best-spent money in the whole $800-billion stimulus package for a variety of reasons, from reducing greenhouse gas emissions to improving the longevity of American industry. A 2009 study by researchers at the University of Massachusetts and the Center for American Progress found that cleantech investments create more employment for less money than government incentives spent elsewhere—a $100-billion investment in cleantech would yield two million new jobs, compared to 1.7 million created by an equivalent tax rebate program or just 500,000 in the oil and gas business. Even without such backing, the wind industry employed more American workers in 2008 than coal mining did (85,000 to 81,000). And the bottom line in a full-cost analysis of the coal industry in West Virginia found that once you factored in the debits incurred by injured workers, wrecked roads and "legacy costs" of cleaning up the mess, the net impact of employing 22,000 people in coal mining was that it actually cost the state's economy almost $100 million every year (this even before you considered the toll exacted on the planet's climate by the burning of all that coal).

And yet the inertial drag of a status quo unable (or unwilling) to see there from here continues to hold back the American economy's Leap. As federal and state election campaigns were heating up in September 2010, for example, the *Des Moines Register* reported that new wind-farm construction in Iowa had completely ceased, awaiting the renewal of a federal subsidy program or a national renewable portfolio standard, both of which were lost to partisan bickering over climate policy in Washington. A TPI official warned that their plan to expand the Newton plant—and possibly even the existing operation—was dependent on a clearer policy mandate. In Toledo, meanwhile, the entrepreneurial zeal of Norm Johnston and his pioneering colleagues in the thin-film business remained tempered by the utter intransigence of the state's utility companies and the Public Utility Commission charged with overseeing them. Al Compaan, a University of

Toledo professor and frequent collaborator with Johnston, told me about the "amazingly complex" process by which he had managed to get a few PV panels installed on his own home's roof and wired up to the state grid. Not only was there no incentive in place to encourage Ohioans to join in their state's great industrial renewal project, but the apparatus of electricity generation in Ohio had adopted a strategy toward renewables that Compaan characterized as "bordering on obstructionist." One of the reasons they were so hostile to new kinds of energy, he told me, is that they'd been burned badly by soaring rates in the aftermath of their embrace of nuclear power a generation earlier.

Or consider the case of solar installations in California, which as I explained in Chapter Three is the heartland of America's cleantech industry. Blessed with a supportive state government, muscular legislation, the risk-happy entrepreneurs and financiers of Silicon Valley, and of course one of the nation's most robust solar resources—that fabled warm California sun—there should surely have been no obstacles remaining to slow California's ascent to the vanguard of the global green-collar economy. The state government even came up with an inventive financing scheme to get solar panels onto household rooftops. The program is called PACE ("Property Assessed Clean Energy") financing. It was intended to allow homeowners to take out low-interest loans from funds managed by local or county governments, paying for the PV painlessly over twenty years as a small surcharge on their property tax bills. The idea spread like wildfire to twenty-two states. But in the summer of 2010, months after the program had secured federal stimulus money to launch in five California counties, the federal government's own Federal Housing Finance Agency and its adjuncts, the mortgage lenders Freddie Mac and Fannie Mae, derailed the PACE program over concerns it would interfere with mortgage payments. The PV loans were effectively liens against the house, and Freddie and Fannie simply couldn't abide the risk of re-mortgaging houses that had outstanding liens on them—even ones backed by the federal government's own stimulus package. The government of California sued the mortgage lenders in retaliation, but for the time being the PACE program was finished.

It's one of those tricky things about The Leap: without a *complete* commitment to the disruptive technique, a full recognition that the priorities of sustainability are fundamentally different from those of the status quo and that what was once risk is now opportunity, it can get mired in a thousand varieties of business-as-usual quicksand.

THE WALMART EFFECT

When Norm Johnston was head of research at Owens Corning in Toledo, his R&D team had T-shirts made up that read: "Bust your ass for fiberglass." The T-shirts, Johnston told me, were an accurate representation of the proscribed limits of his team's imagination—they could innovate like mad scientists, but only in the medium of fibreglass insulation. He mentioned the T-shirts by way of explaining what he thought had happened to that innovative spirit once known as Yankee ingenuity. Johnston: "I think the trouble with the Midwest was, they had all these inventors who did all this stuff, and then it moved into the heavy industry, and they didn't invent the next thing that was coming along. They were so enmeshed in keeping it running and making small, minor improvements that you didn't have the Silicon Valley start-up."

Johnston's point is well-taken: there's never been a shortage of innovative risk-takers in American business, but in recent years they've worked their magic more often in digital communications and financial services than in heavy industries like glass and cars. And even when they've set their minds to essential tasks like energy production, they've been artificially limited, like Johnston's fibreglass team, by the strict boundaries of the existing paradigm. After all, deepwater oil drilling and bitumen refining and hydraulic shale fracking are nothing if not wildly inventive businesses, expanding the very limits of human engineering in terms of complexity and scale. But they exist exclusively to perpetuate the global energy economy's fossil-fuel addiction, to extend the duration of the status quo.

What Johnston is referring to is indeed almost exactly what Thomas S. Kuhn described in *The Structure of Scientific Revolutions* as "normal science." Outside of communications (and possibly biotechnology in the wake of the sequencing of the human genome), the normal, day-to-day work of the conventional economy is still governed almost exclusively by the industrial paradigm established by James Watt's steam engine and Eli Whitney's cotton gin, by Rockefeller's Standard Oil and Edison's Electric Illuminating Company. As Kuhn explains, science rarely enters a revolutionary period, doing so only when acute problems *within* that normal paradigm persist for so long that the pursuit of solutions to them establishes a new paradigm altogether. In the industrial economy, the climate and energy challenges have imposed just such an acute crisis period. Sustainability has emerged as the new paradigm.

In economic terms, sustainability is best understood not as a series of incremental changes to better tune existing business and industrial practices to the harmonies of the biosphere but as a wholly new foundation for the industrial economy—and as a wellspring of industrial innovation not seen since the days of Edward D. Libbey. And such is the scale of its transformative force that sustainability has proven an effective innovation engine even in the absence of significant government leadership. Even without feed-in tariffs or carbon taxes, even without the most basic commitment to a consistent and coherent policy framework on climate and energy issues, even with obfuscation and outright hostility the norm in some industrial sectors and halls of government—even in North America, in other words—sustainability works.

Sustainability as a business principle—*corporate* sustainability, more or less—was in fact made in America. Long before the word had much currency in business circles or anywhere else, let alone any established implementation tools or best practices, Ray Anderson, the CEO of an industrial carpet manufacturing company called Interface, decided pretty much unilaterally to commit his business to making a Leap to sustainability that still has few equals in the corporate world. In 1994, he enshrined sustainability as Interface's new bottom line, giving the business twenty-five years to achieve "Mission Zero." By 2020, Anderson declared, a company whose core product—nylon carpeting with a polyvinyl chloride (PVC) backing—was made almost exclusively from petrochemical byproducts, some of them highly toxic, would have no environmental footprint at all. No more toxins, no greenhouse gas emissions, no waste whatsoever. In 2009—roughly 60 percent of the way through the original timeline—Anderson told his employees they were 60 percent of the way to their goal with the end in clear sight. Not only that, but costs were down and sales up. "This is a better way to make a bigger profit," he concluded.

Possibly the most significant Leap in American business came a decade after Interface's improbable pledge. In 2005, to the utter amazement of the green-minded world, Walmart vaulted to the front ranks of the sustainability movement. The public unveiling of Walmart's sustainability strategy came in a speech by CEO Lee

Scott at the company's Arkansas headquarters on October 24, 2005. In recognition of its import, the announcement was broadcast live to every one of the company's 6,000–plus stores and later shared with its tens of thousands of suppliers worldwide. Walmart's work on the initiative had actually begun a year earlier, with the introduction of new waste-reduction practices at 650 of its outlets and the construction of a hyper-efficient showcase store in Texas. Well aware of the depth of skepticism its sustainability promises would inspire, the company had waited until it had something to show before making any grand pronouncements.

Scott began with a frank recounting of the colossal scale of Walmart's corporate footprint, its extraordinary impact on everything from the planet's health to the baseline practices of entire business sectors. "We are in uncharted territory as a business. You won't find any case studies at the Harvard Business School highlighting answers for companies of our size and scope. If we were a country, we would be the twentieth largest in the world. If Walmart were a city, we would be the fifth largest in America. People expect a lot of us, and they have a right to. Due to our size and scope, we are uniquely positioned to have great success and impact in the world, perhaps like no company before us."

Scott explicitly acknowledged the range of criticism the company was facing. In the planning meetings from which its sustainability strategy emerged, he explained, "we talked about jobs, health care, community involvement, product sourcing, diversity, environmental impact: all the issues that we've been dealing with historically from a defensive posture. What became clear is that in order to build a twenty-first-century company, we need to view these same issues in a different light. In fact, they represent gateways for Walmart in becoming the most competitive and innovative company in the world."

For such a far-reaching speech, Scott's sustainability pitch was impressively rich in precise targets. Walmart would invest half a billion dollars in technological innovations to reduce its greenhouse gas emissions. Its supply chain would be 25 percent more efficient within three years. And then there was the trio of long-term goals at the core of the new strategy: Walmart would, in time, be powered entirely by renewable energy, create no waste, and sell only products that "sustain our resources and environment." There's a stock phrase often passed around in jargon-loving American business circles—*Big Hairy Audacious Goal*—and Scott had just unleashed three of them on the assembled worldwide staff and myriad suppliers of the largest retail enterprise on earth.

When it comes to Walmart, there's no need to hyperbolize. The stats themselves tell the story of a business operating at earth-shaking scale. Walmart rings up more than a billion dollars in sales *every single day*. About 140 million Americans make a purchase at Walmart each week, and it is America's largest private employer. In 2006, the first year Walmart made major purchases of organic cotton clothing, it bought and sold significantly more of the stuff than the entire global supply for 2001.

Owing in part to its gargantuan stature, Walmart has long been understood to be the very definition of the problem—an overgrown behemoth indifferent to its local conditions and impacts (environmental, social, geographical) and openly hostile to any change that might reduce its ability to sell lots of stuff cheaply. Its Supercenters upsized the big box. Its supply chains were fossil-fuel addiction made globally manifest. Walmart subcontracted cheap Chinese labour to produce piles of disposable plastic junk to sell in mammoth warehouses on the car-dependent exurban fringe, gutting the retail strips of traditional downtowns. Walmart was practically a synonym for *unsustainable*. Jeffrey Hollender, the founder and former CEO of green household product maker Seventh Generation, often claimed hell would freeze over before you'd see his company's products on a Walmart shelf. Five years after Lee Scott's big hairy audacious pledge, Seventh Generation dishwashing soap and laundry detergent are readily available in Walmarts across North America. And this is Hollender's take on it nowadays: "What I realized is if you could get Walmart moving quicker and more aggressively in this direction, we'd be able to solve the challenges we're facing much more quickly and much more efficiently. Walmart can move quicker than probably any government on the planet."

In environmental circles, there's a word for a giant, rapacious, growth-obsessed corporation's cosmetic efforts to tout its earth-friendly credentials, and that word is *greenwashing*. You'll find greenwashing at work in the glitzy marketing campaigns of conventional energy giants—most notably BP and its oft-derided "Beyond Petroleum" campaign—but also in the "new and improved" pitches made by the makers of nearly every conventional consumer product a big-box store sells. Walmart's lofty sustainability push seemed, at first glance, like a textbook case of greenwashing: the king of Chinese-made disposable goods promising to change the light bulbs in its energy-hog big-box stores to save the planet.

The reality, though, proved to be much more complex. Yes, Walmart did eventually swap its light bulbs for more efficient ones. And no, it didn't stop building new 150,000-square-foot Supercenters ringed with a family farm's worth of parking lot just over the county line from a more stringent zoning bylaw. But in pursuit of its surprising sustainability pledge, it also began a slow, careful consultation process with every green guru and efficiency expert who would agree to pay a visit to Bentonville. Marc Major, formerly of Blu Skye Consulting—one of the first sustainability advisers to make that trek—told me that Walmart recognized the scope of their Leap from the very beginning. "They talked about this," he said, "as a potential business strategy. Not just as a nice-to-do thing, not just as a bolt-on accessory to the business, but as a central part of the business moving forward."

Walmart saw the chasm toward which its own unsustainable track was headed, in other words, and it understood the necessity of crossing it in a single leap. As it turns out, this suited its self-image—Walmart prides itself, Major explained, on being a "ready-fire-aim culture." It was more comfortable than most companies—especially ones of its extraordinary size—with making decisions in the absence of clear measurements of likely success. This has proven to be a valuable asset at every turn on the long and bumpy ride the company has faced in pursuit of stable, sustainable ground.

Walmart's excessive size and management culture, which favoured flat hierarchies and regional autonomy, created significant challenges on their own. The company's 100,000-plus suppliers around the world, though, have proven to be an even greater hurdle. They come from corporate cultures of their own, operating in many cases within entire business sectors whose boardrooms had never before echoed with the word *sustainability*. Walmart's suppliers had toiled for years to conform to the stringent low-cost model of their biggest customer. And now a whole new organizing principle? Some vague buzzword tinged with the profit-wrecking hues of environmentalism? Wait-and-see was, understandably, a common reaction.

For these and many other reasons, Walmart has had to lead by example. Marc Major again: "Until [sustainability] gets deeply, deeply entrenched into the company and embedded into the performance evaluations and the incentives, it wouldn't be taken seriously by the suppliers. So there's a lag time there. Of course you can't build it into the performance incentives and metrics until you actually have something to measure, so there's a whole sequence of things that has to unfold. First Walmart has to figure out where they're going and what works for them, so they can start walking the talk. Then they need to start spreading the word to suppliers. Then they need to start figuring out exactly how they're going to measure this. Then they need to actually measure it and test those measurements. Then they can actually roll out perform-ance standards for their own employees. Then suppliers will finally start to take it seriously. So it's a multiyear process."

From the very first step—which was persuading the best minds in sustainability to help the company figure out what exactly it meant to be sustainable when you were a $400-billion retail behe-moth—Walmart's Leap required considerable tenacity. Adam Werbach, formerly the youngest president in the Sierra Club's history, made his consulting work contingent on a public relations ban—Walmart could not score easy, empty green points by adver-tising its association with the wunderkind of the American envi-ronmental movement. Instead, Werbach worked behind the scenes, store to store, engaging rank-and-file Walmart employees in discussions about the basic tenets of sustainability and how to integrate them into their work and into their lives. At some stores, this meant organizing better recycling programs or staff discounts on transit passes; at others, it began with weight loss pledges.

One after another, the gurus of green set aside their reserva-tions and agreed to work with Walmart. When the company needed advice on how to reduce its energy use, it enlisted Amory Lovins, a globally lauded energy efficiency pioneer and one of the originators of the very idea of natural capital. Starting in 2006,

Lovins's Rocky Mountain Institute embarked on a radical over-
haul of Walmart's trucking fleet, with efficiency as the primary
goal. Executives from the outdoor clothing company Patagonia,
one of the most respected brands in green retail, were brought in
to help Walmart establish sustainability guidelines for its house-
brand clothing line. When Walmart Canada gathered its suppliers
in Vancouver for a sustainability conference, it invited David
Suzuki—Canada's most prominent environmentalist and a strident critic of Walmart itself—to address the audience.

Walmart soon began to reap substantial benefits. It saw lower
costs down the length of the supply chain, reduced risk exposure
on issues of climate legislation and energy prices, booming sales
of organic milk. By 2010, the efficiency of its US shipping fleet
had improved by 60 percent, not only saving tens of millions of
dollars each year in fuel expenses but also cutting an additional
$200 million simply by packing trucks and scheduling their routes
more carefully. More than half of the waste from its American
retail stores had been diverted from landfill sites by 2009, toward
a goal of 100 percent by 2025. And the company's timing proved
impeccable—Walmart began filling its shelves with green consumer products just as demand for the stuff was exploding.

The American market for green household products tripled
in size from 2005 to 2009. As Walmart rolled out its own sustainability push, online retailer Amazon began pushing for less pack-
aging, Frito Lay started investing in hyper-efficient warehouses,
and the global shipping giant Maersk made noise about eliminating unsustainably caught seafood entirely from its container
vessels. Walmart, for its part, is credited with more or less singlehandedly establishing waste-reducing, triple-concentrated laundry detergent as the new industry standard. It's also a fair bet that
most Americans will purchase their first item of organic cotton

clothing, their first bottle of organic milk, and their first piece of organic fruit at a Walmart.

The biggest hurdle Walmart has faced to date has been the lack of established industry-wide standards for quantifying sustainability. What constitutes a sustainable shampoo? On what scale do you measure the relative merits of competing brands of frozen peas? On a shipment of produce, which is the more important metric — greenhouse gas emissions or food miles? How do you even measure the carbon footprint of a set of patio furniture or a flatscreen TV?

It's not that there were no answers to these questions but that there were no *definitive* ones. These are the sorts of conundrums generally solved by national governments, by international trade bodies, by extra-national organizations like the European Union and the United Nations. Even the largest retailer on the planet soon found itself far out of its depth, and even the most distinguished of sustainability consultant roundtables found it all almost beyond comprehension. But The Leap, once launched, has its own inertial force. Walmart, to the surprise of many doubtful observers, pressed on.

In 2009, surveys were sent to every one of Walmart's suppliers — more than 100,000 companies worldwide — quizzing them on key aspects of their business. The intent is to eventually produce a "Sustainable Product Index" of everything Walmart sells, which comprises a broad swath of everything that is sold in mainstream consumer culture. The highest scorers will lay claim to the best shelf space, and the poorest performers may eventually be turfed out of the store entirely. In the absence of government leadership, Walmart has taken on a role that verges on regulatory — in its coverage of the indexing initiative, *Advertising Age* noted that the company was becoming "a sort of privatized Environmental Protection Agency, only with a lot more clout."

The full impact of that clout has yet to be fully felt, but it will be considerable. Pick your preferred brand of buzzword—it will be a gamechanger, a quantum leaper, a paradigm shifter. Many of Walmart's suppliers have been slow to respond to the indexing quiz, and there remains widespread skepticism about just how quickly and sternly the new standards, whenever they are finally tabulated and whatever they turn out to be, will be enforced. But Walmart's reluctant wards are awake to the idea now, and they are starting to act.

In 2010 Marc Major left Blu Skye to start his own consulting firm, Cleargreen Advisors, one of a growing number of boutique shops launched with the expressed purpose of teaching Walmart suppliers how to adapt and prosper in the new sustainability paradigm introduced by the retailer. "It's the classic sort of disruptive innovation challenge," he told me. "Big companies are loath to destroy their old business model, so new companies are going to have to come in and do it for them to some degree." Such is the impact of the ultimate corporate giant's Leap—when it lands, it gives rise to entire new types of enterprise simply in the charting of its course.

Walmart, meanwhile, continues to soldier on. Its corporate offices are often among the most energy-efficient and waste-free in their jurisdictions (the Canadian headquarters even pioneered Styrofoam recycling in southern Ontario) and some of its newest ventures are genuine marvels of sustainable industry. The company's massive new food distribution centre for western Canada, for example, opened its cargo-bay doors in late 2010 overflowing with efficiency and emissions-reducing tricks—everything from hydrogen-powered zero-emissions forklifts and hyper-efficient LED lighting to airlocks between differently cooled storage areas and between warehouses and truck beds to reduce heat transfer and loss. The building is basically an enormous refrigerator-freezer, and so it also uses the waste heat from its cooling unit to heat the administrative offices and keep temperatures from dipping too low during the frigid winter months. Of course, much of this stuff has been toyed around with by governments and green innovators for years. But here is the Walmart effect: Whatever Walmart does becomes the norm by definition. The Walmart effect renders sustainability *commonplace*.

"Everything that people say is wrong with Walmart *is* wrong with Walmart," Adam Werbach told me. "And so is the opposite. Walmart is just *so big*." This too is part of the Walmart effect, and it explains why principled people like Werbach and Amory Lovins and Marc Major and organizations like the Environmental Defense Fund and Seventh Generation were eventually coaxed to Bentonville. Walmart remains outsized, ungainly, as cursed as any nation-sized apparatus with hypocrisies and blind spots and profound injustices. But there is no larger force in the marketplace, and so there is no single lever of power with a greater potential for transformative action—at least in the corporate world—than Walmart's boardroom.

So consider some recent news from Walmart. In the fall of 2010, the company announced plans to develop small urban retail spaces—20,000 square feet (1,850 square metres) at most, not even one-tenth the size of the average Supercenter—from which to peddle fresh food to downtown customers. Walmart also announced, to the usual round of skeptical harrumphing, that it would be looking to buy local and regional produce to stock these and other stores. Two of the lingering blots on Walmart's own sustainability scorecard were the excessive length of its supply chains and the exceeding difficulty of paying a visit to a Walmart in anything other than a private motor vehicle. Walmart appears—with more incongruous thinking from inside the big box—to be ready to address both of these criticisms. Tiny downtown grocers with local produce and other essentials and no parking lot whatsoever—how very *European* of them, really.

FAST TRAINS & THE SUSTAINABLE LONG-DISTANCE COMMUTE

There's more to a business, of course—and more to its claims to sustainability—than what it does in its boardroom or on its shelves or on the factory floor. There is the place it is situated, its proximity to other businesses and to places people live, to public spaces and essential services. The private sector of an economy also involves the connections between these individual businesses, the networks—physical and professional, but also social and political and psychological—that link these agglomerations of commercial and industrial activity together. When we trace the borders of a discrete economy, we're outlining the limits of such networks. The webs of interconnectivity that define cities and communities are two such essential networks, and I'll discuss those in the next two chapters; energy and communications are also vital networks, and I'll discuss those in the chapter after that. Right now, though, I'd like to make a case for the primacy of the most physical of networks: transportation. The backbone of a sustainable economy might turn out to be a long length of railroad track and a very fast train to fly along it. So let's return to the plain in Spain and ride those rails.

My first taste of the state of the art in high-speed rail came in the first-class compartment of the AVE del Sol, one of the newest routes on Spain's rapidly expanding Alta Velocidad Española system. The AVE del Sol runs from Málaga on the beach-blanketed Costa del Sol to the capital of Madrid. The first complimentary glass of dry Andalusian sherry came as we hit 250 kilometres per hour. On my trip, the AVE del Sol topped out at 302 kilometres per hour over an unexpectedly tasty pasta lunch somewhere on the Castilian plain, though it's been known to reach speeds as high as 320 kilometres per hour. As the Spanish countryside smeared past, it struck me that I'd never travelled across the earth's surface at such a phenomenal speed and that I was among the first generation of human beings capable of doing so.

The train left the station in downtown Málaga at noon sharp, a mere ten minutes after I'd boarded, and arrived at Madrid's Puerta de Atocha station in the shadow of the Prado Museum shortly after 2:30 p.m. I'd travelled about 540 kilometres—slightly less than the distance from Washington to Boston and almost exactly the distance between Los Angeles and San Francisco or between Toronto and Montreal—in two and a half hours.

When I disembarked in Madrid, I was in the centre of the city, steps away from a subway platform, with no need to hunt for a taxi. My carbon footprint was 83 percent smaller than the equivalent flight. There was even the bonus of a warm sherry buzz making the world seem luminous. In all my travels, I'd never before encountered a combination of cost, speed, comfort and convenience this flawless.

In 2010 the AVE overtook France's famed TGV as the most extensive high-speed rail network in Europe. New track continues to be laid at breakneck speed—a link to the French network via Bilbao within a few years, another one west out of Madrid all the way to Portugal, a line to Santander in the far north by 2015. Once it has been fully constructed in 2020, 90 percent of Spain's population will live within 50 kilometres of an AVE station, and Spain will be bound together by probably the most thorough high-speed rail network anywhere on the planet.

The AVE network's godfather, former Spanish president Felipe González Márquez, now looks like one of the world's great transportation visionaries. High-speed rail is fast emerging as a critical infrastructure upgrade all over the world, and Spain is now blessed with one of the best models. Efficient, reliable and enviably extensive, the AVE network has stitched together a country long riven by regional conflicts and reinvented its cities and the relationships between them. Zaragoza, for example, a midsized industrial city halfway between Barcelona and Madrid, is now barely an hour from either end of the line and steals conferences and high-tech business from both—Zaragoza's conference and trade-show traffic has tripled in just its first two years as an AVE hub.

AVE stations have also provided the catalyst for substantial downtown makeovers in small, formerly decaying regional cities such as Lleida (near Barcelona) and Córdoba (near Seville). The Spanish train maker Talgo, meanwhile, finds its services actively courted from Germany to the American Midwest as high-speed rail construction booms the world over. The price tag on the AVE system is an eyepopper—as of mid-2009, it has cost more than €100 billion, with another €100 billion or more to be spent by 2020. About $280 billion in US currency, all told. But to put that in perspective, Eisenhower's US Interstate highway system would cost $429 billion in 2009 dollars. And in any case the compound benefits of the AVE have far outweighed the upfront costs—the Madrid–Valencia line, for example, which cost €6.6 billion all by itself, is expected to create more than 130,000 jobs as new business opportunities and revitalization plans come to fruition at its terminus.

Bullet trains have had similarly revolutionary effects everywhere track has been laid for them. Lyon, France—the first terminus in the TGV network—used the arrival of high-speed rail as the fulcrum in its jump from dour industrial city to model of urban revitalization. The same process is now underway in Lille, a small city in northwest France that is emerging as a hub for fast trains from Britain and Germany as well as the rest of France. When Germany introduced its high-speed services between Hamburg and Berlin and between Frankfurt and Cologne, it reduced air traffic between the cities to virtually nil. And high-speed rail is emerging as the most efficient way to travel between urban centres in increasingly car-clogged and smog-choked China, which has the largest network in the world as well as the one growing the most rapidly—this thanks to a multiyear investment of more than $300 billion.

"It's not a bad investment over the long term, because you save a lot of things" this was how José María de Ureña Francés put it to me. As we sped toward his office at the University of Castilla–La Mancha (UCLM) in Ciudad Real at somewhere near 250 kilometres per hour, he enumerated the savings for me. There was time saved, of course, as well as energy and greenhouse gases—Spain's fast trains are 19 percent more energy efficient than the ones they replaced, and because they are powered invariably by electric motors, they have no smokestacks or exhaust pipes.

But most importantly, you can save whole cities. We were bound for Spain's strongest case in point to date—the slow-fade city of Ciudad Real. I already noted its radical transformation with the arrival of high-speed rail in Chapter Two, but the changes wrought on the city are substantial enough to warrant a return trip.

Until the AVE station was built on the edge of town, Ciudad Real had been bypassed by modern transport infrastructure—it was bereft of trunk rail lines and 50 kilometres from the nearest major highway. "Ciudad Real was isolated from the world," Ureña told me. "But high-speed rail is able to articulate more cities than the plane. The cities at an intermediate distance are the ones that are benefiting more from this system."

Ciudad Real was, in essence, the first unanticipated beneficiary of the compound effects of Spain's infrastructural Leap. When the AVE was first conceived, the nation's rail officials had been focused solely on the big hubs. Ciudad Real wasn't even scheduled for a station until local officials learned there would be a stop at nearby Puertollano and lobbied for one of their own. The Ciudad Real stop was a commuter hub even before Avant trains were introduced specifically for traffic to and from Madrid, 200 kilometres away. As Ureña explained, this phenomenon was repeating itself on one AVE line after another, in every formerly isolated city that has suddenly found itself within an hour's commute of a metropolis.

That one-hour barrier is one of the most enduring norms in human transport. It is a corollary of what is sometimes called Marchetti's Constant, named for Italian physicist Cesare Marchetti, who determined the mean daily travel budget throughout human history has been about an hour. It represents the maximum hike a Stone Age hunter-gatherer would readily make from cave to foraging ground, the average time it took a Greek villager or Roman citizen to walk the breadth of their hometowns, the length of a motor vehicle or transit trip to work beyond which even the most seasoned contemporary suburbanites will start looking for housing (or jobs) requiring less time in transit. On the morning Avant to Ciudad Real, Ureña and I were surrounded by Madrileños who'd been willing to make the daily trek only once the travel time was reduced to under an hour each way.

Our compartment emptied out almost entirely at Ciudad Real, and we followed a crowd of smart-suited professionals through the sleek new station. Not only were people with jobs in Madrid settling in the smaller city—taking advantage of bargain housing prices to buy up older local real estate as well as hand-some new townhouses built near the station just for them—but Ciudad Real was attracting a much higher calibre of professionals, who are commuting out from Madrid. My travelling companion from the local university was one of these, and among the ranks of Avant riders were also top-notch doctors and engineers and grad students who never would have even considered working or study-ing in Ciudad Real if not for the ability to live in Madrid while they did so.

The UCLM campus—Ureña's workplace—was a Spartan cluster of modern buildings just a few blocks from the AVE sta-tion. There, he left me with José María Coronado and Maddi Garmendia, two of his colleagues in the university's new planning department, to discuss the finer points of high-speed rail's impact on Spain.

"That's the biggest revolution that the high-speed train intro-duces is to have an intermediate level." This was Coronado, one of the school's few locally sourced staffers, born and raised in Ciudad Real during its period of slow decline. Everyone compares high-speed rail to air travel, he told me, and it was true that bullet trains could compete on cost and efficiency grounds with air-planes. But the most powerful thing about high-speed rail was that it brought smaller cities into the fast lane of the global economy. "The regional networks—that's the real revolution here."

This, in a sense, is what Ureña had meant about high-speed trains *articulating* more cities. An airplane speaks only to its depar-ture point and its destination. Trains, though, can tell new stories to every city along the track. In Ciudad Real, the emerging story was one of unprecedented self-confidence.

"People say that this is not a city," Garmendia told me, "it's a big town." What's more, she added, Ciudad Real was simply one of many stagnant big towns scattered across the plain. She was from elsewhere in Spain, and she confessed she didn't know exactly where it was on the map when she first agreed to come study at UCLM. The moment the city's name appeared on an AVE schedule, however, it vaulted to "first place in the city network" of the region. It was now a place you could *come to,* a place where you could build a business or raise a family, taking day trips to the capital for meetings or—as many already were—to go shopping on Saturdays. In the wake of the AVE boom, Ciudad Real had been chosen as the crossroads for two major new highways, and a new regional airport had opened not long ago, launching plans to steal air traffic from Madrid.

For the first time in generations, Ciudad Real saw itself as a place in the world, a place worth investing in. Not all the commuter housing deals would pan out, of course, and no amount of new development would transform a tired old burgh on the dusty plain into a thrumming metropolis like Madrid. But then not everyone wants to live amid such bustle. And if parts of modern Ciudad Real had all the charm of a strip-mall community in exurban New Jersey (though substantially better tapas, I'd wager), the elegant old downtown square over which Cervantes kept eternal watch would be the showpiece of almost any city in North America. And there was now a reason, for the first time in generations, to plan to stay.

Coronado: "One of the biggest changes—but it is impossible to measure—is what happened in people's minds." Again that persistent Great Leap hurdle of inaccurate measurement, again a yardstick failing to quantify a quantum leap. There were surely numbers to attach to the singular story of Ciudad Real—daily passenger rates on the Avant, the bump in local GDP and local housing prices, the abrupt halt to the steady downward decline in population that had come to seem as much a part of the city's fabric as the cobblestones on the main square—but how would you put a price in euros on a city's newfound sense of optimism? Could you quantify the value of an esteemed professor or a highly skilled doctor merely by the amount of his salary? Was Ciudad Real a singular phenomenon, a one-off born of that first AVE line only, or could its transformation be mapped out and replicated?

If the fast train fix can be copied, there is nowhere that it is needed more desperately than in North America. Not even one in one hundred trips between cities in the US are taken on trains, the lowest percentage of the world's thirty-two most developed nations. The Acela running between Washington and Boston—the nearest thing to a high-speed line operating in the US today—averages just a little over 100 kilometres per hour, less than half the average speed of an AVE train. This was no accident but rather a product of half a century of deliberate neglect—from 1956 to 2006, the US government spent six times as much on air transport infrastructure and sixteen times as much on highways as it did on passenger rail.

Critics of high speed rail in the US like to harp on its high cost, the huge amounts of tax dollars required to lay track and buy equipment; estimates of the cost of an extensive high-speed rail network in the US range from $140 billion to $500 billion. Such critics, however, are less likely to note that all current user fees— from gas taxes to tolls—account for as little as 51 percent of the operating cost of the country's highways. Owing in part to this generous subsidy, 87 percent of all trips made anywhere in the United States are by private motor vehicle, and 99 percent of those trips arrive at a free parking spot. The cost of providing all that free parking amounts all by itself to an additional subsidy of about $300 billion *per year*. It is not cost nor the vagaries of national geography but habit, bias and priority that have held back high speed rail in the New World. Indeed it was the federally funded Interstate Highway System that initiated the decline of (mostly privately operated) passenger rail services back in the 1950s.

Awake finally to the oversight, the Obama administration has injected $13 billion in stimulus money into developing high speed rail in the United States. This has given a major boost to fledgling projects like the one linking Los Angeles to San Francisco, but it is nowhere near enough to build a real network—the total estimated price tag for just that California trunk line is $45 billion.

Probably the most difficult hurdle for rail in North America is a product of one of those unforeseen side effects of subsidizing the status quo. For fifty years, as highways and wide roads have eaten up public spending and become basically the *only* essential piece of transportation infrastructure, they have radically reordered the priorities of America's cities. Where public streets may once have been seen as multipurpose public spaces, they are now viewed almost exclusively as conduits for cars. One of the delights of high-speed rail in places like Spain is that it transports you from city centre to city centre, but entirely too many North American city centres have nothing to offer the visitor who arrives on foot. Part and parcel of the sustainability project, then, will be a radical redress of the shape and priorities of the urban environment. To make the trains work, we will also have to remake our cities.

< FIVE >

THE LEAP IN THE CITY

FOOTLOOSE IN SOLE CITY

AT SOME INDETERMINATE POINT in 2008, humanity crossed a
vital threshold. It may have been a trainload of workers from
China's interior arriving at the station to find work in one of the
country's massive new industrial cities, or maybe it was a Kenyan
family leaving a destitute farm for an uncertain future in Nairobi.
A kid from the Midwest stepping off a plane at LaGuardia to find
his fortune in Manhattan, or a young Mexican migrant arriving
surreptitiously in Los Angeles. In any case, the weight shifted forever from one side of a fulcrum to the other—for the first time in
human history, more than half the world lived in cities.

A United Nations report that year projected an urban population of 6.4 billion worldwide by 2050—nearly equal to the whole
planet's population today—out of a global total of 9.2 billion.
More than nine billion people, 70 percent of them residing in
cities. Our future, then, if we intend to have one worth investing
in, will be an urban future, and the most vital Great Leap Sideways
may well be the one taken by our urban spaces.

This may sound, on the surface, like a fool's errand. Cities,
after all, have long been the antithesis of living in harmony with
nature. Certainly the definitive images of big-city life in my youth

were portraits of squalor, decay, depravity and crime. And some of the most hopeless of these were images of New York. Escape was the literal goal in the 1981 film *Escape from New York*, and a more figurative or psychological one in sitcoms like *Welcome Back, Kotter* and *Diff'rent Strokes*, in the music of the Ramones and Public Enemy, and in films like *The Panic in Needle Park* and the relentlessly bleak *Taxi Driver*.

Though I knew nothing of it at the time, *The Panic in Needle Park* was a roughly accurate depiction of Bryant Park in Midtown Manhattan in the 1970s (it earned the "needle park" sobriquet because of the popularity of intravenous heroin injection at the time). And the Times Square of *Taxi Driver*, though impressionistic, is not a particularly exaggerated rendering. Times Square was a lurid neon adult playground in reality as well, its sidewalks lined with porn theatres and prowled by petty criminals and prostitutes. New York's municipal government had come within a hair's breadth of bankruptcy in 1975, and a blackout in the summer of 1977 had triggered a twenty-four-hour explosion of riots and looting. The city teetered on the brink of collapse throughout the era. And Times Square and Bryant Park—these two once-vital public spaces, separated by just a couple of blocks—together formed the dark, seedy centrepiece of the city's decline.

The city has been a critical social unit and primary economic engine of civilization at least as far back as ancient Greece (arguably all the way back to the Old Testament cities of Ur and Babylon). And New York was the zenith of the Industrial Age metropolis, the wellspring of a modern nation's prosperity and the repository of its wildest hopes and dreams. But its time, it seemed, had passed. Our brightest future appeared to reside elsewhere—most likely among the wide freeways and curvaceous avenues and tidy shopping malls of booming suburbia.

My own first encounter with Midtown Manhattan just a generation later is a story of a fundamentally different place. A few weeks after the terrorist attacks of September 11, 2001, my wife and I came to New York to visit friends. We found ourselves near Times Square with a lazy autumn afternoon on our hands. We wandered down a cross-street—as I recall, we were trying to find the legendary Algonquin Hotel, thinking maybe we'd pop in for a nostalgic cocktail. Instead, we stumbled upon a wide, quiet lawn of radiant green, capped at one end by some grand stone edifice. At its base lay a broad, tree-shadowed patio—a perfect spot for an afternoon drink. The bar was open, but there were hundreds of empty seats. Half an hour after we sat down, the New York Stock Exchange closed for the day, and the patio was soon packed tight as a hip nightclub with traders from the surrounding towers taking the edge off their market buzz before starting the commute home.

We'd unknowingly taken seats on the upper terrace in Bryant Park at the foot of the New York Public Library. The experience was almost cinematic in its unexpected drama and broad comedy. We talked shop with a couple of young traders whose North Jersey accents were a thing we'd previously believed to exist only as movie cliché. We witnessed fashion statements we were powerless to avoid gawking at. And we left, much later than we'd planned, feeling somehow part of the city in a way tourists rarely do. It was urban living at its best—a couple of random visitors colliding with a horde of locals going about their daily ritual in a vibrant public space perfectly proportioned to host both of them. It was one of those unpredictable, profoundly humanistic intersections so beloved by passionate urbanists of the Jane Jacobs school.

Our serendipitous afternoon notwithstanding, there was nothing accidental about Bryant Park's dramatic turnaround. It began with a group of concerned citizens and local property owners, who formed the Bryant Park Restoration Corporation (BPRC) in 1980 to rehabilitate the crime-ridden square. The City of New York leased the park to the BPRC in 1988, at which point it was summarily closed for a five-year renovation. The park's biggest problem was its isolation, which was by design—when it had been laid out in the 1930s, urban parks were imagined as oases amid the city's gritty chaos, not central nodes in its daily life. Bryant Park had thus been elevated above the street and closed off to its neighbourhood behind high hedges and iron fencing. The BPRC redesign removed many of these fortifications and punched new rights of way through what remained. Fixed benches were replaced with more than three thousand movable patio chairs and tables, turning the park's Great Lawn into a more versatile and informal space. And the Upper Terrace, once the hub of Needle Park's drug bazaar, became a stylish restaurant and watering hole.

A decade later, I'd become a much more frequent visitor to the city, and I'd even absorbed a little of the native New Yorker's contempt for Midtown. I'd come to think of Times Square in particular as a dizzying eyesore, a place with all the charm of a theme park ride's overlong queue and none of the thrilling payoff. If it couldn't be avoided entirely, Times Square was merely to be endured. Which is why my social call one brisk afternoon in the fall of 2009 was all the more remarkable. In intermittent drizzle at grey twilight, I strolled casually up Broadway from Herald Square at Thirty-fourth Street along a pedestrian promenade broken only by the lights at each cross street. And when I reached Times Square I took a seat right in the middle of it.

Times Square was an urban space reborn. For the first time in many generations, its name was no longer an ironic vestige of an age long past—it was a public square again. As I settled into a metal patio chair at a little red café table, one of many scattered across a broad expanse of pebbled, sand-coloured pavement, I did what so many visitors to New York have longed to do as they found themselves jostling along Times Square's narrow, overcrowded sidewalks: I simply stopped and watched the city's pounding heart, decongested at last, as it pulsed boisterously along. At one nearby table, a tourist family took snapshots of themselves; at another, a dark-suited gentleman took a phone call. In front of us, an expanse of empty pavement hosted a quick-stepping parade of pedestrian commuters. A young man stood among them, holding a hand-lettered placard that read FREE HUGS, eliciting many grins and the occasional taker.

The NASDAQ ticker still spat out its endless, frenetic LED stream of market quotes, and the towering ads for soda pop and electronics still brought a neon glare to the space. But as I sat in quiet repose, with room to stretch and exhale, I couldn't help but wonder if Times Square had ever before been this civilized.

If it ever had, it would've been at a time well before the supremacy of motorized transport. For decades, cars and trucks had dominated Times Square like alpha predators prowling the Serengeti. Fully 89 percent of the square's surface area was dedicated exclusively to motorized traffic, while the 350,000 pedestrians who tromped through each day were penned into the remaining 11 percent of the space, rubbing shoulders and bumping hips on the narrow sidewalks as they struggled for marching room amid a tangle of sandwich boards and hawkers and construction scaffolding.

But on May 24, 2009, for the first time ever, Broadway was closed to motor vehicle traffic from Forty-second Street to Forty-seventh. There was little fanfare, and not even much in the way of new construction. Some simple temporary bollards went up to mark off the space, and a few months later the pavement got a coat of epoxy gravel in green, beige and burgundy to differentiate the pedestrian and cycling space from the cross streets still open to motor vehicles. As an afterthought, a local business association scattered a couple of hundred lawn chairs in the empty space. The total cost to the city—even once the comparatively posh metal café tables and chairs were brought in to replace the widely mocked lawn chairs—was $1.5 million, little more than a rounding error on the sums the municipal government spends trying to keep cars moving safely around the city.

As cheap and simple a makeover as the pedestrianization of Times Square was, it inspired a flurry of anticipatory anxiety and outrage. Cabbies predicted impenetrable gridlock, and Broadway theatre owners worried about declining attendance. One *New York Post* columnist, Andrea Peyser, was particularly apoplectic. "In the annals of stupid ideas," she wrote, "this has got to be the worst. Ever."

Chaos, however, failed to ensue. Even the *Post* noted "surprising results" the day after the closure, "with traffic flowing smoothly out of the city during the usually horrific rush hour." The *Post*'s front page that day depicted a Times Square scene so dense with strolling pedestrians it looked like a street festival. A banner headline read, "SOLE CITY: It's the Great Walk Way as B'way Car Ban Begins."

The heated rhetoric is almost understandable, because this Great Walk Way scene marked a fundamental change in the nature of urban life and the priorities of the modern city. The pedestrianization of Times Square is best understood as a sort of final triumphal hop at the end of a much greater Leap, a half-century in the making and ultimately global in scale, that traces its origin all the way to the car-choked streets of Copenhagen, Denmark, in 1962. Before we examine those humble Danish origins, though, let's first take a look at the tangled web of problems plaguing cities around the world—the urban crisis that has made this jump a global necessity.

THE DEFEETED CITY (*SIC*)

When you're hunting for a free seat amid a crowded copse of café tables in Times Square, you probably don't think of your problem as one of mobility. It's not happenstance, though, that the seat you eventually find is there courtesy of New York's Department of Transportation. The solution may have taken the shape of patio seating, but the problem—in Times Square as in urban spaces the world over—was a matter of traffic.

By *traffic* I don't mean the most basic sense of the term, the simple fact of people moving from place to place. I mean rather the more freighted modern term, the *stuck in traffic* sense of the word in which the absence of hassle and danger would be a notable surprise. This kind of traffic defines the modern city and pervades urban living so fully that in most places it's almost impossible to imagine a day's journey without it. And our understanding of traffic is so completely linked to the idea of the automobile that I would've used a qualifying noun—*bike* or *pedestrian* or *bullock cart*—if I'd meant anything other than cars and trucks. Indeed the very idea of using a city street primarily for anything other than moving motor vehicles from place to place would first require an explanation of what is to be done with all the cars.

The tidiest story of our modern traffic conundrum goes something like this. In the first decades of the twentieth century, the automobile went into mass production and revolutionized mobility everywhere it went. People could travel much further, much faster, on whims as frivolous as simply being in the mood to drive. At the same time, the roaring industrial economy was filling overcrowded urban spaces with noxious clouds of smoke, lethal cinders and blankets of choking ash, the stink of pulped wood and smelted metal and slaughtered animals. People of sufficient means—a class that expanded in rapid synchronicity with the industrial economy itself—relocated their residences as far away from the filthy, dangerous inner city as possible. Even as steel-framed skyscrapers in dense glittering clusters were coming to exemplify the modern workplace, expansive homes on ever-larger lots on the urban periphery came to define the modern house-hold. Enabled by the automobile commute, cities grew out as well as up, particularly in the second half of the century, after the birth of the tract suburb.

In the half-century after the Second World War, the spacious suburban home with two-car garage and broad, manicured lawn on a quarter-acre patch of former farmland or wilderness was every democratic citizen's presumed birthright and every immigrant's dream. And because population densities were so low in these new suburbs, and the workplace and shopping mall so far away, the efficient movement of cars from place to place became the ultimate goal of all transportation policy and the top priority of city planning in general. This vision of urban life, car-centred and increasingly traffic-jammed, was understood to be synonymous with the good life, freely chosen in the benevolent free market as the best of all possible worlds. After all, who wouldn't want a bigger house with fancier amenities and lots of room for the kids to safely play? Whose heart is so hard it isn't set racing behind the wheel of a sporty new car at 100 kilometres per hour on a spacious freeway? Doesn't the name itself—*free*way—say all you need to know about where you're headed?

Here, though, we stumble again on the pervasive myth of the rational actor in a free marketplace, and again we encounter the great rubble pile of bias and irrationality described by the behavioural economists. Suburbia illustrates the inverse of two of The Leap's mechanical laws. In much the same way that we can't measure quantum leaps with yardsticks and we can't clearly see the sustainable horizon from the unsustainable side of the chasm, we're also not very good—individually or in groups—at estimating the repercussions of our unsustainable actions and the size of the problems they create. And moreover we're simply terrible at accurately gauging and effectively pursuing our best long-term interests. A key reason for this—one particularly relevant to the choices that created our traffic mess—is that human tic called *arbitrary coherence*, as codified by the behavioural economist Dan Ariely. The "rational" prices we pay for things are mostly random, based on arbitrary "anchors" that can be established by little more than a passing reference to a particular number. (I explained the concept of arbitrary coherence, including Ariely's use of social security digits to convince his students to bid higher or lower on luxury goods, in Chapter Two.)

If we think of the modern urban landscape as a vast, multitiered marketplace, its shape and form a product of countless anchoring decisions regarding housing purchases, employment choices, social pursuits and the myriad means of moving between the sites where these activities occur, we find Ariely's arbitrary coherence writ large. And since the Second World War, the most common and significant anchor giving coherent shape to this whole scene has been car ownership—a sort of base price of admission to the modern good life.

There was a time (or so I've heard) when a world of pure pleasure awaited the suburban motorist. And even as the costs of it all have mounted—time lost in ever-growing chunks to commuter snarls, lives lost to collisions, cities cleaved by supersized highways and the remnant fragments left to wither and decay—the arbitrary coherence of the whole transaction has barely wavered. However dire or absurd, each new cost is simply another line item in the price of living in (or near) a city. You simply *must* have a car to get around—or aspire to own one. Recall the powerful influence of Ariely's "endowment effect"—our tendency to vastly overestimate the value of what we have. The endowment effect renders us so obsessed with what we stand to lose by abandoning the status quo that we can't see the value of what we would gain. The automobile is so central to our conception of a comfortable, convenient life that we can't see the efficiency and usefulness of any other way of getting around, nor the enormous costs of the means we've chosen.

From nearly any point of view other than one fully invested in the arbitrary coherence of the car-centred norm, the actual price of all this traffic is astronomical. The basic maintenance and servicing of roads cost taxpayers $100 billion per year in the United States alone, and by one detailed estimate, the taxes Americans pay on fuel fall 20 to 70 cents per gallon short of covering the total expenses paid out by the government for motor vehicle travel. (By comparison, many European countries collect three or four times as much revenue from fuel and other vehicle taxes as they pay out.) A host of studies in recent years, meanwhile, have attempted a more thorough accounting of the cost of gasoline by factoring in the full range of externalized costs of traffic, including the environmental impact of tailpipe emissions, subsidies to the oil industry, and the skyrocketing security costs of maintaining fuel supply; estimates begin at around $5.25 per gallon and top out at more than fifteen bucks. Or how about this for an irrational state of affairs born of arbitrary coherence? The single most dangerous type of roadway in the United States is the one most prized for its seeming safety—the wide, curving, uncongested arterial road at the city's exurban fringe.

When journalist Tom Vanderbilt embarked on a comprehensive tour of the world of traffic, he peeled back the coherent veneer to uncover a place that was not just arbitrary in its logic but literally insane. His findings, compiled in his 2008 book *Traffic*, reveal the operation of a motor vehicle as "the most complex everyday thing we do." The act itself requires the use of a vast subset of 1,500 distinct skills, many of them so far away from our basic instincts and inborn, time-tested survival skills that, as Vanderbilt puts it, "In traffic, we struggle to stay human." Because we're mostly moving too fast and at too great a distance from each other to permit eye contact, all of our adaptive social cues are stripped away. It's easily the most dangerous thing any of us does with any regularity. And on average, Americans spend more time in this state—overwhelmed, dehumanized, engaged in a bewildering and potentially deadly ritual—than they do having sex or eating meals with their families.

What's more, Vanderbilt discovered that nearly every "common sense" effort at fixing our traffic problem has either made no lasting difference or else deepened the problem. Wider lanes with fewer distractions on the roadside are actually more accident-prone than cramped, crowded ones. Widening highways and building new ones only encourages us to drive more and has a negligible effect on the overall flow of traffic. The more we treat traffic as a discrete transportation problem, the further we get from a durable solution. And in the meantime, the toll all that driving takes on the places we live continues to mount.

The city is a textbook case of a sum greater than its parts, but that larger cumulative total is reached only when the individual parts can be properly added together. Reconfiguring the city for motor vehicles has, by contrast, been a protracted act of subtraction, parcelling off essential urban spaces—residences, workplaces, marketplaces, social spaces—into isolated islands linked only tenuously by traffic-choked roads.

Innovation is the fuel in the urban engine, the socioeconomic force that powers the city, and recent archaeological studies have found that it is a direct product of population density. The great evolutionary and civilizational leaps made by our prehistoric ancestors occurred only in those places with sufficient densities to encourage a brisk trade in ideas between disparate groups. Small wonder, then, that dense, human-scale communities exert an instinctual pull on us even when they've all but vanished from the housing market. Demand for walkable urban spaces in the United States—the birthplace and most welcoming home of the suburbanized, low-density car culture—far exceeds supply. One conservative estimate found that a third of American homeowners prefer to live in walkable communities, but they represent at most 10 percent of the available housing stock. Homes in dense, multiuse urban centres in American cities, even newer areas well outside the downtown core, command premiums of more than 50 percent, while by one estimate the US will have as many as *twenty-two million* excess large-lot homes on the urban periphery by 2025.

The suburban model has begun to fail even on its own terms. The cul-de-sac, the quintessential suburban street form, has turned out to be much more expensive to equip with essential services than any other type of residential street, and it feeds a traffic pattern that increases congestion in the community as a whole by up to 80 percent. Typical suburbanites, meanwhile, spend between 25 and 40 percent of their household budgets on transportation, while those in walkable urban spaces—even those well outside the centres of cities—spend less than 10 percent on average. And since the dawn of the twenty-first century, suburbia has also been home to the largest and fastest growing population of poor people in America. We are paying more to achieve less in a deepening spiral of unsustainable urban dysfunction.

The act of bringing this spiral to its end and restoring balance to the city is the crucial first step—maybe the only essential one—in bringing sustainability to urban life. And it is a deceptively simple process—no more complicated, on the surface, than cordoning off a patch of asphalt and placing a handful of patio chairs on the reclaimed oasis of public space. The automobile turns the public street into a private sphere of fast, dangerous private transport, a transient, negative space that exists only as the conduit between isolated private spheres—home and work, work and store. The solution is to place at least as much value on public spaces as private ones and to put the priorities of people ahead of their cars in the urban hierarchy.

Simple as this transformation might seem, it begins with an act of revolutionary resolve—a disruptive technique, in other words. And it was a genial Danish professor in old Copenhagen who brought that technique to New York.

THE RECONQUEST

Jan Gehl is an architecture professor at the Royal Danish Academy of Fine Arts. As I explained in Chapter Two, he has spent nearly half a century studying the reclamation of urban spaces from the dominion of the automobile, a phenomenon he has taken to calling *reconquest*. From humble beginnings as a researcher counting strolling pedestrians and patio seats on Copenhagen's streets, Gehl has emerged as one of the world's most revered theorists of civic life, disseminating Copenhagen's urban design philosophy and assisting in the re-engineering of urban landscapes around the world.

In Gehl's view, public spaces supply the life's blood of democracy, the essence of humanism and the bedrock of a city's green-minded livability. "Throughout history," Gehl explained, "public spaces had three functions. It's been the meeting place and the marketplace and the connection space. And what has happened in most cities is that we forgot about the meeting place, we moved the market space to somewhere else, and then we filled all the streets with connection, as if connection was the number one goal in city planning, in public space." What he meant was that we replaced public squares with parking lots, enclosed and privatized our marketplaces as shopping malls, and then turned our streets over almost exclusively to rapid transportation by private vehicle. In so doing, we enslaved ourselves to oil, choked ourselves on exhaust, and shattered the public realm where civil society once flourished. Gehl: "It's hardly a coincidence that the First Amendment to the American Constitution emphasizes the right to free speech and to peaceful gathering with your fellow citizens. That is one of the strongest expressions of the importance of the public space."

Gehl's life's work has been the careful study of the first great urban reconquest, which began in Copenhagen in 1962. Like most European capitals, Copenhagen had grown to maturity long before the invention of the automobile. Its downtown is a tangled web of narrow, twisting pathways laid out informally by medieval habit and built to the dimensions of pedestrians and horse-drawn carts. Because few Danes had the money to buy their own vehicles in the first penny-pinched decade after the Second World War, car culture came late to Denmark. Still, it took so little motor vehicle traffic to jam those medieval roads that by the early 1960s downtown Copenhagen was hopelessly clogged. Every avenue and laneway ran thick with streams of cars and trucks, and every square in the inner city had been turned into a parking lot or traffic circle or both. On most streets, pedestrians clung precariously to strips of sidewalk not much wider than the average Dane's shoulders. Copenhagen had long been a city of bicycles, but by 1962 there was talk of banning bikes from the roads in the name of safety and traffic decongestion. The crisis was particularly acute on the Strøget, Copenhagen's primary commercial artery, a meandering chain of narrow avenues between once-grand squares that snaked from city hall to the harbour in an unbroken line of ceaseless one-way traffic.

For a number of years, the municipal government of Copenhagen had imposed a stopgap measure on the Strøget at its moment of maximum crisis—each Christmas, the street was closed entirely to motor vehicles for a few frenetic days of shopping and revelry. In November 1962, the emergency ordnance was brought in early and made permanent. Motor vehicles were banished from the Strøget's pavements forever. It wasn't the first modern European experiment in car-free urban life—a number of German and Dutch cities had closed their main shopping streets to vehicle traffic in the years after the Second World War— but the pedestrianization of the Strøget would prove to be far and away the most significant. It would transform Copenhagen, by stages, from a dour Scandinavian burgh into a thriving metropolis widely hailed as the world's most livable. Copenhagen would become a model for cities from London to Oslo, Milan to Guangzhou, Melbourne to New York. Before all that, though, the car-free Strøget was a local measure, and it was wildly unpopular for profoundly local reasons.

To stroll down the avenue to some quaint, breezy outdoor café, detractors argued, was simply not the Danish way. Copenhagen is a northern city, cold, damp and dark for long stretches of the year. Its residents claimed to yearn only for cozy indoor spaces, for candlelight and heavy sweaters and perhaps a glass of warming aquavit by the fire. The loftiest goal of Danish social life is a concept called *hygge*, which refers to a gently intoxicating mixture of warmth, comfort and close fellowship. It is a pointedly indoor phenomenon. "We are Danes, not Italians"—this was the anti-pedestrianization rallying cry. From the overcrowded pavement of the Strøget in 1962, Copenhageners couldn't see past the unsustainable traffic situation to the sustainable horizon.

The most vocal opponents of pedestrianization were the Strøget's own merchants. If customers could no longer drive to their shops, they insisted, they would simply stop coming. A number of Strøget merchants were so sure of imminent disaster that they closed up shop in the months before the car ban and relocated to a side street. It might say all that needs to be said about the rapid and dramatic success of the Strøget's pedestrian reconquest that some of those same merchants would lead the initiative to expand Copenhagen's pedestrian district to the street onto which they'd relocated.

In any case, the merchant class of downtown Copenhagen did not collapse, and Danes, it turned out, could be as easily persuaded as Italians or anyone else to sit out in the sun sipping a coffee or a Carlsberg. Indeed a new tradition would be introduced before long at outdoor cafés the length of the Strøget (and in time across the nation), whereby café proprietors lay out fleece blankets on their outdoor seats on pleasant but still-chilly afternoons in the spring and fall.

The Strøget, like a great many other European high streets, was returned once again to its natural place as a premier public space in the heart of the city. It was a small leap, really, and it might have remained nothing but a quaint regional story of Danish pluck, were it not for a young architect who started to haunt those liberated spaces in the months that followed.

As is so often the case with a Leap, Jan Gehl's jump was a cognitive one, a disruptive shift in point of view and priorities. In the first years after the Strøget's pedestrianization, Gehl undertook an unprecedented study of urban life. His interest in the public life of the city began after he married his wife, a psychologist, in 1961. "Why aren't you architects interested in people?" his wife's colleagues would often ask him. Stuck for a reasonable answer, Gehl shifted the focus of his research from the built environment to the people using it.

Gehl became an obsessive chronicler of the everyday minutiae of the Strøget. He counted the number of people walking the street's length at various times of day and different times of year, of course, but he also categorized and quantified the myriad ways people occupied themselves—a varied, vital, amorphous urban pursuit he came to refer to as "spending time." How many café seats were there on the Strøget, and how many were filled? How many people stopped to sit on the rim of the fountain at Gammeltorv? What kinds of storefront made people stop and gawk? What sorts of steps and railings invited people to take a load off for a few minutes? What times of day and year did street entertainers draw the biggest crowds?

Gehl's meticulous study—the first thorough data-driven analysis of urban public space in Copenhagen or anywhere else—was published in Denmark in 1971. Virtually every year since, the reconquered urban space of downtown Copenhagen has been expanded or improved in some way. Until then, only a single small branch and one other square had been added to the Strøget pedestrian network. But city bureaucrats finally had the proper tools for measuring the size of the city's quantum leap—reams of Gehl's hard data, attesting to the social and economic value of the reconquest philosophy—and they took to the work with renewed zeal. The primary street network was bolstered with four new pedestrian-only avenues in 1973. Several squares were cleared of cars that year as well, and more were added every few years. In 1980, Nyhavn—a row of old candy-coloured warehouses at one end of the Strøget, separated from the wharf by a thin strip of pavement that was being used almost exclusively as a parking lot—was closed to motor vehicles. Nyhavn is the final block in the whole city to fall into evening shadow, and with the cars cleared away that thin strip of pavement became Copenhagen's premier afternoon outdoor-café destination. It has been thronged with drink-sipping patrons, street performers and strolling tourists nearly every sunny day since. In the mid-1990s, the broad square in front of city hall at the other end of the Strøget, long an intractable snarl of traffic circles and bus lanes, was redesigned. Vehicle traffic was moved to the periphery, and the wide centre of the square transformed into a vital space for cultural and political activities in the city. In addition, Copenhagen is now laced with a growing secondary network of "pedestrian-priority" streets, in which cars are permitted at very slow speeds and must yield to walkers and cyclists.

Since the day the Strøget was first closed to motor vehicles, Copenhagen's pedestrian network has expanded more than sixfold, from 15,800 square metres of pavement to about 100,000. Eighty thousand people now stroll the Strøget on an average summer day, and the wintertime foot traffic—though moving faster and stopping less, as Jan Gehl's regularly updated data attests—falls only 40 percent.

The story of Copenhagen's reconquest, however, is not wholly a measure of pedestrian traffic volume. The real revolution has been in the *quality* of the city's public life. The raw numbers may have sold the city on its Leap, but it's all the fine-grained detail, hinted at by the data but often impossible to fully quantify, that has made Copenhagen a global model of sustainable living. The city's residents, once obsessed with the pursuit of *hygge* behind closed doors, have come to embrace the great outdoors of car-free public space with as much verve as any urban population on the planet.

THE LIBERATED CITY

On a recent visit to Copenhagen, I had a morning meeting at a business park in a distant western suburb of the city. I rode the regional commuter train nearly to the end of the line, anticipating an unpleasant slog from the train station to the site of my appointment. I've stubbornly insisted on using public transit to traverse suburban commuterville countless times before in sprawling metropolises from Southeast Asia to Silicon Valley, and it's always a mistake. I inevitably find myself marooned in a pedestrian-free desert populated by generic clusters of office pods separated from each other by six lanes of high-speed traffic, with nothing even vaguely resembling a sidewalk in between.

In suburban Copenhagen, though, I was a little surprised to find a dozen other commuters emerging onto the platform at my stop, and I was flat-out amazed when I followed their lead to reach not a parking lot but a tidy paved pathway reserved for walking and biking. It was separated from the rushing cars by a wide grassy median, and it wound through pod after pod of low glass office buildings and factories with bucolic ease. There's the whole grand urban reconquest in a single surprising fact: it's *wholly pleasant* to walk through a business park in suburban Copenhagen. The city's Leap has been great enough that it has reconfigured even the industrial wastes of its distant, car-centred suburbs.

Copenhagen is not perfection, not some tidily packaged finished product of flawless city living, because sustainability is a process of change and adaptation, not a destination. Copenhagen is simply the state of the art in urban sustainability, the world's richest repository of best practices, refined and updated with mounting enthusiasm.

"Quality of life"—*livability*, for short—is a highly subjective term. What qualities? Whose life? Measured how? But in any case, Copenhagen now routinely finishes at or near the top of global livability rankings. It placed either first or second on the last three worldwide "Most Livable City" lists published by the jetsetting British journal *Monocle*, for example, and it was named the greenest city in Europe in an exhaustive survey conducted by Siemens and *The Economist*. The Danish capital is about the same size as Detroit, but the average Copenhagen resident lives—lives *well*—using only one-tenth as much energy. The city is a sort of living repudiation of the idea that a low-carbon, car-free lifestyle in a dense city is in any way a kind of sacrifice. Sustainability's hairshirts, it turns out, are cozy and stylish.

For a full generation now, the baseline of Copenhagen's transportation policy has been to keep growth in motor vehicle traffic volumes flat, even as the city grew rapidly. And this simple change in point of view—not to treat increased traffic volume as some inevitable facet of urban growth but to refuse to let it happen at all—has guided a fundamental shift in the city's planning and design. To cite just one unconventional measure for keeping gridlock at bay, Copenhagen's transportation officials have been slowly chipping away at the number of available parking spaces across the city, eliminating an imperceptible 2 or 3 percent each year. At the same time, the city has actively encouraged the growth of other modes of transportation—not just feet on pavement but subways and commuter trains and especially bicycles.

Maybe the most illustrative example of Copenhagen's impressive achievement in the art of green livability is the modest digital counter mounted alongside Norrebrøgade, one of downtown Copenhagen's busiest commuter arteries. The device is a tall, slim slab in black and grey, about the size of a small billboard. Its four LED displays inform commuters of the date, the time, the number of bicycles that have passed over the sensor embedded in the bike lane beside it on the current day, and the cumulative volume of bike traffic that has passed since it was installed in June 2009. The reason the sign is on Norrebrøgade is because it is the test case for a new innovation called the "Green Wave," in which the avenue's traffic lights have been carefully synchronized so that bicycle commuters will hit nothing but green lights on their ride to and from work. The city has introduced this innovation basically because it is not satisfied with its enviable livability. Copenhagen intends to be completely carbon neutral by 2025, and one way it plans to achieve this goal is by becoming the most bike-friendly city on the planet.

In 1996 Jan Gehl and his academic partner, Lars Gemzøe, published a progress report on the Copenhagen reconquest entitled *Public Spaces Public Life*. The study overflows with impressive stats, perhaps none more startling than the city's commuter data. Thirty-one percent of the metro area's residents, the study noted, were by then travelling to and from work by mass transit—the exact same portion as travelled by car. And the largest share—34 percent of all Copenhageners—making their daily commute by bicycle. Within a generation, the motor vehicle traffic that had nearly ground downtown Copenhagen to a halt in the early 1960s was well on its way to becoming the choice of last resort for Copenhagen's commuters.

The bicycle's share of Copenhagen commuting has since grown to 37 percent citywide, with fully 55 percent of downtown residents now using bikes as their primary transportation mode. (Only 25 percent of Copenhageners now commute by car.) Recently, the goal was set to expand the city's legions of cyclists to 50 percent of all commuters by 2013. To this end, bike lanes have been dramatically expanded and improved across the city. The standard Copenhagen bike lane is physically separated from motor vehicle traffic, either by a curb, a line of parked cars or a tree-lined median. At busy intersections, the bike lanes, often as thick with traffic as the roads next to them, are governed by their own traffic lights. When this failed to improve the bike accident figures sufficiently, the bike signals were given priority, switching to green a few seconds before the motor vehicle signals so that the bike traffic is already out into the intersection before anyone in a car can decide to make a right turn. At the most dangerous intersections, right turns for motor vehicles are controlled by a separate signal entirely and forbidden while the bikes have the right of way. (This has all but eliminated the dreaded "right hook," probably the single biggest cause of serious urban cycling accidents the world over.)

Even best-in-the-world bike lanes aren't enough to achieve the city's increasingly ambitious goals all by themselves. "We have sticks and we have carrots and we have tambourines, and you can't reach 50 percent with just carrots," Copenhagen bike planner Niels Jensen explained. "I mean, we have a pretty good infrastructure, and of course it can be better. Much better. But still it's a pretty good infrastructure. And even if we build it complete, we don't believe that you can reach 50 percent." The city was considering the most effective stick—a congestion charge that would impose steep fees on motor vehicles entering the inner city during business hours—but Denmark's federal government has vetoed that measure until 2015 while it considers a user-fee scheme for roads and highways nationwide. Which leaves tambourines, cheerleading and other forms of persuasion from the behavioural economist's toolkit. The digital "Green Wave" sign on Norrebrøgade, for example, reminds cyclists every day that they are legion, and that the city has adjusted the traffic signals to maximize the ease of their collective journey. Like a smiley face on an electricity bill, it's a routine reminder that the city's bike commuters have made the right choice, that they are part of a large and growing movement.

It's also a strong example of the sort of can't-see-there-from-here resistance that can persist even *after* a successful Great Leap. Jensen again: "The Green Waves for cycling—that's something we have been fighting here for many years. The engineers said that it's not possible to do that. You can't make a Green Wave for let's say ten or twelve signals, coordinate them, because the speed of the cyclists is too uneven, it varies a lot. But when we tried it, it worked perfectly well. So it has changed what is possible to do."

The net result of all this, Jensen noted, is to create a city where cycling becomes automatic, the default option. "It becomes like breathing" is how he phrased it. I heard almost the exact same description from the bike enthusiast who brought me to see the Green Wave counter in the first place—Copenhagen filmmaker and biking advocate Mikael Colville-Andersen, who'd only settled in the city when he was in his twenties.

By the time I met him, Colville-Andersen had become a

consultant to cities around the world on Copenhagen's approach to biking, as well as the proprietor of two well-trafficked blogs that documented its evolution day to day. He had a funky cargo bike leaned up against the park bench where we sat, watching the thick flow of morning commuters pedalling by on Norrebrøgade. Here's Colville-Andersen on his introduction to cycling in Copenhagen: "When I got off the train and down to my friend's house, he said, 'Alright, there's two things you need to know, Mikael. One is that FC Copenhagen is now your football club, and you can't decide that, okay?' And the other one was, 'You need a bike.' That was just a necessity of life here."

He paused to point out a particularly stylish young woman biking by. The noted absence of Lycra racing gear and generally casual vibe of Copenhagen's bike crowd is a recurring theme—Colville-Andersen considers it critical to cycling's impressively steep growth curve in the city. "Here, the bicycle is a vehicle," he explained. "It's a tool. We have 500,000 people who ride every day, and I always say we don't have any cyclists in Copenhagen. None of them identify themselves as a cyclist. They're just people who are getting around the city in the quickest way."

As with great design generally, urban design is at its most exemplary when it is mostly invisible, intuitive, inevitable. *Like breathing.* Fortysome years after flirting with a cycling ban, Copenhagen had designed a bike transportation network with that kind of unconscious ease to it—as powerful a symbol as any of the success of the city's Great Leap. And the process, it turns out, is easily translated to languages other than Danish. Colville-Andersen even has a word for it, a verb to describe the act of making a Great Urban Leap. It's the name of one of his popular blogs on the subject. *Copenhagenize.*

COPENHAGENIZATION

For their fiftieth wedding anniversary, Jan Gehl and his wife decided to take a self-propelled tour of Gehl's life's work, a sort of mobile review of the Copenhagen urban sustainability model. They got out their bikes, I mean, and they went for a good long ride. Gehl: "My wife and I, in our early seventies, we did our 20 kilometres through the city, through all of the nice places in the city. On our bikes, in leisurely tempo, and a good style — on safe bicycle lanes — and had a wonderful dinner at an outdoor café. Which was one of seven thousand outdoor seats. And all the bicycle lanes and all the outdoor eating has happened while we were married. We could not have done that forty-five years ago."

Simply spending time — it might be the paramount example of the understated revolutionary force of the whole Copenhagenization process. Imagine almost anything called to mind by the word *urban* — from a debate across a Parisian café table to the teeming bazaars of Delhi or Marrakesh — and the image it inspires is one of people spending time. Unmeasured and unvalued until Gehl started tracking it statistically, this practice of spending time turns out to be precisely the sort of incidental interaction of people in public space that differentiates a thriving city from a dying one.

Just as Copenhagen had embarked on the rapid expansion and enhancement of its public spaces, and Gehl began assembling his array of statistics tracking urban vitality, cities all over the world were encountering grave crises in the health of the public sphere. They didn't always realize that this was the nature of the problem, though, at least not at first. The crisis instead may have been initially understood as traffic congestion or urban decay, violent crime or the drug trade, the "donut city" problem of a downtown drained of its vitality to feed growth at the periphery, a dwindling tax base or crumbling infrastructure. Recall the near-broke New York of the 1970s, its government going bankrupt and its public squares turned into warrens of vice—it was becoming a place in which people didn't want to spend time. Its public sphere, broadly defined, was in crisis.

Though mostly unmeasured, this public sphere is not an incidental feature of the city. It is rather its lifeblood. It is the wellspring of all social capital. When Francis Fukuyama described social capital as the *sine qua non* of democracy, he was referring to the many processes of civic engagement in the public sphere that build a healthy political culture. The regulatory failure that permitted the financial meltdown of 2008 was a failure of the public sphere. The externalization of the real cost of our energy use—resulting in both our addiction to fossil fuels and the climate crisis that addiction has caused—is at base a failure of the public sphere to properly account for the public costs of private enterprise. And many of the most acute problems of the modern city were caused by the privatization of the public sphere, starting with the conquest of public streets by private automobiles.

The historian Tony Judt has argued that "the disintegration of the public sphere" is the defining crisis of twenty-first-century democracy—a self-reinforcing and thus deepening crisis, particularly for the current generation of youth growing up in societies devoid of a functional public sphere. Judt's *Ill Fares the Land* is worth quoting at length on the subject:

> If public goods—public services, public spaces, public facilities—are devalued, diminished in the eyes of citizens and replaced by private services available against cash, then we lose the sense that common interests and common needs ought to trump private preferences and

individual advantage. And once we cease to value the public over the private, surely we shall come in time to have difficulty seeing just why we should value law (the public good par excellence) over force . . . In an age when young people are encouraged to maximize self-interest and self-advancement, the grounds for altruism or even good behavior become obscured. Short of reverting to religious authority—itself on occasion corrosive of secular institutions—what can furnish a younger generation with a sense of purpose beyond its own short-term advantage? . . . If we don't respect public goods; if we permit or encourage the privatization of public space, resources and services; if we enthusiastically support the propensity of a younger generation to look exclusively to their own needs: then we should not be surprised to find a steady falling-away from civic engagement in public decision-making.

Or, to put it in Copenhagen's terms, how would you learn the value of great public spaces—how would you understand how critical it was to invest in them—if you'd never spent time in one? Such was the situation for a wide swath of the urban world just as Copenhagen's public-space renaissance was hitting its full stride, and so Jan Gehl began publishing his urban design ideas for audiences outside Denmark. The first English translation of his 1971 study of Copenhagen appeared in 1987 under the title *Life Between Buildings*, and it inspired reconquest campaigns in cities around the world. Gehl's expertise was soon in high demand, and he realized that in documenting his hometown's public life, he'd developed a toolkit that could be easily used to reinvigorate public spaces and build sustainability back into cities anywhere.

"Cultures and climates differ all over the world," he once told an interviewer, "but people are the same. They will gather in public if you give them a good place to do it."

The global reconquest has taken Gehl—and, later, the urban design firm he established to meet the growing demand for his services—from Oslo to Zurich and from São Paolo, Brazil, to Guangzhou, China. He worked with the city of London in the wake of its massively controversial congestion charge to enhance its newly decongested urban spaces, and he redesigned the harbourfront in Pittsburgh to be a "100-percent location," where people live and work and play all hours of the day and every day of the week. In every case he's found that following the same simple principle—the development of quality public space in places where there are lots of people—has worked as a catalyst for reconquest. And he has encountered essentially the same resistance to his initiatives every time.

Consider the very first step Gehl often recommends, which is the physical reclamation of some portion of the city's streets from the dominion of the automobile. Total pedestrianization is not always prescribed—sometimes simply building wider sidewalks, removing parking spaces and reducing traffic volumes can do most of the work of Copenhagenization. But in any case Gehl inevitably runs into the same litany of caveats and counterarguments. Traffic will go berserk. People will flee the space in droves. And businesses, in particular, will never be able to find customers in this strange new world.

Gehl: "In all the years I've worked, I've never come to any city anywhere without somebody pulling me aside and saying, 'You must realize, my good man, that this is contrary to the spatial culture in this particular place.' Could be Canada, could be New York—especially New York—could be Australia. All the places—even in all the Danish provincial cities, going from one to the other—you'll always be told that in this particular little region and corner of the country, we have a rather special way of using our cars here which you must realize. And then things were changed and you heard nothing afterwards. That's typical. And when it has been recorded, there is solid proof that to treat people gently is good for business."

In Brighton, England, Gehl Architects redesigned a key commercial street, reducing automobile traffic by 93 percent, increasing pedestrian traffic by 62 percent, and upping the volume of people "spending time" by a factor of six. Gehl helped Mexico City conceive and execute its first modern cycling infrastructure, laying out more than 300 kilometres of new bike lanes. In Rotterdam and Sydney and Wellington, New Zealand, Gehl and his colleagues have counted people strolling, sitting, cycling, spending time. Without fail, the Copenhagenization process has proven useful in places with nothing whatsoever in common culturally or geographically with a Scandinavian harbour city built on a medieval street plan. *Cultures and climates differ all over the world, but people are the same. They will gather in public if you give them a good place to do it.*

Perhaps the hardest test for Copenhagenization's axioms has been the city that considers itself the exception to every rule, the ultimate metropolis—New York. Jan Gehl's whirlwind relationship with the Big Apple began in November 2005 with a lecture at New York University and a meeting with civic leaders to discuss the city's urban design. Before he left, he was interviewed by an enthusiastic executive from a local engineering firm named Janette Sadik-Khan. Just over a year later, Michael Bloomberg appointed her commissioner of the New York Department of Transportation (DOT), and by 2007 Gehl and his colleagues were counting walkers and gawkers on the streets of New York City. They determined that New York was a world-class walking city in terms of pedestrian numbers and latent potential, but it was an incoherent, dysfunctional mess in terms of pedestrian infrastructure. Fully 30 percent of the sidewalk surface along the three busiest miles of Broadway, for example, was covered over with scaffolding, and a mere 3 percent of the "at rest" space on a key shopping artery in Soho was dedicated to pedestrians. (The lion's share of it was a parking lot for cars and bikes.) Some of Gehl's findings beyond Manhattan were especially surprising. Who'd have suspected, for example, that Flushing Main Street in Queens saw more pedestrians each day than Copenhagen's pedestrian-friendly Strøget? But its sidewalks, a mere half the width of the Danish model, were overcrowded 83 percent of the time, impeding not just walking traffic but safe and efficient transit use.

Gehl's survey was published in early 2008, and by summer the reconquest was underway. For three consecutive Sundays that August, a 7-mile stretch of Park Avenue and the Bowery, from Central Park to the Brooklyn Bridge, was closed to motor vehicle traffic. More than 150,000 New Yorkers thronged the liberated street, building support for the broader campaign. Street by street and sidewalk by sidewalk, Sadik-Khan and her speedy redesign crews transformed Gehl's recommendations into reality. Car-choked concrete expanses became modest public squares at Herald Square in front of Macy's, at Madison Square at the foot of the iconic Flatiron Building, in a small patch of nameless, derelict parking space in Brooklyn. The re-engineering of stretches of Broadway—including the full pedestrianization of Times Square—not only created vibrant public space on the city's primary thoroughfare but allowed for smarter traffic-light timings on east-west cross streets, improving motor vehicle traffic flow throughout Midtown Manhattan. (Northbound taxis traversed Midtown 17 percent faster on average after the closure.) A bus rapid transit (BRT) system was launched to improve commuting crosstown and beyond. Ninety miles of new bike lanes were designated in just the first year of the new program, precipitating an unprecedented 35 percent spike in bike commuting (well on its way toward a goal of tripling bike traffic in New York by 2020).

Here's Sadik-Khan on the strategy at work: "It's great to have a great idea. 'World class streets for a world class city!' Who can argue with that? But getting it done really was the difference. And so we developed this rapid implementation team here, so that we could transform pavements into plazas in a matter of weeks. With just a paint can and a paint brush and some planters, we were able to grab underutilized pavement and give it back to people."

If the shock of a car-free Times Square garnered the most headlines (and inspired the most groans), the most thorough Copenhagenization of New York might be along Ninth Avenue, which runs arrow-straight up the west side of Manhattan. Ninth Avenue is a broad commuter artery carrying one-way traffic south out of the centre of the city—the sort of high-speed automobile channel that has always been especially dangerous and forbidding for pedestrians and cyclists. Using a loosely codified set of design principles for implementing Copenhagen-style smart growth called "complete streets," twenty blocks of Ninth Avenue were reconfigured as an everyday functional counterpart to the Times Square marquee. To turn the car-centred avenue into a complete street, a smart bike lane was built along one side, separated from motor vehicle traffic by a mix of medians, concrete planters and parked cars. (It was the first physically separated bike lane ever built in New York, and bike traffic shot up 57 percent within a year of its construction.) A range of medians and other "pedestrian refuges" were installed at every intersection, serving both to slow down motor vehicles on cross streets and physically narrow the space pedestrians have to traverse to cross the street by more than 30 percent. At the complete street's southern end, triangular patches of old pavement and cobblestone have been hemmed in by concrete slabs and planters to cordon off Gansevoort Plaza as a pedestrianized square. After generations as a space almost exclusively for cars, the pavement of Ninth Avenue has been reclaimed as a public space for all. It has also become a model for citywide complete street redesign.

The tools of Copenhagenization are sufficiently common-sensical and universal that a great many cities around the world have liberated themselves without Danish assistance. Nevertheless, the same basic techniques and processes are generally at work — and the same biases, as well. Portland, Oregon, for example, is every urban designer's preferred example of a formerly car-dominated American city that has waged a thorough and successful battle against the automobile. In Portland's case, the catalyst for change was a ferocious political fight in the 1970s to stop the levelling of a downtown neighbourhood to make way for a freeway. The victors in that battle soon discovered many of the same tools their Copenhagen colleagues did. They rehabilitated and inaugurated a few public squares. They developed good public places for people to gather in. They expanded mass transit and built safe, dedicated, often physically divided bike lanes — more than 300 miles of them to date, for the same price as a single mile of freeway. As a result, bicycle use in Portland tripled in the first decade of the twenty-first century, and Portland's transit system, which nearly went bankrupt for lack of passengers in the late 1960s, now carries one of every eight of the city's commuters to and from work each day.

In Montreal, the city's public sphere reinvestment found its initial inspiration in the city's longstanding tradition of closing streets for grand summer festivals. In 2008 a twelve-block stretch of Ste-Catherine Street—the city's closest analogue to Copenhagen's Strøget—was closed to motor vehicles for the whole summer. Around the same time, the municipal government began developing a public bike-sharing system similar to the one pioneered in Copenhagen (and later expanded upon in Paris and Barcelona). The Montreal system's designers took care to address the shortcomings of the first generation of systems. Paris's Vélib' bikes, for example, were easily broken, so Montreal's bikes are built on a durable one-piece aluminum frame. In Barcelona, bikes had a tendency to migrate to the bottom of hills and never return to the top, so Montreal's system is modular, with locking stands that can be moved to meet roving demand. The resulting system—Bixi by name—was assembled from scratch in just eighteen months and launched in the spring of 2009. It was an overnight success: not only has Bixi quickly emerged as a highly visible symbol of the city's deepening commitment to urban sustainability, with more than five thousand bikes in operation by just its second year and a 99.7-percent in-service rate, but it has become the market leader as bike-sharing systems spread around the world. After just two years on the market, Bixi systems have been installed in London, Toronto, Minneapolis and Washington, D.C., and there are Bixis on order for Boston and Melbourne.

This urban bike boom is just one facet of a broader global movement toward Copenhagen-style livability. As I noted earlier, popular demand in the US for homes in walkable, human-scale communities far exceeds supply, and such housing commands a premium wherever it has been built. In one study, the simple fact of being located within walking distance of entertainment, shopping and other amenities added between $4,000 and $34,000 to the value of an American home; in Belmar, the pioneering New Urbanist district in the Denver suburb of Lakewood mentioned in Chapter Two, property values were as much as 60 percent higher than the surrounding neighbourhood, while homes in a similar development in suburban Washington, D.C., were valued 50 percent higher than those in less walkable parts of the community.

In the developing world, as well, smart urban growth has become a widely adopted tool for broader improvements in quality of life. Efficient new mass transit systems in cities like Bangkok and Delhi have become powerful symbols of urban ambition, while in Bogotá and Medellín (as discussed in Chapter Two), pedestrian walkways, bike lanes and BRT were critical tools in crime prevention and poverty reduction as well as urban renewal.

These cases duly noted, Copenhagen remains the most revered model for urban sustainability worldwide. And so to fully understand how Copenhagenization works, let's take a closer look at the city that has had the longest and deepest experience with the process: Melbourne, Australia.

COPENHAGENIZATION DOWN UNDER

In June 1978, there appeared in *The Age*, Melbourne's prestige daily newspaper, a vitriolic analysis of the city's urban design. "Effective city planning has been almost unknown in Melbourne for at least thirty or forty years," wrote Norman Day, *The Age*'s architecture critic. "For the ordinary Melburnian, that means our city has been progressively destroyed. It no longer contains the attraction and charm it once had." The essay's headline pointed toward the root of Melbourne's problem. AN EMPTY, USELESS CITY CENTRE, it read.

Melbourne was, in other words, an archetypal example of the "donut city" pattern that had dominated the growth of New World cities since the Second World War. The exigencies of the automobile and the suburban tract home had emptied out downtowns in booming metro areas from the Canadian prairie to the American heartland to the southern coast of Australia, as people and their tax revenue rushed to the low-rise, car-centred periphery. Melbourne was a particularly acute case: a small, central municipality surrounded by a broad and fast-expanding ring of separate suburban boroughs. The boundaries of the City of Melbourne itself contained less than half as many residents as it did at its 1954 peak, and the central business district (CBD) was almost completely bereft of noncommercial life. The CBD's total residential population was barely 1,000, and its tall office towers were linked by "skybridges" that sucked still more life from its streets. In addition, many of the wide Victorian avenues of Melbourne's gridded downtown had been turned over to through traffic that traversed the core at high speeds en route from one suburb to another.

Today, Melbourne might well be the most fully rehabilitated donut city in the world. The inner city bustles day and night, its broad sidewalks thick with foot traffic and its laneways overflowing with cafés and funky little shops. At the southern edge of the CBD, crowds gather on the expansive steps of Federation Square, the landmark plaza studded with stylish restaurants, galleries and performance spaces that was inaugurated in 2002. No city has worked as closely for as long with Jan Gehl—his involvement in the civic life of Melbourne has spanned more than thirty years —and so Melbourne is also the poster child for Copenhagenization. It provides incontrovertible proof that the tools of Danish urban design can be applied successfully to the streets of even the most car-obsessed New World metropolises.

The reconquest of Melbourne—its Leap from donut city to global model of urban sustainability—would in time require a thousand big changes and tiny tweaks to the fabric of the city, but it began with two running steps. The first was the election of new governments at the local and state levels in 1983, both of which came to power with explicit revitalization mandates. It was broadly understood that the status quo no longer served the city; people and public space simply had to be put ahead of cars if the city was to have any future at all. Working with a range of consultants—eventually to include Jan Gehl—the municipal government developed a new master plan and began charting its new course.

One of the key consultants, Rob Adams, was installed in a new position, director of city design, and charged with the task of coordinating activity in disparate city departments toward the common goal of revitalizing the city as a whole. Adams would prove to be an even more critical figure than Gehl in Melbourne's reconquest. In the first years of his new job, Adams busied himself with a laundry list of minor details: installing better surfaces of iconic Melburnian bluestone on the sidewalks, cajoling downtown developers into building more and better "active frontages" for the street-level facades of their buildings, planting more trees streetside.

The next stage in Melbourne's Leap—the point of no return, when it truly launched itself from the car-centred, unsustainable side of the chasm to the sustainable Copenhagenized side—started in 1991. It began with the partial pedestrianization of Swanston Street, the Melbourne CBD's most important north-south thoroughfare. Streetcars and service vehicles were still permitted to use the street around the clock and it would reopen to all traffic in the evenings, but for much of the working day it was liberated from motor vehicle traffic. "We had 26,000 cars thundering through the centre of the city," Adams recalled. Now they had virtually none. This "grand gesture," as Adams referred to it, was symbolically important, even if it was only a minor transformation at street level. Naturally, the neighbourhood's merchants held up their old yardsticks and estimated that the closure amounted to a disaster roughly the size of a retail apocalypse. Adams: "The retailers were up in arms, we were going to kill them. Well, we've doubled the number of pedestrians walking past their doors. You know, you don't shop from a motor car—not at 60 kilometres an hour, you don't."

In the wake of this first victory, Melbourne's reconquest quickened its pace. Adams brought in his old friend Jan Gehl (who had taught at the University of Melbourne in the late 1970s) to assemble the statistics and make the case for the next phase of the plan. A 1994 report, *Places for People*, co-authored by Gehl and the City of Melbourne's urban design and strategic planning departments, established "benchmark data" to measure the success of the coming changes, set targets for the city's public life to be achieved by 2001, and proposed strategies for reaching them. As in Copenhagen, Gehl's first contribution was simply to provide measurement where none had previously existed.

But Gehl served a second purpose, possibly the more critical one. Australians talk often of their chronic "tall poppy syndrome"— their tendency to hack down fellow Aussies whose ambitions grow too high—so Gehl, as a distinguished foreign expert, could make the case for boldness where a local official couldn't. Adams again: "Jan's role here was not in actually writing the strategy—he never did that—but in assisting as a sort of an international mentor that could actually sometimes act as a voice for what we were trying to do, and therefore gain recognition from the local people that this wasn't a bad way to be going."

In addition to fewer and slower-moving cars, the report recommended more residences, more outdoor cafés, more and better public spaces, quieter trams, and integrated street furniture. All of this would come to pass, and then some, with startling speed. Outdoor café seating shot up by 177 percent over the next ten years, and public space grew by 71 percent. The long-neglected City Square got a smart new makeover, and the swish new Federation Square made its debut. Weekday pedestrian traffic was up 39 percent across downtown, and evening foot traffic had doubled. The 1994 report recommended increasing downtown Melbourne's population from about 2,000 to 4,000 by 2001; by the time of the 2004 follow-up report, more than 9,300 people lived in the downtown core, and the total number of apartments in the area had grown by more than 3000 percent from the 1982 level. Newspaper kiosks, water fountains, public toilets and information pillars were all built to the same design specs, underscoring the renewed sense of integrated street life and civic pride. In 2003, just twenty-five years after dismissing downtown Melbourne as an "empty, useless city centre," *The Age* described it as "a city few would have imagined thirty or even ten years ago." Gehl called it "the Melbourne miracle."

There's probably no stronger symbol of the nature of that miracle than Melbourne's laneways, which have been transformed from unloved back alleys for service vehicles into the very heart of the city's street life. The laneways began life as a sort of correction to a planning error; when the city's downtown grid was laid out in the mid-1800s, it was built with overlong east-west blocks, so small paths were cut into the blocks, providing shortcuts for pedestrians and, in time, pleasant shopping arcades. In the age of the automobile and the office tower, however, the neglected laneways had been reduced to service corridors, places for delivery trucks and garbage bins. When Jan Gehl conducted his 1994 survey of Melbourne's street life, he found that just 8 percent of the 3.7 kilometres of the city's laneways were "accessible and active." The *Places for People* report strongly urged the municipal government to reconquer this forgotten public space.

Rob Adams and his team were particularly vigilant on this point. The city's "laneway improvement program" obliged new and refurbished buildings alongside laneways to include active frontages and put huge incentives in place for existing developments to open their laneway-facing facades to retail activity. The impact was revolutionary: by 2004, 92 percent of the city's laneways were "accessible and active," which only hints at the scale of the change. Melbourne's laneways aren't just active—they are perpetually *thrumming*. They're lined with stylish little boutiques and shops and packed with cafés and bars. There are grandly restored Victorian arcades in the laneway network, but there are also funky little warrens enlivened by graffiti art and hip music. The old cracked concrete between buildings has been replaced in many laneways with pleasing brick or bluestone, but often as not it is barely visible for all the café tables and chairs and stools that fill the space. By day they offer up coffee and lunch to hordes of office workers, and by night they are the preferred launch pads for evenings out in Melbourne's boisterous core. The laneways zigzag throughout the city centre, as if a broad Italian piazza has been unravelled into a thin strip and strung around the city like garland.

Melbourne's lanes also illustrate a critical lesson about Copenhagenization: It is a broadly applicable disruptive technique, but it is not a one-size-fits-all urban model. When it adopted the Copenhagen point of view, in other words, Melbourne did not import the physical geography. Cobblestones were not laid on

Melbourne's streets, and its buildings did not get primary-coloured paint jobs in the style of Copenhagen's old harbour warehouses. Instead, Copenhagenization cast Melbourne's existing infrastructure in a new light. The unloved vestige of its laneways became its greatest asset. But they are distinctly Melburnian, not a universal fix. Here's how Rob Adams explained it: "A lot of people who come to Melbourne say, 'We love the lanes. Now, we've got to copy these lanes.' Well, you know, that's fantastic they want to copy them, but unless your city's actually got them already, it's going to take you decades to get people to put lanes back. So we were lucky . . . The challenge is to get people to realize you just can't pick up one model and transport it to another city. You can pick up the *principle* that we're going to make the city more livable."

It was mid-2008 when Rob Adams told me this, and he had no intention of easing up on his campaign for change. He'd just moved into an office in the municipal government's elegant new tower, which was far and away the greenest building ever built in Melbourne. It was solar-panelled for both electricity and hot water, generously sunlit and efficiently lightbulbed to reduce its energy use for lighting by two-thirds, and outfitted with nighttime "purge windows" to air-cool the building and reduce the air-conditioning load by a fifth. It was intended to inspire the city's next Leap.

"The 1980s was about livability—we've done livability," Adams told me. "You know, we can vie with the best in the world about a livable city. Our agenda now is sustainability. But ironically, the criteria used for livability and sustainability are very similar. So the good news is if you convert to a sustainable model for a city, it's actually going to become a better place to live in. Because increased densities, mixed use, connectivity, local character, all the things that we did to improve the livability of the city are exactly the same things you need to do to improve the sustainability."

When people gather in public—which they do, as Jan Gehl's aphorism informs us, wherever you give them good space to do so—there's more to the scene than just the urbane joy of it. More space for people means less space for cars, fewer tailpipes coughing carbon dioxide. People on foot use transit more often and play and work within walking distance of the places they live. There are plazas from Imperial Roman times that are as functional today as they were then, apartment blocks older than the internal combustion engine that still provide top-quality living space. The same has never been said (and never will be) for freeways and off-ramps. When the people come to the reconquered city, they may come for the livability, but they stay because the scene can sustain itself. They stay because there is public space to *be* in. Public space is the physical location for civic life, social interaction, the nurturing of that elusive but precious commodity called social capital. It is out of such raw materials that community is built. And community, both as a physical place and as a social force, is a vital ingredient in The Leap to sustainability.

< SIX >

THE LEAP IN THE COMMUNITY

POWERLESS

WHEN HARVARD UNIVERSITY political scientist Robert D. Putnam set out to define and quantify "social capital"—that network of formal and informal associations, professional and personal relationships and reciprocal engagements by which an enormous amount of society's critical institutions get built and the world's business gets done—he recognized it would be a slippery concept. His own summary description acknowledges social capital's ephemeral nature. "The term social capital emphasizes not just warm and cuddly feelings," Putnam wrote, "but a wide variety of quite specific benefits that flow from the trust, reciprocity, information, and cooperation associated with social networks. Social capital creates value for the people who are connected and at least sometimes for bystanders as well . . . When a group of neighbours informally keep an eye on one another's homes, that's social capital in action. When a tightly knit community of Hasidic Jews trade diamonds without having to test each gem for purity, that's social capital in action. Barn raising on the frontier was social capital in action, and so too are email exchanges among members of a cancer support group. Social capital can be found in friendship networks, neighborhoods, churches, schools, bridge clubs, civic associations and even bars."

As for what social capital is worth, that's a figure sometimes best calculated by the cost of its absence. Let's return to New York City on the night of July 13, 1977, for a stark case in point. At around 9:30 that evening, lightning struck one of the city's electrical substations, sparking a chain reaction that plunged all five New York boroughs into darkness. In an instant, seven million people were without power. Traffic ground to a halt and thousands were trapped in subway trains. Emergency vehicles tried in vain to get to the neediest, while the police scrambled to maintain calm.

There was a fairly recent precedent for the event, a familiar script to fall back on: in 1965, an even more widespread blackout had paralyzed New York. And it had been met by the city's resilient populace with co-operation, voluntarism and the widespread sharing of vital resources. It had been an inspirational exercise in peace and goodwill. A vigorous trade in social capital, in other words.

In the intervening decade, however, much had changed. The city had endured a period of steep social decline and financial chaos. For the first time ever, New York's population was on the wane. There were not enough police officers on the payroll to keep the city safe and not enough dollars in the coffers to keep roads surfaced and subways clean. Whole commercial districts of Lower Manhattan had hollowed out almost entirely, leaving block after block of empty warehouses; the trade at the docks—New York's commercial life's blood since the days of the Black Ball Line—had moved to New Jersey and beyond. In some of the poorest neighbourhoods in Brooklyn and the Bronx, where social supports had withered away along with the shrinking population base and tightening municipal purse, entire blocks of apartments had been left empty, as landlords, unable to extract rents from the destitute, abandoned their real estate as worthless.

July 13 was a stinking hot night in the midst of a roiling summer dominated by the mounting tensions of civic bankruptcy, social decay and the hunt for a serial killer who called himself "Son of Sam." When the lights went out, New York became two entirely different cities. In the neighbourhoods where social capital was still abundant, a repeat of the 1965 blackout ensued. Neighbours shared flashlights and food, volunteers set themselves up in the streets to direct traffic or headed down to the subway with emergency crews to help in the rescue. A headline in the *New York Daily News* the next day told the story of this side of New York: SPUNK, CHEER SHINE THROUGH.

The more widely told story of the 1977 blackout, however, was the one *Time* magazine referred to in its cover story the following week: NIGHT OF TERROR. Within minutes of the power outage, the stressed social infrastructure in the city's toughest neighbourhoods gave way entirely. The ghettos of New York exploded. Almost literally so: more than one thousand fires were lit that night and the following day before power was restored. Looters plundered thousands of stores. Beneath the tracks of the elevated train on Broadway in Brooklyn, fourteen contiguous blocks of businesses were ransacked and set ablaze. In the end, almost 4,000 New Yorkers were arrested, and the damages would eventually be tallied at $300 million—more than half of this total caused by looting and arson. This was the cumulative value of the social capital lost over the previous twelve years.

So what then, ultimately, is social capital? It is the joint trust account that bankrolls the building and enhancement of community. And when the reserves dwindle too low, all the critical infrastructure of community—the social trust, co-operation and shared vision from which society is made and Leaps are launched—falls apart. Before there can be a Leap, then, there must be a community, a place well-stocked with social capital.

(COMPLETE) STREET VALUE

Here's another way to think about the value of social capital. Find the most vibrant parts of a city, the places where everyone from the surrounding area goes to shop or see a show or splurge on a good meal. There you will almost invariably find diverse retail streets fronting on wide sidewalks, parks and public institutions, transit hubs and bike lanes, homes and offices right next to and right on top of stores.

There are a variety of terms for this agglomeration of stuff to do—mixed-use development or transit-oriented development, Smart Growth or New Urbanism, walkability or livability or (urban) sustainability. Not long ago, some number crunchers and software whizzes patched together census data and the kind of local business information embedded in Google Maps into an algorithm called "Walk Score." This helpful if somewhat crude measuring tool assigns a one-to-a-hundred ranking of the ease of walking and the number of destinations worth walking between in a given neighbourhood.

Some savvy realtors have started adding Walk Score to their property listings, because walkability serves as a sort of shorthand for the things that actually inflate the sale price of a home: walkable neighbourhoods with great public spaces, where as much or more happens on the street or at the local coffee shop or pub as in the basement rec room in front of a flatscreen. Walkable neighbourhoods promise diversity—of incomes, backgrounds, uses and points of view—and they provide the means by which these diverse elements can commingle, cross-pollinate, multiply and amplify their worth. Walkability is shorthand for social capital, and people are happy to pay hard cash for an abundance of the stuff, because it makes community grow.

Community emerges everywhere people gather, of course, because we are social animals by nature. Despite their highly uninspiring contexts, there is community in refugee camps and in the poorest slums, and in the aisles and parking lots of Walmart Supercenters (which serve as a vast, informal network of RV camps across America). The point of the mixed-use urban development, though—its added value, if you will—is that it *nurtures* community.

We understand this instinctively. Human society has provided for this need throughout history, and it has been the fundamental building block of human habitation from the tribal village on up. The sudden absence of community, as in a refugee situation, is immediately understood as an emergency. (Indeed, a big part of what international aid does is to reconstruct the pillars of community in a safer space than the one being fled.) When a decline in community happens gradually, however, by tiny subtractions and separations like the ones visited upon the North American suburb, the crisis can come to look like the most placid of norms.

As a result of this fragmentation, much of the compound interest of sustainable community has been lost. In such circumstances, allegorically speaking, old folks taking their morning constitutionals at the shopping mall never see what the kids on skateboards or shooting hoops are getting up to, and the preacher rarely trades notes with the teacher, and the shopkeeper is a long commute away from a conversation with the mayor about how business has been since the new bus routes were introduced. The Great Leap Sideways for communities across North America often begins with the reunification of community's farflung parts, the re-accumulation of social capital.

This process is already underway in many North American metropolitan areas, though often as not in a piecemeal, fragmentary way that mirrors the original separation. Strip malls have been retrofitted for residential and commercial uses as well as retail ones, and structures built for chain fast-food outlets now house ethnic eateries owned by recent immigrants. A fading strip mall in Phoenix, Arizona, becomes a stylish destination so trendy it makes souvenir T-shirts, while a similar structure in Boca Raton, Florida, is converted into a mixed-use residential complex for seniors. Across America, at least a dozen former Walmarts have become churches. In each case, isolated pockets of private, generic retail have been transformed into something closer to integrated multipurpose public space.

In their textbook on this process, *Retrofitting Suburbia*, architects Ellen Dunham-Jones and June Williamson argue that even the booming trade in technological surrogates for community has only enhanced the value of the real thing. "Public spaces are crucial for supporting the public life that binds a community," they write. "But does community building today rely on public space? Many critics and commentators contend that the political and cultural roles of physical public space have been replaced by the media, by shopping and by the virtual world of cyberspace. The old distinctions have been obliterated by television, cellphones, Webcams and blogs. Yet, rather than substitute for public space, they appear only to have fed a greater desire for direct experience of connectivity, especially in the suburbs."

There's probably no better illustration of this point than the "meetup." Almost anywhere on the internet where the like-minded and socially inclined have congregated, the online interactions and conversations have eventually inspired the organization of a flesh-and-blood gathering to strengthen the digital community's bonds and expand its purposes. People meet up to talk pop culture trivia, share hobbies, explore obsessions and fetishes. But there are also meetups to build political campaigns (internet-arranged meetups are credited with providing vital early momentum to Barack Obama's presidential run) and to build community in a physical sense. In this digital age, the meetup has often become a precursor to the process, an aggregator of social capital ahead of the spadework of community building.

Consider the case of Oak Cliff, a neighbourhood on the southern fringe of downtown Dallas, Texas—an inner-belt suburb whose history tells a sort of shorthand story of the crisis of community in North American urban life. Oak Cliff was one of Dallas's first satellite towns, founded in the late 1800s as a railroad suburb and annexed by the larger municipality in 1903. The community prospered throughout the first half of the twentieth century and then reached its peak in the roaring postwar years. An explosion in new housing and new lifestyles and institutions transformed it into a quintessential Baby Boom suburb, the living embodiment of the lifestyle that would later be sentimentalized as an American ideal in the TV show *Happy Days* and films like *American Graffiti* and *Grease*.

Tract houses with single-car garages went up along Oak Cliff's streets, and amusement parks, drive-in theatres and fast-food restaurants lined its boulevards. (The term "drive-in restaurant" was coined by an Oak Cliff restauranteur, whose barbecue joint was locally famous for its leggy "carhops" on roller skates.) By the end of the 1950s, the trolley tracks that had long linked Oak Cliff to the rest of the city were torn up, in final acquiescence to the supremacy of the automobile.

In the early 1960s, Oak Cliff's fortunes shifted dramatically, beginning with a vicious school desegregation battle that instigated a "white flight" to newer suburbs further afield. Though pockets of prosperity remained, Oak Cliff's story became mostly one of decline through the rest of the century, told most often as an adjective attached to some of Dallas's worst crimes—*Oak Cliff murder, Oak Cliff drug raid.*

Low rents, empty spaces and old urban infrastructure often serve as magnets for the young and artistically bent, and in recent years Oak Cliff's mix of these elements inspired the beginnings of a community revival. In art galleries and hip bars, a new story of Oak Cliff began to emerge, spilling over onto blogs and Web sites. Little caches of social capital started to fill the neighbourhood's underused spaces. Community, though, needs welcoming street-scapes in which to truly thrive, and many of Oak Cliff's most promising avenues had been gutted by car traffic and bad zoning. Oak Cliff yearned for *complete streets.*

In April 2010, on the occasion of the second annual neighbourhood art crawl, a local non-profit called Go Oak Cliff joined forces with Bike Friendly Oak Cliff, a cycling advocacy blog, to stage a sort of meetup where they could address this need. There was a particularly promising two-block section of Tyler Street lined with great old prewar storefronts, a good sidewalk, some sympathetic local businesses. The trouble was the three lanes of fast-moving traffic, compounded by a planning mess that had zoned one side of the street only for residential uses and the other side only for light industrial. Businesses along Tyler were unable to put up awnings or put out seats, and some stores remained empty because smaller enterprises would be unable to supply sufficient parking to meet the zoning requirements. When the new bike shop in the neighbourhood had staged a street party the previous summer to celebrate its opening, Dallas police had broken it up, telling the organizers in no uncertain terms that the streets were for cars, not people.

Under the guise of a temporary "art installation" called "Build a Better Block," the non-profit group and the biking blog transformed a two-block stretch of Tyler Street into a complete street, at least for one pleasant weekend in April. The better-block builders had less than $1,000, a truckload of simple supplies and a cadre of volunteers. They painted a lane on the street in bright green and stencilled some bike symbols on top of it and used a row of parked cars as a buffer, and they slapped some thick white stripes down to make crosswalks. They widened sidewalks and built a median using potted plants and trees as barriers, and they set out café tables and chairs. The local pizza place built a patio out of surplus wooden shipping pallets, and the better-block gang established a handful of "pop-up businesses" for the weekend: Wigwam Flowers, the Philosophia Café, an art studio for neighbourhood kids. They painted murals and strung up lights and unfurled a banner across Tyler that read, "Hey Dallas! This is how to build a better block!"

All day and into the night, locals and art crawlers strolled, sat, lingered and chatted. Kids zoomed through on bikes, and street musicians performed. Car traffic trawled past at substantially lower speeds than usual on the two narrow lanes that remained. The bookstore had some of its best sales days ever. For a short time, all of Oak Cliff's nascent social capital had sufficient space to come together and build a community.

Jason Roberts of Go Oak Cliff provided an ecstatic summary for a documentary crew's cameras as the event unfolded in the background: "We've got the first complete street in Dallas. As you can see, it's pretty popular around here. We didn't have to hire consultants from other faraway places to make this happen. It took us a day. And all we did was slow the street down. We made room for everybody— for cars, for people, for bicycles. That's all we've got to do. We changed the psychology of the street. We changed the economy of the area."

In the months to follow, the better-block builders consulted with city officials about making the changes permanent and launching a plaza conversion trial in Oak Cliff, and they worked with two other Texas cities on replicating the better block. They learned— re-learned—and then taught their neighbours that community is not difficult to build and social capital reserves are never exhausted. They simply need a space—a complete street—in which to thrive.

THE RUINS OF THE UNSUSTAINABLE & SUBURBAN UTOPIA

There are few human landscapes as resilient as a well-made urban street. Gut the neighbourhood or let it crumble or bomb it into ruins, sprinkle it with broken glass and garland it in garbage, but if it is a good street and there are people nearby, it will recover. It will draw social capital to it like a magnet. It will become, time and again, the heart of a community.

Abandoned urban space is never more than a few good ideas away from thriving community. It can even be manufactured more or less on demand—provided, that is, the demand comes from within rather than without. This is the lesson—one of them, anyway—written on the streets of perhaps the most successful suburban development project of its time, a neighbourhood built on Cold War ruins south of the Black Forest city of Freiburg, Germany. A sainted place that has come from nothing to stand as the very model of sustainable community in less than twenty years. A place called Vauban.

"The ruins of the unsustainable," the futurist Bruce Sterling has said, "are the twenty-first century's frontier." Vauban was such a ruin, a French army base outside of Freiburg operated for forty years as part of the defence of West Germany against the Soviet menace. With the fall of the Berlin Wall and the demise of the Soviet Union, the base was summarily abandoned, leaving a ghost town made primarily of military barracks.

Freiburg's municipal council decided within a year of the French withdrawal to redevelop the site as a new residential district. But even before a development plan could be properly discussed, the vacant streets of the old base had attracted new residents. They parked camper-vans and trailers in the empty spaces between military buildings, establishing makeshift homesteads. The generic German term for their vehicles—*Wagen*—would lend the place a new nickname: *Wagenberg*. The *Wagenbergers* were soon joined by students from Freiburg's esteemed but space-constrained university, who petitioned the city to convert some of the empty barracks into dormitories. After an interregnum of protest and heated debate, the *Wagenbergers* were permitted to stay and ten of the barracks were turned over to the students' union for retrofitting. Meanwhile, other interested parties—would-be residents, that is—formed their own collective voice, a sort of lobbying group they called Forum Vauban.

The new neighbourhood, whatever it was to become, would not be the singular vision of a deep-pocketed developer or a micromanaged top-down master plan. This would prove to be perhaps the most critical detail in the whole Vauban project. It would be a collective, grassroots endeavour, the product of the social capital of its aspiring residents as well as the financial capital of its owners and the political capital of its overseers. This somewhat accidental approach to suburban redevelopment was the essence of Vauban's

Leap—a shift from expert studies and precise controls to the unpredictable, ad hoc wisdom of the general population. In digital-communications circles, they call this "crowdsourcing," and Vauban was in a sense the first crowdsourced neighbourhood design of the twenty-first century. In more conventional terms, Vauban was an exercise not just in residential development but in community building. The result of the process is a place so flawless in its conception and execution, so careful in its attention to detail and so welcoming in its general aspect, that it's difficult to imagine how it could have come together without the guidance of some grand overarching vision.

Quartier Vauban, as it is formally known, is a collection of more than a dozen distinct subdevelopments arrayed along two main thoroughfares. If there were standard city blocks in Vauban, the community would perhaps fill sixteen fairly tight ones. It was built in three phases from 1998 to 2008, and it is now home to about 5,000 residents. There are ten converted barracks buildings for students and many tidy rows of new midrise flats and townhouses, as well as a cluster of handsome live-work buildings and a permanent space for the *Wagenbergers*. The energy allotment required by the units in the new buildings is at most 30 percent of the German average, and a district heating plant at the community's edge burns wood chips efficiently for hot water and space heating. One side of the heating plant provides shade for a community chicken coop, where residents can collect fresh eggs for 50 euro cents each. Or they can just bring their kids—30 percent of Vauban's residents being under the age of eighteen, an astounding number for a community in rapidly aging Europe—to play with the chickens. Much of the story of Vauban's extraordinary Leap in sustainable community-building lies in details like this one. Barely ten years old, it has the general feel of a community that has been there forever. It is lived in, cared for, refined, *adored*.

I was taken to see the chicken coop and everything else by a Vauban couple who typify the place demographically. Gesine Bänfer and Ian Harrison are in their early forties, with three energetic daughters. They are musicians who specialize in playing near-obsolete medieval instruments, performing together at folk and classical festivals around the world. Their two older daughters attend the Rudolf Steiner (a.k.a. Waldorf) school across the creek from Vauban proper, and the youngest is at the kindergarten in the shadow of the neighbourhood parking garage; both the school and the garage are crowned in solar panels. Like more than half of Vauban's residents, Bänfer and Harrison don't own a car, so they receive a sort of rebate in the form of the avoided purchase price of their parking spot in the solar garage. (Parking spaces in the garage retail for around €20,000, so this is no small savings.)

This is the most famous detail about Vauban—midway through the development process, Forum Vauban and the city decided together to plan the community with limited road access and without permanent parking spaces adjacent to the buildings. Residents who wanted cars could park them in the garage at the community's edge, and the considerable land this freed up in the community itself could be used for public space, walking and biking paths, transit, playgrounds and parkland. Primarily on the merits of this extraordinary sacrifice—suburban living without a car!—*Time* magazine named all 5,000 Vauban residents to its list of 2009 "Heroes of the Environment." This amuses the hell out of many of those residents, because the car-free thing is such a small detail, really, in the grander community scheme. And in Vauban, it is no kind of sacrifice.

My tour of Vauban began at the kindergarten. The building itself is a low-slung, primary-coloured series of attached, self-contained classroom units, each with its own patio and garden, like a row of holiday condos. Vines hang from trellises for shade, and there's a communal cob oven out in the rear courtyard where the kids learn to bake. The previous week, Bänfer told me, the kids had used the oven to roast the potatoes they'd grown themselves in the school's garden. As you do in Vauban when you are five.

As we strolled Vauban's wide, car-free main drag amid a makeshift parade of kindergarteners and parents heading home for lunch, Bänfer and Harrison took turns pointing out the sights. Here was the old barracks thoroughfare, reborn as a central promenade for vibrant suburban life. The tramline running alongside us had opened in 2004, just as the neighbourhood was starting to fill in. The space between and around the tracks was covered in a lush blanket of grass—to reduce noise, not just to look pretty—and trams whisked Vauban residents the 3 kilometres to Freiburg's cobblestoned and mostly pedestrian-only downtown core in about ten minutes, passing through a thirteenth-century stone gate and linking up with the wider transit network at several points along the way. (Freiburg's transit system is as thorough and efficient as any I've ever found anywhere—especially remarkable considering that this is not some broad-avenued metropolis but a regional city of 220,000 built around a cramped medieval core.)

We passed an expansive square with a community centre on one side and an elegant café on the other. A little further along, we came upon the *Quartiersladen*, Quartier Vauban's bustling general store, its windows crammed with handbills and notices. "This is the absolute classic village shop," Harrison said. "The spider in the web." When he and Bänfer return from one of their performance tours, they always check in at the general store to hear the latest news and find out whether their subletters behaved themselves.

At regular intervals we passed sidestreets lined with residential buildings, the spaces in between given over to jungle gyms or walking paths lined with park benches or, in one case, a communal brick oven. The most common development scheme in Vauban was a neat line of a half-dozen conjoined apartment blocks, narrow buildings four or six storeys tall, each one outfitted and trimmed to the specifications of its residents. The mix of styles and facades lent the young neighbourhood a sense of maturity rarely seen in a new residential development. In the early days of Vauban's reconstruction, prospective residents had formed *Baugruppen* ("building groups") to work together with architects, engineers and the city to determine the specs of each block of flats. The city established certain basic guidelines—the energy efficiency standard, for example—and each *Baugruppe* worked on its own to meet those standards.

As the first wave of Vauban residences was being built in the late 1990s, Bänfer and Harrison decided to pay a visit one day, more or less to gawk. "It was just a boring Sunday and we went out to have a look what's going on here," Bänfer explained. She'd grown up in a small village, and she loved the little creek running along the edge of the neighbourhood. All the buzz that day was about a fancy new *Passivhaus* complex just completed, so they went to have a look.

"We didn't really know what a *Passivhaus* is, we had no idea," Bänfer said. "We heard rumours about it." Though still newfangled in those days, "passive houses" have become one of the most celebrated trends in German architecture. These are structures designed to soak up sunlight and trap its heat zealously, greatly reducing the building's overall energy needs. The first passive house went up in Darmstadt in northern Germany in 1991; today, there are more than 15,000 passive house buildings worldwide (most of them in northern Europe), including twenty in Vauban.

Between the creek and the eco-conscious design, Bänfer was entranced, so she and Harrison wandered over to a notice board to study the financing. Bänfer told Harrison she couldn't imagine Bohemian artists like them being able to afford to live there. A woman standing nearby overheard and asked if they would like to join a *Baugruppe*. Soon they were working together on design details, architectural plans, the programming of the community space around their section of Vauban land. They learned about a favourable government loan scheme in place for young families, and Harrison's parents kicked in a modest down payment. More than a decade later, the woman from the notice board is their neighbour in a row of meticulously efficient *Passivhausen*. Harrison: "The community is much older than the houses, because we were planning for two years with these neighbours before we moved in. So when we moved in, we knew the neighbours on both sides."

The collaborative financing and design process thus turned out, almost by accident, to be a powerful investment tool for *social* capital. The results were evident at every turn. I stayed in the community for nearly a week with my family in a rental apartment, and I felt like we'd have been ready to start hosting dinner parties if we'd stayed just a week or two more. Literally within five minutes of arrival—while I was still unloading our luggage—our four-year-old daughter had been invited into a game of pickup soccer with the neighbourhood kids. She also learned to ride a push scooter on Vauban's car-free streets. One evening there was a rollicking block party in the laneway between buildings the next block over from ours; in the one beyond that, we discovered an expansive fort in a copse of trees. Meals at the local café were languorous affairs, with kids kicking balls around in the square while the adults finished off their wine. The next tram to go into town for dinner or shopping was never more than a few minutes' wait. From recycling to buying local produce to parking your bike, the sustainable choices were also the most obvious and intuitive, the *easiest* ones to make. In Vauban, sustainability was not an overlay or an afterthought; it was the foundation of the whole community.

Toward the end of my walking tour with the Bänfer-Harrisons, we'd turned down a back street. We came first to the cogeneration plant with the chicken coop in its shadow. A little farther along were low-rise office blocks containing studios and live-work spaces, and the University of Freiburg's *Studentendorf* district of repurposed barracks lined much of the rest of the street. It terminated at *Wagenberg*'s permanent home. The old caravans and trailers had been arranged along either side and up meandering side lanes, stitched into the larger community as effortlessly as the students and the live-work artisans and knowledge workers and the Bänfer-Harrisons with their low-energy *Passivhaus* and medieval instruments and angelic trio of fair-haired girls.

"I'm constantly amazed this exists," Harrison said. He was referring to the *Wagenberg* homes, but as far as I'm concerned it described the whole incomparable Vauban scene. It was all enticing enough at face value, of course, the green buildings and the lush grounds, the creek and general store, the pathways and whisper-quiet trams. But the real magic of Vauban wasn't that it was so enviable but that it seemed so *inevitable*. Community will happen anywhere, given sufficient time and enough passionate people, but Vauban had proven that it would emerge vibrant and durable and all but fully formed, almost overnight, from an urban space designed with sufficient care—and enough trust in the people who gather there to let them build it to their own specifications. Trust, after all, is an important form of social capital, maybe the most vital one, and the community's Leap is propelled by it.

There's a tendency to think of trust as something ephemeral, not just beyond measure but beyond manufacture. Vauban is a compelling argument to the contrary. To a considerable extent, you can design a community to encourage trust, simply by building it to human scale and human needs and keeping it open for people to engage in and define for themselves. The revolution in Vauban isn't particularly technical—the energy technologies and efficiency tricks that give it less than a quarter the standard German carbon footprint are hardly unique. It isn't even a design innovation so much as a careful copy of the most successful model of sustainable urban development yet created—the one I encountered nearly everywhere I went in Europe.

Consider the urban form at work in Vauban. It's a simple and straightforward design, actually: buildings three to six storeys tall, a dense but not crowded mix of townhomes and apartments, room (and permission) for small-scale retail and office space and live-work units, and lots of public space adaptable to a range of uses, with significant swaths of it car-free or at least indifferent to ease of automobile access. I'd found pretty much the same system in place when my family and I rented a flat in ultra-livable Copenhagen. It was in a neighbourhood called Vesterbro on the western fringe of the inner city, just beyond the main train station—an old working-class community, home to the city's red-light district, now midway through a significant revitalization. The buildings in the area were again mostly three to six storeys, and there was a mix of uses on each block, excellent transit, and plenty of great public space. Our apartment, for example, was in a building that shared a wall with the ramparts of the old royal shooting grounds, which had been converted into the best children's playground my daughter had ever laid eyes on. It was also a great walking and cycling route to the excellent shops up on Vesterbrogade.

Later, in Spain I noticed that this urban form readily scales downward. You find it in the proportions of the landmark Plaza Mayor in Madrid—the centre of a dense, bustling metropolis built mostly to similar specs—but you also find it along the narrow lanes and modest squares of hilltop towns in the Andalusian country-side. In Segovia it had even been integrated with a two-thousand-year-old Roman aqueduct and medieval fortress atop a Castilian mountain ridge.

In each case, this is the default urban form not because of visionary planning or an overabundance of municipal wealth but simply because it works. It suits people, makes them feel welcome on the streets and encourages them to come together to build liv-able neighbourhoods. It nurtures both commerce and community. This model is the single most successful template for urban sus-tainability yet extant. It has survived depression and war and total social collapse. It has adapted itself to the automobile age and the digital age. And it's the best urban model currently available for a low-energy, low-emissions lifestyle with an enviably high quality of life.

The standard European urban form is indeed a striking exam-ple of how to build resilience into a manmade system—the vital sustainability feature that enables a place to endure in a rapidly changing social, political and physical climate. My temporary home in Berlin was a downtown neighbourhood called Prenzlauer Berg, and it provides a particularly convincing case in point.

There might be no single neighbourhood in the world that has been as fully ravaged by the twentieth century's worst excesses as poor Prenzlauer Berg. Its capsule history reads like a litany of the most egregious sins of the industrial age. Prenzlauer Berg was initially developed as a working-class residential district back in the mid-1800s. At the start of the twentieth century, it had many of the telltale markings of a tenement slum, and it was all but deserted in the final years of the century after the fall of the Berlin Wall. In the years in between, it endured more than its share of the terrors visited on Germany as a whole: rioting and murder during the failed Communist revolution of 1918, the pogroms of Nazi brownshirts in the dark years before the Second World War (the *Wasserturm*, the community's iconic water tower, even used for a time as a makeshift concentration camp), Allied bombing and Red Army invasion, and then forty years of slow-grind exhaustion under the boot of the East German police state.

By 1989, Prenzlauer Berg was a place so bereft of sustainable life that many of the neighbourhood's elegant old flats were abandoned fully furnished by East Germans fleeing west when the Wall came down. The neighbourhood's apartments and warehouses were soon occupied by squatters and artists, at which point the well-known post-industrial makeover from ruin to Bohemian refuge to upscale mixed-use enclave proceeded apace.

Prenzlauer Berg has been reborn, just twenty years after complete bankruptcy, as one of the most livable neighbourhoods anywhere in the world and a wellspring of vibrant community. It is home to boutiques and innovative small businesses and a thriving café culture. It's the neighbourhood of choice for young families, with wide sidewalks and carefully constructed bike lanes providing some of Berlin's most complete streets. It's minutes from the city centre by subway and efficient new light rail transit (LRT), and each Saturday, it hosts the best farmers' market I've ever overindulged at. In the shadow of a sombre statue of Käthe Kollwitz, whose paintings chronicled the harrowing violence of Berlin's darkest half-century, Prenzlauer Berg puts on a weekly community-building showcase of sustainable eating.

I could go on for some time about the Markt am Kollwitzplatz. The bread, the fresh-picked wild chanterelles, the olive oil pressed on site, the luscious stacks of robust fruit and vegetables, the currywurst lunch with beer poured from a tap and served in a real glass despite the take-out counter. But to do so would really be to restate a well-known fact about Europe, which is that the food's spectacularly good. And moreover that the *culture* of growing and eating food in Europe has mostly skipped the most severe deprivations of modern agribusiness, meaning that even the most workaday green grocers and mini-markets and take-outs deal mostly in what is regarded elsewhere as gourmet food.

This should come as no surprise, since there are few ways in which we have failed our communities in North America quite as thoroughly on the sustainability front as the way in which we supply them with their daily bread.

A FIG TREE GROWS IN BROOKLYN

A black and white photo printed in *The New York Times* during the New York City blackout of 1977 tells an ugly story of Bedford-Stuyvesant, better known as Bed-Stuy, a predominantly black and Latino community in Brooklyn. The picture was taken on Broadway in broad daylight the day after the lights went out; sun pokes through the holes in the elevated train tracks overhead, lending an incongruously bucolic aspect to the scene. In the foreground, a young, shirtless African-American man holds aloft a large, pillar-shaped ornamental furnishing of some sort, balancing it precariously over his head as he marches past the photographer. Another man in the middle distance is wrestling a new mattress across the street. The looting of Bed-Stuy's prime retail strip is in full swing.

In the background is a scene that looks almost festive. The street is thick with kids running here and there, and the sidewalks overflow with pedestrians. There's a kind of community here, or the remains of one, but it is so lacking in social capital that it is evidently trying to right the balance in pilfered merchandise. For one hot afternoon, the neighbourhood is celebrating a kind of prisoner's liberation from its poverty.

Life in Bed-Stuy has mostly improved since that desperate summer day in 1977. Crime has gone steadily down and property values up as thirty years of growth and mounting affluence have pushed well-off New Yorkers outward from Manhattan across one formerly blighted Brooklyn neighbourhood after another. The impoverished precincts of Bed-Stuy remain, however, and residents there continue to live in a kind of isolation from the rest of the city that is most starkly demarcated by access to fresh, nutritious food.

There are parts of New York—the Upper West Side of Manhattan, Greenwich Village, Park Slope in Brooklyn—where seemingly every edible thing on the planet can be obtained for the right price. But in recent decades, neighbourhood greengrocers and full-service supermarkets alike have mostly avoided poor urban districts in New York and beyond. Their absence has been filled by convenience stores and fast-food outlets selling sugary, fatty junk food, and discount markets dealing mostly in heavily processed, nutrient-deficient goods. One recent study found that fully three million New York residents "live in areas severely in need of fresh-food options." Many residents in such places have essentially nowhere to go within walking or reasonable commuting distance to meet their daily nutritional needs. There's even a generic term for such places. They're called *food deserts*.

In a classic Brooklyn brownstone five blocks down a side street from the stretch of Broadway that burned in the blackout, the Brooklyn Rescue Mission stands as a small oasis in the food desert of Bed-Stuy. Since 2002, Reverend Robert Jackson and Reverend DeVanie Jackson, a husband-and-wife missionary team, have run the place as a refuge and food bank. When they began, they operated on the standard food-bank model: they solicited cash and food donations from the community at large, packed the stuff into parcels and handed it all out to the needy who showed up on their stoop. But sometimes Reverend Robert would look out the back door at the chainlinked vacant lot behind the mission house and wonder whether it couldn't be doing a bit more for the community. He'd grown up in the urban jungle of Queens, but he'd spent enough of his childhood on his grandparents' farm in Alabama to know how much bounty an empty expanse of flat land could give. "People said, 'Turn it into a parking lot and make money,'" Reverend Robert told me. "I said, 'I think it has just as much value as a farm.'"

In 2005, just in time for spring planting, the Jacksons obtained permission from the city to plant a garden in the vacant lot. They dubbed the space Bed-Stuy Farm. They cleared the garbage and weeds, turned over earth that had seen nothing but neglect for a generation, and built raised soil beds. They planted strawberries, grapes and melons, tomatoes and cucumbers, lettuce and fresh herbs, plus rows of traditional African-American staples like okra and bitter melon and collard greens. A couple of times they came out in the morning to find that the locks on the gate had been cut in the night and the fledgling garden smothered under construction debris, so they cleaned out the trash and nurtured the plants back to health. Within a few years, that formerly derelict patch of Bed-Stuy, not much bigger than a neighbourhood basketball court, was yielding seven thousand pounds of fresh produce every year; on an average day at the peak of the harvest, the Brooklyn Rescue Mission handed out about a hundred big sacks overflowing with fresh, nutritious food.

The Jacksons' Leap—the simple conviction that the earth could provide sustenance even in the food desert of a ghetto—soon began to yield unforeseen compound benefits, as well. Grandparents came with their kids, introducing them to soul-food standards that had all but disappeared from local diets. The Jacksons began to offer gardening and cooking workshops and evening tasting parties with live music. AmeriCorps (the US government's national community volunteer program) deployed a couple of workers to help with the weeding and picking, and the United Nations sent a delegation from its sustainability conference in Manhattan to see what the Jacksons were doing. In 2008, for the first time in anyone's memory, there was a weekly farmers' market in Bed-Stuy, with the rescue mission's excess produce as its anchor.

To come upon Bed-Stuy Farm today, set amid the dusty concrete and chainlink and crumbling brick of a Bed-Stuy residential street, is to discover a literal oasis. Raised planting beds boxed neatly in wood are thick with tall plants in countless green hues, accented by explosions of pink and orange flowers. Flower boxes and pots line the fences, and a brightly coloured mural has been mounted on one wall. Grapevines climb up an old concrete dividing wall on one side of the lot and hang down from the power lines above.

When Reverend Robert took me on a tour one radiant autumn morning in 2009, he finished beneath the expansive canopy of a squat fruit tree. When he and his wife first cleared the lot, he explained, there was only a single thing worth saving, "one little scrawny stick" still clinging to life amid the rubble and weeds. They left the branch intact and built the new garden around it. They fed it and nurtured it, and by the second year it had sprung new branches and grown fat with leaves. "Try the sugar ball," Reverend Robert said, pulling down a branch to pluck a plump fig. I took it from his hand and popped it in my mouth, where it exploded in a burst of rich, sticky sweetness. I'm no connoisseur, but it was the best fig I'd ever eaten, not to mention the freshest. We wondered for a moment at its provenance. Some long-ago Italian immigrant's garden, perhaps. A sort of miracle, in any case: where there'd been desert just a few years ago, a fig tree now stood in Bed-Stuy, bearing impossibly succulent fruit.

Bed-Stuy Farm is not alone in its crusade to restore life to America's food deserts. Similar operations—some as charitable missions, others as for-profit enterprises—have sprung up in cities around the country, from La Familia Verde across town in the South Bronx to City Slicker Farms in Oakland, California. Growing Power Farms in Milwaukee serves a customer base of 10,000, selling tilapia from a downtown fish farm in addition to greenmarket standards. Detroit's hollowed-out inner city has so much new farmland that its growers formed a co-op to market their produce. Philadelphia's Greensgrow Farms is one of the oldest and most successful urban farms. From an acre of farmland on the site of an abandoned steel factory in hardscrabble North Philly, it rings up about half a million dollars in sales each year peddling produce to local restaurants and the 300 members of its Community Supported Agriculture subscription system. (One of its most popular items is "Honey from the Hood," produced by its on-site bee colony.) In my local farmers' market in Calgary, a stall called Leaf & Lyre made its debut in 2010, selling leafy greens, herbs and fruit grown in a sort of distributed farm consisting of dozens of backyard gardens across the city. And farmers' markets themselves have gone from fringe to *de rigueur* in recent years, particularly in the hippest urban neighbourhoods. By the harvest season of 2009, there were more than 5,000 farmers' markets up and running in the US, up from just 1,700 fifteen years earlier. And these thousands of scattered urban farms and local markets merge with a broader trend in food consumption that has begun to reshape even the produce sections of the biggest supermarket chains. *Local, seasonal* and *organic* are the markers of a booming business in sustainable food. The global market for organic produce, for example, doubled in size from 2003 to 2008 and now rings up more than $50 billion in total sales.

For all of this, the Brooklyn Rescue Mission's fig tree is still best understood as a symbol among a great cluster of symbolic gestures. These small urban enclaves of sustainable food procurement are an exception that still has to find its way to some sustainable norm. The mainstream of food production, in the meantime, remains committed to a system of industrial monocrops grown in artificially over-fertilized soil, kept alive by petrochemical pesticides, tended, harvested and distributed by an oil-addicted processing system, and maintained by a vast web of perverse subsidies. This is a fundamentally unsustainable food production system, a sort of cheap food bubble propped up by low-cost fossil energy. It is inefficient and wholly lacking in resilience, and it now teeters on the brink of total failure.

The signs of the crisis are nearly everywhere our food is grown. In the US, for example, a single farm on marginal Midwestern land better suited to ranching might receive more than $200,000 in federal subsidies in order to grow corn to feed to cattle or chickens in some distant feedlot (or increasingly to produce corn ethanol fuel at a ratio of energy inputs to energy outputs that barely exceeds breaking even). The corn-fed livestock in turn gobble up 70 percent of all the antibiotics consumed in America just to stay alive long enough to make it to slaughter in high-density "concentrated animal feed operations." These lots have turned into breeding grounds for antibiotic-resistant bacteria. Weeds in high-yield farmers' fields across the country and around the world, meanwhile, are rapidly developing resistance to the ubiquitous pesticide Roundup.

The picture's no rosier beyond America's borders. Climate change brought abnormally high temperatures to Russia in the summer of 2010, leading to widespread wildfires and destroying a fifth of the wheat harvest from the world's third largest grain exporter. Russia responded with an export ban that helped drive wheat prices up nearly 90 percent for the year. Across the board, global food prices increased threefold from 2006 to 2008 as the costs of fossil fuels and other inputs skyrocketed—this after fifty straight years of decline from 1950 to 2000, the golden age of fossil-fuelled agriculture. Australia's Murray-Darling Basin, which feeds water to 60,000 growers in a $30-billion annual industry, no longer has enough water to flow all the way to its mouth four out of every ten days; the Australian government has begun offering farmers direct buyouts if they agree to quit agriculture entirely, to free up more water for the country's parched cities.

In the Punjab region, India's breadbasket, farmers are using three times the amount of fertilizer as thirty years ago. The glaciers feeding the region's rivers are rapidly melting, leading to water shortages and ever-deeper wells, and pesticide-resistant insects have also begun to rear their ravenous heads. The state agricultural council has baldly declared its agribusiness "unsustainable and non-profitable" and warned of permanent barrenness across much of Punjab within 15 years. In neighbouring Gujarat state, farmers receive free electricity to pump groundwater to their crops, an annual subsidy whose value routinely exceeds that of the harvest it fuels; Gujarati farmers are being paid more to pump scarce water to their fields, in other words, than those fields can produce in food sales. More than 90 percent of all the water that continues downstream from India into Pakistan's agricultural heartland, meanwhile, is used for irrigation there—and that water is doubly vulnerable, both from ecological pressures and from hostilities between India and Pakistan, two nuclear-armed countries who share the Indus watershed based on a tenuous fifty-year-old treaty.

A ruinous fungus called black stem rust has devastated crops across Africa and Asia in recent years. California's Central Valley, which produces a quarter of America's fruits, vegetables and nuts, has been plagued by drought, and both it and the South Saskatchewan Basin that feeds Canada's prairie wheat-growing heartland are highly vulnerable to long-term chaos due to changing rain patterns and vanishing glaciers. There are virtually no commercial fisheries anywhere in the world free from risk of collapse this century. And in the meantime, something at least a quarter of everything grown in America is lost to rot or waste before it can reach a plate.

To put it mildly, then, the crisis facing the world's food supply will not be solved exclusively—nor even primarily—by a Bed-Stuy Farm on every block. Except for those living nearby, Bed-Stuy Farm's power is, as I said, symbolic. The same goes for other urban farms and farmers' markets, avowedly "natural" grocers and the rest—they indicate a widespread desire for sustainable food, but they don't necessarily possess all the tools for building it. Consider: using current industrial agricultural methods, the city of New York requires a patch of farmland 150 times the size of Manhattan to feed itself. According to one report, that could be reduced to a factor of about 46 under state-of-the-art Dutch high-density farming employing hydroponic and organic methods—a step in the right direction, but not far enough to suggest Manhattan (or any other major urban centre) could reasonably host all its own food production. In our urban future, the community—any community—will by necessity be reliant on an agricultural hinterland for some significant portion of its sustenance. Fortunately, there are strategies emerging to adapt the hinterland to more resilient food production.

As in urban design, twenty-first-century food production will likely rely on density and efficiency to transition to a sustainable model. Houweling Nurseries, which started its business in the highly fertile Fraser Valley outside Vancouver, has built a next-generation greenhouse operation near Los Angeles that points in one critical direction of food-supply innovation. In essence, Houweling has applied the design innovations of the *Passivhaus* to the greenhouse. Its two new greenhouses, each of which covers 20 acres, opened in spring 2009. They zealously capture rainwater and dew, filtering and recycling it to reduce overall water requirements by 20 percent. The tomato plants inside are stacked in midrise hydroponic towers that produce 15 percent more produce than a conventional greenhouse and twenty times the yield of a conventional field. The plants require no herbicides, very small amounts of pesticide and only half the usual fertilizer; an adjacent 2-MW solar power plant supplies electricity. The greenhouses verge on self-sufficiency, and they suggest that farming's sustainable heartland might one day be situated in something more like a suburban industrial park than a vast field of loam. Houweling's greenhouses constitute a mere pilot project at present, its yield mostly symbolic in the shadow of California's $36-billion agri-business industry. But the project demonstrates, in any case, that conventional agribusiness *can* innovate along sustainable lines.

What's more, conventional agriculture has already demonstrated a willingness to shift rapidly and in impressive volume to more efficient farming techniques, even in the absence of high energy prices or climate chaos. Over the past generation, for example, thousands of farmers the world over have adopted an organizing principle that was pure laboratory experimentation as recently as the early 1960s—a practice called "no-till farming." The crisis of conventional agriculture is to a significant degree a crisis of soil fertility—the annual growth in fertilizer use and increasingly desperate hunts for more water caused by the loss of good topsoil—and no-till farming is essentially a radical soil conservation effort, capable of reducing soil erosion by more than 90 percent.

Farmers—particularly sustainability-obsessed ones—will often say their primary crop is soil. Just a single inch of fertile topsoil can take anywhere from 300 to 1,500 years to develop; for as long as there have been plows, however, conventional agriculture has encouraged the squandering of this precious resource by turning the soil over before planting, leaving it vulnerable to being blown or washed away. Modern American agriculture began with the invention of a new kind of machine-tooled plow by a Midwestern inventor named John Deere in 1837, and the Dust Bowl—a catastrophe of soil depletion that swept across the North American prairie in the 1930s—nearly ended that agribusiness model. Much of the innovation in agribusiness since has focused on replacing lost topsoil with fossil-fuel inputs that replicate its life-giving bounty each spring. As a snapshot of how conventional agribusiness functions today, consider the heavily farmed valleys of eastern Washington state, where 70 percent of farms have lost at least a quarter of their topsoil, and one in ten farms have lost *all* of it; the state's entire agriculture industry would collapse inside a year without petrochemicals.

In response to the perpetual crisis in soil fertility, farmers around the world have proven receptive to the no-till concept, and American farmers uniquely so. Beginning in the early 1970s, no-till farming expanded slowly at first, as the technique demonstrated its effectiveness year to year. From 1990 to 2004, no-till adoption tripled in the US, and it now governs 22 percent of American cropland. (The global total is 7 percent.) As a result of this and other "conservation tillage" techniques strongly incentivized in US farm policy, soil erosion on American farms declined by 42 percent from 1982 to 2003.

Under a no-till regime, fields are not cleared at the end of the harvest. Instead, crop residues are left to cover over the field as a mulch, halting soil erosion almost completely, returning nutrients to the soil and slowing the runoff of water and chemicals to a trickle. The residues also provide food and cover for wildlife; in Iowa, for example, no-till fields attract four times as many species of nesting birds as tilled fields. Instead of turning over the soil the following spring, no-till farmers use specially designed planting equipment to punch holes through the mulch for their seeds. This technique requires up to 80 percent less fuel and 30 to 50 percent less labour, and cuts capital and operating costs in half; it also sequesters substantially more carbon dioxide than tillage systems, making it doubly helpful for climate change mitigation. The only significant downside is that no-till farms require more herbicides than tilled farms, which has helped hasten the spread of herbicide-resistant weeds. Since 2008 the Rodale Institute has been working with agriculture programs at several American universities to develop an "organic no-till" system that replaces herbicides with "cover crops"—specially selected non-commercial crops grown in fallow fields to keep weed populations down until planting and to provide habitat for pests while the cash crop grows. Early trials have been encouraging enough to suggest the promise of mostly erosion-free, low-input, carbon-sequestering agriculture at industrial scale might be viable within a generation.

Other big-idea innovations of this sort are in the experimental stages of development around the world. At Iowa State's Leopold Center for Sustainable Agriculture, pioneering organic farmer Fred Kirschenmann is leading investigations into "biological synergies" that could greatly reduce agriculture's reliance on artificial inputs. The Land Institute in Kansas is several years into a multi-decade study of "perennial grain cropping"—the breeding of high-yield grain crops that self-propagate as readily as weeds each spring. And Cornell University's International Institute for Food, Agriculture and Development has developed a new management system for rice production dubbed the "System of Rice Intensification," which has upped yields by 50 percent using 50 percent less water at a quarter the cost in rice paddies from Vietnam to Mali. Agriculture is an inherently conservative business, and farmers the world over are loathe to make big changes except in the face of urgent need; as the climate and energy crises intensify that sense of urgency for the next generation, these experiments may well find converts as far and wide as no-till farming has in the previous generation.

No-till farmers, for their part, aren't resting on their laurels. Having made one Leap already, they're maybe better prepared than most in their profession to take another. I know of one in particular, a young, ambitious farmer in the cozy little farm town of Jefferson in northwestern Iowa. After a generation growing corn and soybeans and some specialty Asian beans for export on his no-till farm, David Ausberger has introduced a perennial to the mix: the wind. And one of its most profound benefits is how well a community grows in its shadow.

FIELD OF AMERICAN DREAMS

Even if you're not from Iowa, there is something immediately familiar about its small towns. The proportions of the tidy town squares, the clock tower spiking above the town hall, the baseball diamonds and amphitheatres in the municipal parks, the broad arrow-straight avenues with their canopied sidewalks and sturdy brick houses on either side with American flags flapping from the verandas. This is the landscape of Superman's Smallville and Andy Griffith's Mayberry and Marty McFly's Hill Valley. This is the Anytown, USA, of Hollywood lore, the seedbed of the American Dream.

And here's David Ausberger, ready for his close-up in Jefferson, Iowa. Happy family man, farmer's son and farmer-entrepreneur, cultivator of no-till corn and soybeans on a broad patch of healthy Iowa loam. A big, wide-shouldered body beneath a wide friendly face and an accent as flat and unassuming as the Iowa plain. A handsome home just a few blocks south of Jefferson's tidy town square. Basketball hoop hanging off the garage, toys strewn about the porch and all across the driveway by his two boys, a big goofball Lab jumping up on the guests no matter how many times you tell him *Down, boy*. When people anywhere use the phrase *pillar of the community*, they mean a guy like David Ausberger. He's the archetype. And so it's worth listening closely as he reframes the technical specifications on the American Dream for the twenty-first century.

"It seems like there's a few people in small towns that kind of make their mark on things, and then there's a lot of people that do a very good job and, you know, ten years after they're gone, you may or may not remember them. And then there's a lot of people that don't do anything. They just could come and go, and that's that. But I guess I wanted to be one of those people that kind of made a mark a little bit. And I had a relative that founded American Athletic, which makes balance beams and large gymnastics equipment, mats and that sort of thing, that you see in the Olympics. And I thought that was always kind of a cool story. You know, here's this guy from the middle of nowhere in Iowa, and every Olympics you see 'American Athletic' on the side of that balance beam. I'm not innovative enough to build my own exercise equipment, I guess, and this was a way kind of on a smaller scale to do something right. At the time it looked like wind power was a good way to go, and hopefully it'll remain that way."

This was Ausberger, explaining how he came to own a wind turbine out on his uncle's farm on a ridge just north of Jefferson. His turbine was one of seven on Hardin Hilltop, a great big Suzlon-brand 2.1-MW power plant standing on a concrete base, installed a few years back to spin in the stiff breeze that so often howls across northwestern Iowa. Together the seven turbines comprised the Hardin Hilltop Wind Farm, the first community-scale wind energy installation ever built in Iowa, which started feeding electricity to the grid in 2007.

From the point of view of the national grid, it's an incidental thing, a mere 15 MW of clean energy amid hundreds of thousands fired by fossil fuels. But the new wind farm electrified Ausberger's hometown of Jefferson in more ways than one, and its import reaches far beyond northwestern Iowa. What had long been something done only far away on a scale beyond the town's grasp—power generation—became local and intimate. And what had seemed a marginal idea speaking mainly to a different set of values—those treehuggers with their green energy—became commonplace and commonsensical at the scale of the vaunted American family farm.

Communities often form (or reform) around a singular sense of purpose, whether a common religion or ethnicity, a leader's charismatic vision or a company's single-minded industrial project. And in the global sustainability movement, small rural communities have proven to be uniquely adept at pioneering the big transitions that later emerge at much larger scale on urban streets and in the halls of national parliaments.

Several of the world's first full-scale jumps to energy regimes entirely free of fossil fuels—and still among the most thorough—occurred amid small, isolated farming villages on the Danish islands of Samsø and Aerø. Denmark's national wind program, which supplies more than 20 percent of the country's electricity, began with small installations of just a few turbines, built in many cases by small agrarian co-operative groups. The rural township of Eden Mills in southern Ontario—best known for its literary festival—has dedicated itself to becoming Canada's first zero-emissions community and a living lab for the rest of the country. There are similar efforts afoot in closeknit communities worldwide, among them the English village of Ashton Hayes, the Scottish intentional community of Findhorn, and the Svanholm ecovillage in Denmark.

These small communities often serve as sustainability's Petri dishes, test sites for The Leap, because of certain characteristics that make them particularly suited to such change. The first is an abundance of social capital, often formed organically out of the small population base and enhanced by years of necessary collaboration. (The Danish farm's common practice of placing its excess produce on a wooden shelving unit at the roadside for sale, operated on the honour system with a cash box placed next to the wares, is as perfect a manifestation of social capital as you'll find anywhere.) Second, the scale of these communities helps to establish the *feasibility* of change. Remember the experiments of the behavioural-economics pioneer Robert Cialdini: behaviour change is most likely when it is framed in terms of something most of the people around you are already doing, whether it's fellow hotel guests reusing their towels or neighbours reducing their energy use. In small rural communities, feasibility is sort of inborn—if something is happening in such communities, it is feasible for the whole community almost by definition.

At the same time, small rural communities—agrarian ones, especially—are by nature cautious and calculating. Farms operating year to year on predictable seasonal changes and daily routines don't welcome sudden change, and the community leaders raised in such places don't generally get those positions because they leap at every new fad. Small farm towns are rife with the behavioural economist's status quo bias and endowment effects and an oversized portion of cultural cognition; they are models of risk aversion and change resistance.

For all these reasons, The Leap's scope and uncertainty wind up sort of amplified at this Petri-dish scale. There's an incongruity to big change in such places that can readily inspire imitation further afield, as if they've demonstrated the feasibility of change for *anyone* by their very improbability. This is what David Ausberger meant when he marvelled at the name of a local business *from the middle of nowhere in Iowa* appearing on an Olympic broadcast. How'd *that* happen? And come to think of it, how did an Iowa corn farmer become a wind-energy pioneer? The answer traces the arc of a community's Leap in microcosm.

In Jefferson, the "idea man," as Ausberger calls him, was a

local farmer named Bill Sutton, who got to talking to a local engineer with some experience in Iowa's fledgling wind industry, a reserved older gentleman by the improbable name of Tom Wind. The state government had put some modest tax breaks in place for community-scale wind power but had done precious little to make it happen, so Sutton approached Wind with the idea that the ridge that ran across his farm north of town would be perfect for a few wind turbines. Wind admired Sutton's enthusiasm but doubted his plan—the political and economic culture of Iowa just didn't seem anywhere near ready for small-scale, distributed energy production. "We started on blind faith," Wind told me. "Or no—less than faith. There wasn't any faith on my part. I thought this was a ridiculous waste of time and money. But I said, 'I'll give it a shot.'"

Wind and Sutton started talking up the plan around town, looking for $5,000 buy-ins from a few other farmers so they could put up a meteorological tower on Hardin Hilltop to see just how good the wind was up there. Eventually there was a meeting of interested parties, a sort of straw poll as to whether each was ready to make that single leap across the chasm—that mental gap that said Iowa family farmers do not build power plants. The initial buy-in was just five grand, yes, but who knew how much capital each partner would have to raise to get a turbine built? Here's how David Ausberger remembers his leap: "I kind of looked around the room, and I was the youngest guy, and I'm sure that I had the smallest bank account. And I thought, well, it sounds like a crazy idea. And Bill said, 'You know, it could cost a million dollars apiece.' And I thought, well, I'm going to stick around just to see how far this goes."

There would come to pass a great deal of technical and legislative wrangling. There were trips to the state house in Des Moines, even a sojourn or two to Washington, D.C. Grant applications would need to be written, paperwork filled out. When it came time to finally order turbines, the Hardin Hilltop group wanted Danish-made Vestas windmills—"kind of the Cadillac name in the industry," as Ausberger puts it—but the whole global business was booming so much you couldn't get a Vestas at any price, and everyone wanted minimum orders in the dozens or hundreds, not the seven measly turbines they needed in Jefferson, Iowa. So in the end they went with turbines from Suzlon Energy—an Indian wind turbine manufacturer, of all things—which would deliver the first of its turbines ever to be installed in the US. The whole project was dubiousness compounded by uncertainty, bureaucratic hurdles and technical obstacles. But there'd been that initial Leap, seven Iowa farmers with $5,000 each and their word—a commitment of social capital as well as cash neither made nor retracted lightly.

When time came to begin construction, Ausberger soon encountered the anxiety that arises from the difficulties in properly measuring The Leap. The smallest hurdles could look insurmountable. The way the wind farm was structured, each partner owned his own turbine as a separate corporate arrangement, and David Ausberger's was the first to go up. The crane doing the installing was bigger than any the local crane operator had ever used, and at one point he was sort of showing off and wound up getting the thing stuck in a ditch. When the blade apparatus was finally lifted into place, it got within inches of the hub before anyone realized the rigging was all wrong. On one tense afternoon, Ausberger felt a tightening in his chest over some technical mix-up, and he found himself looking at the 48 tons of rebar and quarter of a million dollars in poured concrete sitting in the middle of his uncle's cornfield and wondering if he could turn a wind turbine's foundation into a basketball court or something.

The drama of it all, though, had a surprising side effect, as The Leap's compound impact reverberated especially powerfully at community scale. Hardin Hilltop Wind Farm became not just an engineering project or power plant but a civic landmark, something everyone in Jefferson felt invested in. Ausberger: "Half the county was on the gravel roads, just sitting around, watching all day. I told my wife, 'You know, we've got to have our kids out here selling hot dogs and hot chocolate'—she didn't want to do that. But it was just a public spectacle."

There were out-of-state ironworkers buying meals at the diner and Indian executives checking in at the local motel, Danish and German engineers gassing up rental trucks at the service station. There was one old-timer who drove out every morning and parked his Cadillac right in the middle of the site and sat there reading his newspaper until someone finally went over and asked him to make way for the construction equipment. And long after the jetsetting installation people went home, the town still felt connected to those wind turbines the same way a guy like Ausberger did when he saw the local gym mats on TV. "The town has ownership in it, and they really are interested," Ausberger told me. "I go to get gas at the gas station and invariably somebody's going to say, 'Well, what's wrong with tower number two, you know?' 'I don't know I haven't been out there.'"

The final chapter of The Leap at Hardin Hilltop will stretch across another generation, and it accrues compound interest with each passing season. The financing of the wind farm was built around a deal known as the "Minnesota flip" (after the place where it was first struck), in which an equity partner joins each turbine's owner to co-own the turbine. Because the equity partner puts up substantially more capital, it receives the lion's share of the revenue and tax breaks for the first number of years. Once it has earned back its money, the ownership arrangement "flips" back to the individual owner. David Ausberger has already made back his $5,000 and then some, but he's waiting on that flip, which he figures will arrive just in time to put his three kids through college.

As to what they might study, Ausberger reckons they could do worse than looking into the wind business. He sees these technicians out at Hardin Hilltop, twenty-two-year-olds from elsewhere in the state loving their work and making great money, and he sees a fine career path for someone from Jefferson. He even bugs the other six owners of the Hardin Hilltop Wind Farm about maybe setting up a scholarship to send someone from Jefferson down to Iowa Lakes Community College to learn to be a wind-farm technician. "I keep telling people around here that have kids that are graduating that don't really know what to do, hey, you know, if they know computers, which they all do at this point, and they are a little bit outdoorsy and a little bit mechanically minded but maybe not wanting to work in a factory or a garage or something like that—man, go into that industry."

I heard a similar story from Barry Butler, the head of the engineering department at the University of Iowa. Once, on a visit to a big wind farm in northern Iowa, Butler met a young technician who couldn't stop talking about his work. He'd quit what he thought was his dream job—managing the hunting department at Cabela's, a mammoth big-box outdoor equipment store—to fix wind turbines. "That was my dream job until I learned about becoming a turbine technician," the kid told Butler. "This is better. Because I'm outdoors, I get to go out to the towers. I go up, every day I'm up looking around, checking things out. Working on the machinery."

Here was another voice in the community, rewriting the American Dream for the twenty-first century. The only remaining thing is to build the infrastructure to support it, to wire it up to the rest of the country, bring it to national scale. To reimagine the grid itself, in other words.

< SEVEN >

THE LEAP ON THE GRID

DUMB GRID

IN THE LATE NINETEENTH century, Pearl Street in Lower
Manhattan—birthplace of Jeremiah Thompson's Black Ball
Line—became the home address for another far-reaching industrial transformation. Inside a brick edifice on Pearl Street, just a
few doors down from Thompson's old counting house, six "Jumbo"
dynamos assembled by Thomas Edison's Electric Illuminating
Company (named after P.T. Barnum's legendary elephant) began
pumping out electricity in September 1882. The wondrous new
service of electrification attracted fifty-nine customers in its first
month and had more than five hundred by the end of its first year.

At first, Edison's half-dozen steam engines served retailers who
used electric lights as a novelty to attract new customers. Soon,
though, the manifold uses of electricity began to reveal themselves, and this dynamic new energy source became an essential
tool for the ice houses and streetcars of increasingly modern New
York. Electrical lines snaked out from Edison's Pearl Street power
station across the city. In pursuit of the proximate goal of bringing
light to Manhattan, Edison invented the electrical grid.

Edison's grid soon became a necessary precondition for twentieth-century industrialization, and the benchmark—along with

running water—of a society's position on or off the humming track of modern life. Much has changed in the intervening century, but certain critical details of today's most sophisticated electrical grids remain identical to Edison's prototype. They are still predominantly juiced by steam turbines sent spinning by fossil fuels. They are still structured in a hub-and-spoke design, with a large central power generator feeding a series of snaking wires in a one-way flow. And the primary goal—if not the only one—of the businesses that make the electricity is to increase consumer demand. By design, the conventional grid has a vested interest in excess, waste and resource depletion.

The grid's Leap requires a complete reinvention of the entire system. It involves a wholesale switch from nonrenewable fossil fuels to waste-free renewable sources, an exchange of the hub-and-spoke arrangement for a web of multisized nodes akin to the internet's reinvention of telecommunications, and the replacement of the demand-driven profit model with one built to reward hyper-efficiency. A *smart grid*, in other words, a twenty-first-century design to supplant the mostly deaf, mute and blind one designed by Thomas Edison. It's a substantial Leap, one of the biggest, but like any other Leap, it begins with a simple, wildly disruptive technique: the recognition that there is nothing rational about any energy market on earth and no generating cost fully paid by the rate per kilowatt-hour listed on any given electrical bill.

To be sure, there has been no shortage of accounting prowess directed at correcting the inaccuracies, distortions and biases of energy pricing into a single standardized measure. One of the most common and authoritative such measures is the "lifetime levellized cost" or "levellized life-cycle cost," which attempts to factor in all the capital inputs, labour and fuel procurement costs, upgrades and inefficiencies and the rest over the entire life of a power plant in order to produce a single "real" price to compare to other power plants and fuel sources. These are useful stats, to be sure, but only within the existing energy paradigm. They do nothing to address the staggering externalities that are exhausting the planet's nonrenewable resources and straining the biosphere's capacity to support modern industrial life itself. The inertial weight of the current system is perhaps best indicated by the fact that almost every "levellized" cost accounting comes to the tidy econometric conclusion that burning coal is the cheapest way to make electricity in almost every jurisdiction. The "rational" result of our best conventional measurements for the cost of power production is that the most destructive fuel source available is the most beneficial one to use.

The errors and omissions embedded in these calculations are enormous. One study of coal power in the US found that if you factored in just the externalized costs of its carbon dioxide emissions, from climate change to mining accidents, you'd be looking at a surcharge of 9 to 17 cents per kilowatt-hour, doubling or tripling the price and making it far less economical than wind power. (Another study noted that the levellized cost of wind power was inflated by data from outmoded small-scale turbines.) Even the most efficient modern coal plants would generate power 2 cents more expensive if emissions were included in the price—a surcharge that would equal, all by itself, the federal subsidy that makes wind power competitive with coal in the US. Factor in carbon capture and storage—the technological basis for "clean coal," complete with multibillion-dollar R&D budget—and the price jumps another 10 cents, into the range of current solar power, whose price has plummeted every year of this young century. In the US, about 40 percent of the coal burned to make electricity is mined in the Powder River Basin of southern Montana and northern Wyoming, an area that is officially *not* a "certified coal-producing region," meaning that it remains exempt from federal leasing rates for coal production that were established in the early 1980s. This alone amounts to a hidden subsidy of somewhere between $130 million and $220 million per year. And none of this even takes into account the environmental cost of *mining* the coal. What would be a fair surcharge, for example, on the removal of an Appalachian mountaintop and the permanent reconfiguration of the ecosystem in the valley below as it fills with rubble and chemical waste?

The list of faulty accounting expands as other "economical" fuel sources are taken into consideration. The subsidies alone are awesome in scale. Worldwide, the fossil fuel industry received $312 billion in subsidies in 2009—more than eight times the amount given to renewables. What's more, levellized costing involves substantial guesswork about the future cost of fossil fuels, with estimates that sometimes date to the age of $10-a-barrel oil. The levellizing process also fails to account for the far greater stability of supply and price attached to renewables. Establish a "risk-adjusted" levellized cost that factors in the enormous fluctuations, uncertainties and emerging emissions charges for fossil fuels, and the sound economics of renewable energy would soon be readily apparent. Multiple studies of nuclear power, meanwhile, have revealed a web of subsidies, incentives and investments that amount to what one Vermont Law School researcher has dubbed "nuclear socialism," propping up continued support for a fuel source that is already at least as expensive as solar PV (the priciest renewable source) even in jurisdictions without any targeted support for solar. (An example: a Duke University study found that solar and nuclear would both come to North Carolina's grid at about 14 cents per kilowatt-hour, with solar trending downward from 30 cents in the late 1990s and nuclear spiking upward from about 5 to 7 cents over the same period.)

"The main reason clean energy is more expensive than dirty old energy is because the electricity game is not played on a level field"—this was how the situation was summed up in *The Wall Street Journal*, a newspaper not known for its hostility to business as usual. "Critics of government support for clean energy decry 'market manipulation,' when in reality what's manipulated is the current state of affairs."

Levellized costs and benchmark prices for conventional power represent the behavioural economist's status quo bias written into the fine print of every consumer's electricity bill. By ignoring the embedded costs and mounting risks of conventional fuels, underestimating the toll taken by fluctuating prices and failing utterly to account for environmental and social impacts, we massively overvalue the electricity we've got, and we regularly overestimate the expense of changing to clean fuel sources. We fret over the loss of cheap coal-fired electricity, failing to see the enormous gains to be had—not just economic but social and environmental—by switching to renewable sources.

What's more, we've so thoroughly habituated this cluster of biases that we deem it rational. It's rational for coal producers to exploit loopholes and rake in subsidies to keep their costs down and then use the money they've saved to pay lobbyists and front groups millions of dollars to obfuscate the realities of climate change and the potential of renewables to guard their market share. (All by itself, the American Coalition for Clean Coal Electricity—a "grassroots" front group backed by thirty-eight prominent conventional energy companies, including several of America's largest coal companies—spent $30 million on its advertising and lobbying campaigns during the election year of 2008; as one solar company manager once put it to me, the imbalance is such that the lobbying and marketing budgets of coal companies are close to the equal of the operating budgets of many fledgling renewable energy companies.) And it's rational to fund R&D on next-generation nuclear and carbon capture technologies—both of which are unproven and solely future-tense—at the expense of augmenting renewable technologies that already work but await economies of scale. It's rational to build a robust energy policy environment not just well-suited to fossil fuels but often written to the precise specifications of the industries that produce them, while equipping the renewable industries only with clunky, inconsistent and abysmally implemented policy slivers. It's rational to assay this steeply slanted moonscape of a marketplace, judge it to be open and level, and dismiss renewable energy as simply unable to compete. The result is an economic travesty and an ecological tragedy.

Actually, here's the result in a single, stark factoid: In the summer of 2010, there was not a single new wind energy installation being developed in the state of Iowa. In the midst of the worst American economy in generations, as hundreds of billions of dollars in stimulus and bailout spending was being stuffed into the furnaces of American industry to try to get the fire roaring again, just over a year after the president himself stood in front of an Iowa wind turbine factory and mapped out the logic of the business and the necessity of clean power, all but hand-picking Iowa's wind industry as the flag-bearer of American recovery and renewal—despite all of this, the wind industry in Iowa was completely stagnant. Iowa's grid was second in the US in terms of electricity volume and first per capita, with almost 20 percent of the state's electricity produced by wind turbines. Thousands of new jobs had already been created, capable young folks were flocking to the state's trade schools to pursue dream careers in the wind business, and farmer-entrepreneurs had begun to dream wind-powered American Dreams wherever the breezes were strong enough. In the long-ago boom times of early 2008, there'd been forty trucks a day navigating the interstates and rural routes of Iowa to deliver wind turbine components to waiting fields. And yet by the summer of 2010 no one could see the wisdom any longer of investing their green American dollars in another power plant to catch that abundant Iowa wind.

Why? What cataclysm had visited the byways of Iowa that summer to so thoroughly upend the economics of wind energy? In a word: price. Cost competitiveness. The almighty business case. It'd blown away in a maelstrom of partisan politicking ahead of the 2010 midterm elections, which had delayed and then shelved legislative renewal of the federal tax credit that sealed the business case for wind power in Iowa.

The business was nearly market-ready all on its own, even with the field tilted so sharply toward fossil fuels — even with no binding, long-term commitment at the state or federal level to secure the market for investors, the kind of thing governments had been doing for power companies almost since the birth of the grid to provide a stable market for new power plants. Even without a feed-in tariff or national renewable energy portfolio standard, even without a carbon tax or cap-and-trade program or anything at all to suggest that the downstream impact of fossil fuels was something to be scored on the negative side of its balance sheet. Even without federal money to upgrade the grid in order to deliver more of that clean Iowa electricity to hungry markets in urban centres like Chicago further east. Even in one of the worst policy environments of any industrial nation, it *nearly* made sense to pump millions more into wind turbines in Iowa. But the line between profit and loss was thin enough that it needed the small boost of a tax credit on each turbine installed. And when the credit's renewal failed to emerge from the vicious Washington climate of the summer of 2010, the wind industry in Iowa ground to a halt. Officials at the very wind turbine plant in Newton where President Obama had so boldly declared the dawn of the clean energy age in America warned that the future of the whole plant depended on policy initiatives to make the market more secure for new investment. Again: This is the least any industry asks, let alone one that promises to build the clean-powered electrical engines of a second industrial revolution.

In America in the summer of 2010, though, the price still wasn't right. The grid was just too dumb.

THE SUN TEMPLES OF ANDALUSIA & OTHER WONDERS OF THE GREEN WORLD

The smart grid is, at present, a conjecture, a laboratory experiment, a vision and the toolkit to make that vision manifest. I'll come back a bit later to the vision and the impressive schematics emerging from some of those labs. The toolkit, though, already contains some wonders of its own. And there might be none more impressive in its sheer monumental grandeur than the Solúcar Solar Platform in Andalusia. On a wide, flat expanse of sun-baked plain just west of Seville, Spanish engineers have reimagined Thomas Edison's Pearl Street dynamo as a futuristic sun temple.

To come upon the platform over a gentle rise covered in olive trees is to think, for a moment, that you've discovered an other-worldly launch pad or a sci-fi movie set. Three high spires dominate the platform, great concrete wedges the height of the steeples on Gothic cathedrals, each with a deep indentation at the top like a gaping eye. They are surrounded by hundreds of broad mirrors the size of barn doors, which gleam in the Andalusian sun like beacons. The mirrors concentrate sunlight on the opening at the top, where a steam turbine has been mounted—a machine the same in its basic operations as Edison's own. After 120 years using the sun's stored energy (in the form of fossil fuels) to spin turbines and make electricity, the Solúcar Solar Platform is home to steam turbines that harness solar power directly. From a technical standpoint, at least, there's no need to ever again build one dependent on the earth's dwindling reserves of fossilized solar energy.

I visited Solúcar on what was by local standards an unseasonably cool and cloudy September day, which meant it was merely very warm and there were occasional breaks in the blinding glare emanating from the mirrors. There are tricks the towers and their mirror beds play with the light that I'm reasonably sure have never existed on earth before. When the sun's rays first re-emerge from behind the clouds to hit the tilted panels, for example, the light is concentrated at a spot several dozen feet in front of the spire's eye at the same altitude. It appears for a long moment as if the spire has somehow extended an energy field in front of it to catch the sunlight. This is because when the sun ducks behind clouds for a long enough interval, the mirrors automatically tilt away from the spire's peak so they don't reheat the turbine too quickly when the sun returns. (Much of the R&D work on the solar towers is now focused on developing materials that can withstand rapid and intense heat fluctuations.)

My guide explained the fine details as we ascended through an elevator in the base of the tallest solar tower to survey Solúcar from the observation deck at its midpoint. This was PS10, the oldest tower, completed in 2006 and capped by a 10-MW turbine. In just three years, the design had already undergone two further iterations. From the viewing platform, my guide pointed to the similarly sized tower closest to us—PS20, a 20-MW power plant. Then she directed my gaze to a squat grey tower in the distance— AZ20, just completed, also with 20 MW of output but at half the size. A whole generation's worth of cost-cutting efficiency had been developed in just three years. Though the solar towers were not yet market-ready, they still made for an impressive triptych of the pace of solar innovation in Spain.

The "platform" idea is more conceptual than literal—Solúcar consists of six individual power plants that could each be tethered to the Spanish grid on its own anywhere the sun shone bright and often enough. They were built by a company called Abengoa Solar (a subsidiary of the Spanish energy giant Abengoa), and were one of its first big technical breakthroughs in the wake of the cost-levelling impact of Spain's feed-in tariff. In addition to providing 300 MW of solar energy for the Spanish grid, Solúcar is conceived by Abengoa as a springboard from which to launch a great technological Leap in the solar business.

The three spires—which Abengoa calls "solar towers" and are referred to generically as "heliostats"—generate only 50 MW of that power. The real workhorses are the parabolic trough concentrators—long, gutter-like assemblages of U-shaped reflective glass that concentrate solar heat on a tube of liquid mounted at the U's focal point, thus to power a steam turbine. These are known generically as "concentrating solar thermal power" (CSP) plants, and they are the most market-ready technology developed thus far at Solúcar.

In fact, Abengoa's parabolic troughs have worked so well that the company has already cut deals to build two more CSP plants an order of magnitude larger in the Mojave Desert. Development has begun on a 280-MW plant in Arizona and a 250-MW plant in California, as part of the leading edge of a nascent worldwide

boom in CSP. In the final months of 2010, California alone commissioned a half-dozen CSP plants at similar scale, including
three solar towers to be constructed by the California solar company BrightSource to specifications similar to Abengoa's Andalusian
monoliths. Meanwhile, eSolar—a California-born entrepreneurial venture with backing from Google, among others—has partnered with the German steel producer Ferrostaal to build heliostats
in China and India similar to Abengoa's solar towers.

All told, the US Southwest has flat, sun-baked land in sufficient
abundance all by itself to host an estimated 7,000 to 11,200 gigawatts
(GW) of solar thermal energy production—somewhere between
twenty and forty times the amount currently generated by all of
America's coal plants. What's more, CSP is cost-competitive *now*,
even in the legislative morass and skewed energy market of the
United States. A study by Severin Borestein at the University of
California's Energy Institute, for example, found that electricity
produced by this emerging wave of utility-grade CSP plants will
connect to the grid at prices per kilowatt-hour similar to juice from
new gas and coal turbines.

A world of sustainable wonders of similar scale and bright
promise has emerged in pretty much every energy marketplace
where renewable energy has been given a fair shot—or even just
a marginally less unfair one. Windy west Texas provides a particularly dramatic example, its open plain filling with turbines
so quickly that on one particularly breezy day in March 2010,
fully 19 percent of the electricity on the 6,000-MW grid powering America's second most populous state was produced by the
wind. (The annual average for Texas is 6.2 percent.) Nationwide,
wind was the fastest-growing energy source in America for most
of the last decade.

In Britain, until recently a renewable energy laggard by

European standards, the launch of a revamped policy in 2010 —
including a steep feed-in tariff for wind power — instigated a substantial offshore wind boom. Week to week through the spring of
2010, one megaproject after another was announced under the
banner of *world's largest*, culminating in June with a 576-MW
wind farm to be built by a trio of German firms off the coast of
Wales. It won't be finished until 2020, however, so for now a
300-MW wind installation in the English Channel, which started
feeding electricity to Britain's grid in September 2010, will wear
that crown.

After Portugal passed its feed-in tariff, wind power grew by a
factor of seven in less than five years. The country is now a net
energy exporter, and Portuguese wind energy companies operate
a great many American wind farms. There are big solar thermal
investments in Algeria and Israel, wind farms sprouting up in open
fields from Turkey to India, substantial new geothermal plants in
Iceland and Indonesia. And that's without even mentioning the
clean-energy colossus that exploded out of nowhere to take the
world lead in solar and wind and electric car manufacture (and
much else) around 2009. In addition to all its manufacturing
might, China also leads the world in the installation of solar thermal heating systems — about 150 million Chinese homes use the
sun's energy to heat their household water. (I'll come back to
China in more detail toward the end of this chapter.) The industrialized West, meanwhile, remains the pacesetter — around 2008,
for the first time since Edison wired up his coal-powered turbines
to that very first electrical network, more new renewable energy
was being wired into the grids of Europe and America than new
power from coal, gas and nukes combined. The grid of the twenty-
first century, it now seems certain, will not look like the one that
powered the twentieth.

OF PARKED CARS & POWER PLANTS

Denmark was one of the first societies to leap headlong toward a sustainable economy, and it remains an ambitious pacesetter. The small nation's biggest jump, however, is only just preparing to launch.

As I discussed in Chapter Two, the Danish government decided in 2007 to expand the portion of its national electricity supply coming from renewable power—which in Denmark comes almost exclusively from wind energy—to 50 percent by 2025. This was considered a rash move even by Danish standards, and it flew in the face of a great howling chorus of conventional wisdom about the natural limits of renewables. Wind in particular is notorious for the headaches it causes by its fecklessness—the interminable intermittency problem born of breezes that suddenly rise and dissipate just as quickly, and that often blow stronger at night, when nobody needs electricity, and die down during the day, when everyone does. Denmark's *current* wind load is indeed a constant challenge for its grid operators, who manage it only by balancing their loads with steady, predictable hydro power generated in Sweden and Norway. And even still there are times when the Danes have to pay their neighbours to buy their excess wind power. Plus one of those neighbours, Germany, has of course embarked on its own massive wind-farming project of late, so not only was it no longer a reliable customer for excess Danish juice, it was now filling those load-balancing lines running up to Sweden and Norway to somewhere near capacity. New Danish wind energy will therefore have to be used in the main by the Danes themselves, and so the conundrum of Denmark's green grid has become a question of storage.

A consortium of blue-chip companies and institutions has been duly assembled to address this challenge. It is led by the

German electricity conglomerate Siemens, and also includes IBM, DONG Energy (Denmark's largest power company), the Technical University of Denmark, the Danish Energy Agency and a host of smaller firms. The group looked at every storage device the modern world had to offer—next-generation batteries and hydrogen fuel cells, pressurized air, the advanced liquids and molten salts used to store solar thermal energy. Each one, though, was either too expensive to build out to national grid scale or far too inefficient—or often both, wasting too much power in the conversion from electrical flow to storage medium and back again. Here's Anders Troi, the senior Siemens engineer on the project, summing up the findings of the preliminary investigation: "Basically we have reached the conclusion that the storage media has to be there already for some other purpose."

They needed something ubiquitous, something people already bought and used in great numbers. Something that often sat around for hours at a time, especially at night, so that it could also double as a storage system for thousands of megawatts of electricity. They seized on a novel solution, derived from another ambitious Danish sustainability target: electric cars. As soon as electric vehicles (EVs) were available on the mass market, the government intended to put huge incentives in place to encourage their purchase. As I noted earlier, new cars are ferociously taxed in Denmark, adding somewhere near 200 percent to the price tag; these taxes are to be waived entirely for EVs. Green-minded and economically minded Danes alike are thus likely to switch in a hurry to the new vehicles. If one in ten of the cars and small trucks currently on the road were swapped for electric-powered ones by 2025, there would be at least 200,000 EVs in Denmark. (The current target of the tax rebate scheme is for around 100,000 by 2015.) They'd be driven on average for less than 40 kilometres at a stretch and sit idle in garages and parking lots and roadsides for twenty-two hours or more most days. Parked cars everywhere—a vast, distributed storage system for a new kind of electrical grid.

By process of elimination and the steady logic of their due diligence, the Danish team had settled on building the first national-scale prototype of the hottest idea in cleantech, one just beginning to generate thundering waves of hype and attract dot-com-like piles of venture money the world over: the smart grid. Often referred to, in evocative metaphorical shorthand, as "the energy internet," the smart grid has emerged in recent years as possibly the most exciting technological advance since the advent of digital communications. Or, more precisely, the most promis-ing *application* of digital communications since the internet itself, since the smart grid is not so much a technology as the integra-tion of several new ones from formerly disparate fields. The smart grid combines renewable power generation; two-way energy flows; hyper-efficient building design; robust, ubiquitous and instantane-ous digital communications; and distributed power generation into an entirely new way of making and using (and buying and selling) energy. Its development has been exquisitely timed, emerging at almost the exact same moment that electric cars have finally entered their mass production phase and inspiring techie minds to exhilarating flights of inventive fancy.

One of the most cohesive of these visions to emerge so far is the product of a design charette convened in late 2008 by the Rocky Mountain Institute (RMI), the energy think tank headed by efficiency guru Amory Lovins. RMI gathered together execu-tives and engineers from high-tech titans (Google, Cisco, IBM), major automakers (Ford, GM, Nissan) and energy behemoths (Duke, PG&E, Bonneville Power), as well as electric-car innovators such as Tesla Motors and Better Place, academics from MIT and Berkeley, and other potential stakeholders. They called it "Smart Garage." For three heady days, the assembled tech elites sized up the challenges and opportunities of a smart-grid system built around an electric vehicle in every garage. The detailed report that emerged takes note of all manner of tricky technical and market hurdles for the concept, but it begins with a plausible near-future scenario that is a perfect encapsulation of the disruptive promise of the smart grid and the future-is-now, sci-fi-made-manifest giddiness it inspires.

Here's the Smart Garage vision of the good life that awaits us just around the corner in 2025:

> A typical day might go something like this: after work, you drive home in your plug-in hybrid, pull into the garage, and connect your vehicle to a power cord that connects to your house. Your car and house "shake hands"—the car tells your house the state of its battery, and the house's energy management system figures out how best to charge your car. The car then spends part of the night recharging on cheap electricity that comes from a new big wind farm. In fact, your car charges in sync with how fast the wind is spinning the turbines—guaranteeing you are only getting "green" electrons. In the morning, you check your home energy dashboard to review the status of your car's charge, and you happily drive to work in your vehicle, which uses electricity most of the time. If your commute takes a few extra turns, an efficient little biofuel, gasoline, or diesel engine comes on to provide extra range.
>
> You get to work, drive into the parking lot, and plug your car into another electric charging system. It

automatically recognizes your car and links to your credit
card and your utility account. Your car and utility share
information in both directions—how much electricity the
battery has or needs, how much it costs (now and perhaps
later in the day). Based on the preferences you previously
set online, your car and utility decide the best, cheapest,
and greenest way to get the energy your mobility requires.

Say it's a hot summer day, and electricity is in high
demand and more expensive. Based on your preferences,
the utility and the vehicle converse. The car declines the
day's charging because the price is extremely high. In
addition, the utility would prefer to draw power from the
car and pay its value back to your credit card. The price
is right, so your car, seeing a juicy "carbitrage" opportunity, decides to use its electrical storage to earn you some
money. At 5 p.m., you climb into your pleasant, pre-
cooled car and drive home mostly on advanced, environ-
mentally-friendly biofuel.

This is the emerging value proposition of the smart grid.
Imagine a car that fuels cheaply overnight and then makes you
money while it's sitting in the parking lot the next day. Imagine
your home as a power plant, your car as its battery pack, and the
garage at home or at work as your own personal electrical substation. Imagine power meters running backward to tally your profits, and appliances that only do their most energy-intensive work
when power is at its cheapest. Imagine yourself as an energy producer, not just a consumer. Much like our recent shift from
phones mounted on walls for voice-only calls, and TVs used solely
to watch whatever happens to be on at that instant, to our digital
world of ubiquitous and omni-directional information flows and

blog postings and mobile-phone picture uploads and text messages broadcast from each of us to everyone else, the electrical grid is on the threshold of a brave new digital age. And it is truly delirium-inducing.

Here's Michael Brylawski, the Rocky Mountain Institute's point man on the Smart Garage seminar, summing up its findings: "It's hard to see an infrastructure play that has so many potentially simultaneous benefits—oil, security, climate, jobs." Here's John Doerr, the venture capitalist who led early investments in Google and Amazon, framing the smart-grid opportunity a little more ecstatically on *60 Minutes:* "Clean energy could be the largest market of the twenty-first century."

There's much more already to the smart-grid boom than fantastical scenarios and breathless hype. By one estimate, it was already a $69-billion industry in 2009, and market analysts believe it will nearly triple in size by 2015. Breakneck growth like that attracts venture capital and R&D investment money in nine-digit lumps. The Chinese government has been particularly enthusiastic, pledging to pour more than half a billion dollars into smart grid infrastructure projects over the next decade, in addition to the huge investments it has already made in renewable energy and EVs. Private American investors, not to be outdone, have been equally lavish in their affections for smart-grid gizmos. In 2008, Kleiner Perkins—John Doerr's venture firm—established two funds with more than a billion dollars in total to invest primarily in cleantech, and many of its first major investments were in smart-grid companies. (Silver Spring Networks, for example, which develops energy management software and equipment, received $75 million from Kleiner Perkins.) Indeed cleantech was second only to biotech in attracting venture money at the peak of the global economic crisis in 2009.

From bare-bones basics like smart meters to next-generation near-perpetual motion machines, the smart-grid mania has stirred up a whirlwind of cleantech R&D activity. The smart meters themselves are the most widely deployed smart-grid technologies to date. At base, these are devices that can measure power flowing both into and out of a building, enabling distributed, small-scale electrical generation of the sort being done by hundreds of thousands of German homeowners, among others (and allowing for it to be properly rewarded). As many as 40 percent of European households will be outfitted with smart meters by 2012, including virtually all of the homes in Sweden and Italy. By the same date, there will be as many as 40 million smart meters installed in the US.

Smart-meter installation, though, is merely the smart grid's prep stage. More recent developments have focused on making meters wireless-enabled and network-ready—something more akin to a small internet server than an Edisonian spinning-dial meter, complete with a host of clever new software applications. Google's recently launched Power Meter widget, for example, allows a computer or handheld device to communicate with smart meters, gathering "near real-time" data on energy consumption; future versions of such apps would, for example, permit homeowners to shut off their dishwashers or turn down the heat remotely if there was a sudden electricity price spike. General Electric, meanwhile, has unveiled a storage device it calls "Nucleus" and an EV charging and networking tool called the "Watt Station" to allow smart meters, digital appliances, car batteries and information widgets on mobile phones to work together. And a California company called Envision Solar has developed the Solar Tree, a shade apparatus for large parking lots that integrates PV panels, smart meters and EV connections into a single quickly deployed unit.

This all assumes, of course, that the local power company has introduced time-of-use pricing, which would take into account the actual price of conventional energy at peak periods. On most grids, the oldest and least efficient plants provide the power during periods of absolute peak demand, at a cost two or even three times the actual charged rate per kilowatt-hour; distributed renewables—and the stored energy in an EV's battery—would be particularly appealing at these moments. Fully 45 percent of the power plants connected to the US grid represent excess capacity waiting idle for absolute peaks such as the hottest day of the summer; as I noted in Chapter Two, just a 5 percent decrease in peak demand across the US, a target that could be reached effortlessly through modest efficiency improvements and smart-grid technology, would eliminate the need for 625 power plants by 2025. Time-of-use pricing has begun to emerge in leading-edge jurisdictions like Ontario and California, and it is generally understood to be a vital legislative precondition for the development of the smart grid.

Some of the most frenzied market activity in the smart-grid field to date has centred on the compound benefits produced by the decentralized grid—particularly residential-scale cogeneration by small combined-heat-and-power (CHP) units. These are the first appliances to bring the future-tense fantasies of the smart grid into the everyday reality of a household basement. There are three of these entering the mass deployment stage: EcoBlue, developed through a partnership between Volkswagen and a German energy company called LichtBlick; the WhisperGen, designed by New Zealand's Meridian Energy and mass-produced in Spain by Mondragon, the world's largest workers' collective; and the Bloom Box, developed with Kleiner Perkins money by Bloom Energy of Silicon Valley. All three are built around the same basic concept: they burn natural gas very efficiently to both heat and power a home, networking with a smart meter to do so only when fuel is cheapest and then sell excess energy back to the grid at peak times.

These mini-CHP units aren't renewably powered and they do produce very small amounts of greenhouse gases. But because they are ready for installation in practically any building with a gas furnace and because they make such enormous strides in efficiency, they may prove to be a powerful bridging technology. Years before EVs and real-time energy pricing systems are deployed at mass-market scale, WhisperGens and EcoBlues may have already accomplished much of the legwork of encouraging smart-meter installation and distributed power generation.

EcoBlue is the most straightforward of the three. It uses a standard Volkswagen engine running on natural gas to generate power on demand, piping the waste heat from the combusted gas to warm the building. The first EcoBlues have already been installed in homes and small apartment buildings in Hamburg, and an initial production run of 100,000 started selling to the wider German market in the coming years.

The WhisperGen and Bloom Box represent a bigger jump in terms of technological sophistication and impact. I'll come back to the Bloom Box's extraordinary ambitions a bit later; for now, let's look at the WhisperGen. The core technology driving the device is a Stirling engine—a hugely efficient engine design first developed almost 200 years ago that uses tiny amounts of fuel to run for hours, delivering space heat as its primary activity and a steady stream of electricity as a sort of waste product. The City of Calgary's subsidiary energy company, Enmax—my local utility— is testbedding the WhisperGen in North America. In fact its former CEO, Gary Holden, tore the natural gas furnaces out of his own house to demonstrate the effectiveness of the WhisperGen in the fierce Canadian winter.

Here's Holden on the value he sees in household Stirling engines: "The proposition that I speak about most often is a scenario where you have a plug-in hybrid car in your garage, and in the middle of the night when your lights are off and your TV's off and everything, your demand is low, you take the power from your Stirling engine to your car and you drive to work each day. It's actually a benefit that even solar power doesn't create, because you're generating electricity in the off-peak hours, and the synergy that has with plug-in hybrid vehicles is amazing. And so then you get into payback periods that are just unbelievable. You'll be paying the whole equipment decision off in months, because you're offsetting some of your power bill during the day when it's running, and you're offsetting a huge fuel bill in your vehicle during the night . . . I think it's such a good technology that it's easy for me to picture, you know, twenty years from now, every single single-house dwelling or apartment block would be inherently built around Stirling engines."

While Enmax's experiment is still at the test market stage—one finding to date has been that the larger homes and colder climate of western Canada require larger units than the WhisperGens being made for the European market—the British energy firm E.ON is rolling out a much broader program. In early 2010, E.ON signed an exclusive deal to be the sole importer of WhisperGen to the UK, where it estimates every unit could turn a profit of more than $500 per year selling electricity back to the grid.

The real genius of the smart grid, in any case, is more in the integration of components than in the whiz-bang design of any one piece. And so in progressive-minded communities across America, local utilities and agile cleantech companies have begun to demonstrate the viability of the whole system. The most ambitious of these is now underway in the Chicago suburb of Naperville, home of one of America's last wholly municipally owned utilities. With the help of an $11-million federal grant, the local grid is being upgraded and 57,000 smart meters installed for time-of-use pricing, a substation is being specially optimized by Siemens to work with small-scale solar plants, and residents will have wireless access to real-time usage and cost data, with incentives for reducing their peak-demand consumption. The net benefit to the local economy has been estimated at $34 to $52 million.

Admirable as these fledgling projects are, they lack the national scope of Denmark's smart grid. Indeed part of the reason Siemens has invested so heavily in the Danish project is that it provides the most extensive test bed for components and systems that are intended to find worldwide application. And the Danish team is not unaware of the potential import of its work, saddling the project with a clunker of a name — Electric vehicles in a Distributed and Integrated market using Sustainable energy and Open Networks — just so they could call it EDISON for short.

The EDISON team has discovered much the same thing as smaller and less thorough projects around the world: The tools are already there. "When you look at the technologies needed to implement this" — this is Anders Troi of Siemens again — "we already have a lot of the systems." The meters exist and so do the cars (though not yet in sufficient numbers). The software and the appliances and the networking hubs need some refinement, but then this is the sort of work companies like Siemens excel at. There are "secondary grid" kinks to be worked out — this is the part of the system running from the neighbourhood substation to the household outlet for the EV, where much of the management of real-time supply and demand will occur — but this too is a surmountable challenge for a Siemens engineering team. And the incentive, moreover, is enormous. For the entire first century of the automobile, the electricity business had only a marginal role to play. In a smart grid, where electrons move from wind turbines and solar panels to household appliances and the batteries of cars, the whole business model is fundamentally altered, opening up a massive new market for electricity companies.

It's no accident, in other words, that a German *electricity* firm snagged the lead role in EDISON. As Troi puts it: "Here we have a situation where we can replace fossil fuel in cars with electrical energy. So all the electrical companies on the European side, they say, hey, here we have the possibility of having a higher market share of the energy. The petrochemical industry, they should be scared here."

Ending the hundred-year-reign of oil-fired internal combustion engines remains a few steps down the path. For now, the EDISON project is focused on building an elaborate real-world model of its smart grid, construction of which has begun on the remote Danish island of Bornholm. A small fleet of fifteen EVs have been delivered, and the island (population: 40,000) already has enough wind turbines installed to generate 40 percent or more of its power from wind; it has only been producing about half of that amount, though, because of the intermittency problem. Using car batteries to store the excess wind power, the EDISON team launched the test project in September 2011. There are plans for a smart grid test in Copenhagen, as well.

Even before it has been implemented, though, the EDISON project has begun to gather solid evidence of The Leap's compound benefits. Contrary to widely held beliefs that an increased renewable energy share is bad for grid stability, EDISON's research has shown the opposite. Batteries — even a widely distributed web of them — respond much more quickly than coal plants or even big hydropower facilities to fluctuations in the electricity flows. As Troi notes, "This is a much better solution from a technical point of view in terms of use for regulating the grid, stabilizing the grid." A study by the National Renewable Energy Laboratory in the US found similarly that wind power becomes more reliable as the amount of it increases on the grid, whether smart or not—this by way of proving that there were no technical hurdles to generating as much as 30 percent of the Eastern Seaboard's power from renewables.

And all this is just what's possible with *existing* technology. With billions flowing into smart-grid R&D labs, the next generation of equipment holds the promise of even greater rewards. Bringing the smart grid, for example, to the billion-plus people in the developing world who've never been connected to any grid at all.

THE GREAT LEAPFROG

Let's return to the promise of the Bloom Box. The company that developed it, Bloom Energy, embodies both the opportunity and the challenge of the smart grid—and indeed the whole cleantech industry, if not the entire sustainability paradigm. Bloom was one of the first and largest cleantech firms to receive venture capital from Kleiner Perkins, and because of the firm's previous success as a primary financier of the internet business, Bloom has become a flag-bearer for the notion that cleantech represents a sort of Web 3.0 situation—the next big thing not just in energy but in information technology, and far bigger in potential impact.

All but the wildest internet evangelists would likely admit, under cross-examination, that there is nothing a mobile phone or laptop or iPad does that is actually essential to life on earth. Whereas the smart grid aims to provide some pretty basic necessities—energy, cooking fuel, refrigeration and mobility and the rest—and has the potential to do it all better and more efficiently than existing technologies. Homes and cars that power themselves and earn a little on the side when you're away from them, an end to fossil fuel dependency and climate chaos, a whole new way of wiring (and saving) the planet—this represents a business opportunity without parallel.

The road to universal application, though, is a harder one for a game-changing clean energy device than for a slick piece of software. Google, Kleiner Perkins's all-time greatest hit, required just $25 million in funding and a couple of dizzy years to get to globally traded, revenue-generating ubiquity. Bloom Energy has already needed eight years and $400 million, and it will need many millions more before it reaches the mass marketplace.

The smart-grid equation, then, involves much higher risk and far greater challenges in pursuit of a bigger marketplace with enormous rewards. It's the kind of thing conventional energy bureaucrats instinctively shy away from; it is manna to Silicon Valley entrepreneurs.

So: the Bloom Box. What it is, in essence, is a very dense stack of hydrogen fuel cells made out of materials much less expensive than the precious metals that have gone into previous generations of fuel cells. The Bloom Box takes in fuel and pumps out power—almost any kind of fuel, and a very impressive amount of power for the amount that went in. Stack more fuel cells in the box, you get a bigger power station. The Bloom Boxes currently up and running—mainly at the headquarters of marquee Silicon Valley companies like Google and eBay—use natural gas or biogas, producing electricity at a lower cost than conventional sources with 60 percent less greenhouse gas emissions. The five Bloom generators at eBay came with a price tag of $800,000 each, but they saved the company $100,000 on its power bills in just the first nine months of operation.

Any fuel turned into electricity anywhere, with less ecological impact and smaller energy bills—the intrinsic and enormous value of a proposition like that is why guys like John Doerr are talking up cleantech and smart grids as the greatest business opportunity of the twenty-first century and potentially the salvation of all humanity. "The Bloom Box"—this is Doerr—"is intended to replace the grid for its customers. It's cheaper than the grid. It's cleaner than the grid." And its inventor, former NASA researcher K.R. Sridhar, believes its greatest impact may be in places with no grid whatsoever, places never reached by even the simple wires of Edison's nineteenth-century illuminating company. Places like his country of birth—India.

There are about 500 million people in India whose homes have no electricity, and another billion people in the same situation worldwide. Sridhar would like to see their first bulbs lit by his Bloom Boxes. "I quit doing my NASA work because I believe this particular technology can change the world," he told *Businessweek.* "Just like developing nations leapfrogged over fixed telephony to mobile, we think our technology will allow developing nations to do the same thing for electricity."

In the same way cheap mobile phones rendered telephone wires obsolete before they could even be strung up in many parts of India, the global cleantech boom presents an opportunity for a Great Leapfrog in sustainability—one that is already underway. The Indian Leapfrog began with small demonstration projects: a flawlessly executed hyper-efficient conference centre in the techie quarter of Hyderabad to introduce green building concepts, SELCO's trailblazing social entrepreneurship bringing simple solar PV systems to India's poorest villages. But sustainability's

inherent logic has begun to trickle up. There is the crazily audacious National Solar Mission that I mentioned in Chapter Two,
of course—the Indian government's plan to build out 20 GW of
solar power, a generating capacity greater than all the solar PV in
the world as of 2008, in just ten years. Tata, the massive Indian
manufacturing conglomerate, has long been a leader in the production of solar hot water heaters, and in 2012 it will start selling
electric cars—first in Europe, where the market for EVs is particularly robust, with eyes on the global market. That first green building in Hyderabad has become the hub of a nationwide boom in
green construction, with more than 150 buildings—everything
from a Tata Motors factory to a Mumbai hospital now certified
by the Indian Green Building Council. And to the utter amazement of anyone even passingly familiar with the country's tendency to make boondoggles of outsized infrastructure projects, the
Delhi Metro opened on budget and three years ahead of schedule
in 2005, and continues to expand at record speed.

India is far from alone in its Leapfrog. The appeal of cleantech's best tools easily hops borders, finding useful application
from North Africa to South America. Morocco, for example,
brought Africa's largest wind farm online in 2010, a 140 MW installation that is part of a $3-billion cleantech program whose goals
include generating more than a third of the country's electricity
from solar sources by 2020. Ambitious renewable energy programs
have also been launched in Brazil and Argentina. The Brazilian
government auctioned off $5.5 billion in green energy contracts
in 2010, which will add 2,900 MW of renewable power to its grid
by 2015; an Argentine study of perpetually breezy Patagonia, meanwhile, estimated that it could provide 200,000 MW of wind power,
which has the Argentine government mulling over a substantial
expansion of its fledgling wind industry.

Probably the most audacious Leapfrog is the one underway on the outskirts of the oil-rich city of Abu Dhabi in the United Arab Emirates. In 2006 the municipal government introduced plans to build a showpiece of sustainability 17 kilometres outside the city—an emissions-free, waste-free, car-free model town called Masdar. The $22-billion project, with overall design by renowned British architect Norman Foster, is intended to provide homes for a population of 40,000 and office space for 50,000 workers in 1,500 businesses, as well as a sustainable technology institute developed in co-operation with MIT and a mass underground "personal rapid transit" system equipped with individual transport pods. Foster's design uses natural cooling to reduce the energy needs by more than 50 percent from the Emirati norm, with the remaining power to come from a range of solar technologies. Masdar's first phase—including the institute and a 10 MW solar plant—has already been built, and Abengoa Solar will be bringing its concentrating solar technology to the Arabian desert to add another 100 MW of solar energy by 2012. Though skepticism remains widespread about Abu Dhabi's ability to deliver on all its promises, Masdar demonstrates at the very least that the logic of sustainability makes sense even in a petrostate.

Symbolically speaking, though, there may be no stronger indication of the speed and transformative power of the Great Leapfrog than the name brand on the wind turbines spinning above those farmers' fields outside Jefferson, Iowa. The name, as previously noted, is Suzlon, and the company was founded in Pune, India, by Tulsi Tanti, the scion of a textile industrialist. Launched in 1995 in a country with no wind industry—indeed no modern wind turbines—Suzlon has grown under Tanti's guidance into the largest wind turbine maker in Asia, installed 5 GW of wind power in India alone, and opened offices and R&D facilities and factories in Germany, the Netherlands and the US in addition to its eight manufacturing facilities in India itself. Suzlon's global sales office is in Denmark, and possibly its most treasured turbines spin over farmland in Iowa. In wind energy, India has leapfrogged past the branch-plant, cheap-labour, tertiary-market phase to take a prime spot at the very forefront of the industry.

In cleantech generally, the relationship between developing and developed world is not entirely one-way, and there are parts of the developing world that clearly have no intention of dutifully following along the First World's 150-year path from steam turbine to wind turbine. China, in particular, gives every indication that its goal is to be the world leader in the manufacture of the essential tools for the Great Leap.

Modern China does almost nothing slow or small, and so the numbers generated by its Great Leapfrog are truly awesome in scale. As I noted earlier, China became the world's leading manufacturer of solar panels and wind turbines in 2009. It outspent the United States on cleantech that year as well, at a rate of nearly two to one. The world's largest wind turbine factory is a Vestas facility in northeastern China, and a single Chinese PV maker, Yingli, went from near zero to a one-third share of California's solar panel market in a single year (2009 again). There are already more than one million jobs in the Chinese renewable energy industry, and it grows by another 100,000 or more each year. China is building some of the world's fastest trains—a long-distance train running between Beijing and Shanghai as well as the more famous one that runs to Shanghai's airport on levitating magnets at world-record speeds—and it is laying out the world's most extensive high-speed rail network. Often as not these days, the key components of the second industrial revolution arrive stamped "Made in China."

The EV business is the most dramatic illustration of China's burgeoning green industrial might. As America's Motor City contemplates turning half its downtown into farmland, the Detroit of the twenty-first century is emerging in the industrial heartland of southern China. An alliance of sixteen automakers and electric-vehicle parts manufacturers, many of them operating in the region, have formed an alliance dedicated to building a million EVs every year before the end of 2015. The target may well be reached before that date—BYD, the biggest Chinese carmaker, transformed itself from a battery manufacturing subsidiary of more famous brand names into the global leader in EV production in less than a decade, and it sold 500,000 cars in 2010 alone. BYD made its first international sales in Denmark in 2011, and its stated goal is to be the world's biggest automaker by 2025. Warren Buffett, widely considered the shrewdest investor in American finance, owns 10 percent of the company.

Like much of the developing world, though, China sends mixed signals on sustainability. As it builds EVs and solar panels at record paces, it also mines and burns coal at a rate never before seen on earth. The World Health Organization estimates that more than 600,000 people die prematurely in China each year due to air pollution; on one particularly smoggy Beijing day in the fall of 2010, the US Embassy, at a loss for adjectives, described the air quality in the city as "crazy bad."

China and India and many other parts of the developing world are urbanizing and industrializing far too quickly to be mindful of details like clean water and healthy working conditions, and their poverty and dislocation problems far outweigh loftier sustainability goals in their planning. Since 1990 the number of Chinese living in extreme poverty has declined by about a quarter of a billion—an achievement that Chinese officials surely size up as more than sufficient justification for its pollution problems. There is much to criticize about the Chinese approach to development—its appalling record on human rights, civil liberties, labour law and environmental stewardship, to name just the four worst offences—but there's also much to learn from a country that has chosen simply to build the industrial basis of an economy less dependent on fossil fuels, instead of dithering endlessly about the supposedly dire costs and purported scientific uncertainties around climate change and peak oil.

The best hope for developing nations is that pacesetting China takes The Leap's core lesson to heart. Not only do economic development and increased prosperity not have to come at the expense of the planet's health, there will be no long-term economic success in China or anywhere else unless sustainability becomes the new bottom line, and resilience the new design paradigm.

Because China's tightly controlled government is so heavily centralized and secretive, it is difficult by design to read the country's intentions and long-term goals. But the best available evidence suggests that China's greenhouse gas emissions will continue to grow until around 2030 or so before beginning to fall. On the other hand, the Chinese government has said it wants to draw 15 percent of its energy from non-fossil fuel sources and reduce the intensity of its carbon dioxide emissions—the volume emitted per unit of energy produced—45 percent by 2020. If the Chinese path of renewable energy adoption follows the German lead, might its energy bureaucrats discover that those targets can be reached faster than expected, with unanticipated and wholly positive ancillary benefits for the country's economic health and quality of life? The five-year plan running from 2011 to 2015 includes a comprehensive "plan for ecological growth." That could turn out to be a gloss on a growing cloud of coal smoke, but it could also indicate that renewable power plants and electric cars have provided the best way to leapfrog past the oil-addicted West into the lead position in the twenty-first-century economy.

Or consider this take on the situation, from Republican congressman Bob Inglis of South Carolina, as he left his position on the House Committee on Science, Space and Technology, defeated in the 2010 election by a more conservative Republican and replaced on the committee by brazen deniers of the reality of climate change. "I would also suggest to my free enterprise colleagues—especially conservatives here—whether you think it's all a bunch of hooey, what we've talked about in this committee, the Chinese don't. And they plan on eating our lunch in this next century."

The twenty-first century, in other words, will belong to those countries that have made the Great Leap Sideways.

< EPILOGUE >

THE LEAP NOT TAKEN

THE SUMMER OF THE SPILL & THE MYTH OF BUSINESS AS USUAL

IF THE SECOND HALF OF 2008 marked the first convergence of this century's defining crises—the moment when the fundamentally unsustainable nature of our economic, ecological and energy systems appeared in the same frame—then the summer of 2010 might best be understood as their fusion point. The crises, once distinct, were now a single inextricable mess, a deep chasm to be crossed as soon as possible. And business as usual was never more visibly a track headed directly at the precipice with no idea how to clear the gap. This was the most extraordinary aspect of the tumultuous summer of 2010: business as usual, in its desperation, revealed itself to be the engine of the most radical and perilous leap of all into the unfathomable deeps, the leap we simply cannot take.

The catastrophic blowout of BP's Deepwater Horizon oil rig was the predominant symbol of that troubled summer, a headline rewritten daily that spoke in staccato bursts to a much broader crisis. In a tragic, explosive moment that stretched with some cruel admixture of mounting alarm and tragicomic absurdity across weeks and then months, the BP spill revealed the staggering scale of the risk built into business as usual and our dizzying proximity to the precipice.

It had taken only a single malfunction, a comparatively minor detail in the construction of one wellhead's concrete casing, to send the entire operation over the edge. It landed on the oil-clouded sea floor in a place at the very limit of human technical capacity, a place of longshots and best guesses and untested experiments, where each day's failure to solve the problem sent another 57,000 barrels of ruinous crude oil gushing into the open sea. It was just barely hyperbole when a Sierra Club official described the BP spill as "America's Chernobyl"—not only for the cataclysmic ecological damage to the Gulf of Mexico, but also for the way it awakened a somnolent, oil-dependent public to the fragile and mindbogglingly complex system that kept the engines of their status quo humming steadily along at 86 million barrels per day.

When most people think of oil, they likely think first of the neighbourhood gas pump, maybe also the scroll at the bottom of the business news channel quoting that day's price for a barrel of the stuff. Perhaps they imagine hydraulic pumps mounted in scaffolding or black gold erupting geyser-like from the Arabian desert or a great hulking steel platform moored in some choppy faraway sea. Until the summer of 2010 they certainly did not imagine a murky green-grey image of ruptured pipe streamed online from 5,000 feet (1,500 metres) beneath the surface of the Gulf of Mexico, nor the fantastical notion of a borehole burrowed out by remote control that extended from that inhuman depth another 13,000 feet (4,000 metres) beneath the ocean floor. A great taper-thin Matterhorn of a drilling rig more than 3 miles tall, built to tap an oil reservoir less than one-hundredth the size of the East Texas Oil Field (still the largest ever found in the United States outside Alaska). A machine to drill into the centre of the earth—this is a science fiction scenario, the world-conquering fantasy of some cartoon villain, or maybe more generously the featured experiment in some extreme engineering show on Discovery. It is not, in any case, business as usual.

From late April until the breach was permanently sealed in September, the status of the ruptured Deepwater Horizon well was daily international news. The world looked on, shock at the cataclysmic scale turning to horror at the ecological toll and fury at the glib incompetence of the official reaction, tar-soaked pelicans and stiff-lipped oil executives alternating with aerial images of the impossibly large stain spreading across the surface of the Gulf. There was real tragedy here, a discrete and multifaceted catastrophe with heroes and villains and too many victims to name. But in some greater sense we were also participating in something more symbolic and transcendent—a sort of cleansing ritual. The billions of residents of the global village, members all of a tribe called Oil, watched the ritual sacrifice of more than 200 million gallons of precious crude, a bloodletting to atone for a daily sin seventeen times as large. Cap *this* gusher, so that all the world's fossil fuel problems would be solved, could at least be *solvable*. But of course the capping ritual meant virtually nothing to the overall flow of petroleum to the world's engines, nothing at all to the steady uptick in parts per million of carbon dioxide in the earth's atmosphere. Staggering as the size of BP's spill was, it was but a fraction of a fraction of the size of our addiction, a puddle on the track of a roaring status quo.

The Deepwater Horizon well gushed oil for 87 days, during which time humanity consumed more than seven billion barrels of oil. More than 1,500 BP spills' worth. Such is the scale of business as usual in the epic final act of the fossil fuel age. Deepwater Horizon was one of nearly 4,000 offshore oil and gas platforms operating in the Gulf of Mexico alone in the summer of 2010, and the Gulf is but one deep-sea oil field. More than a thousand more drilling rigs operate in the Campos Basin off the coast of Brazil, some in even deeper water—the basin's richest offshore reserves rest beneath 6,500 feet (2 kilometres) of ocean and a crust of unstable salt just as thick; the construction cost of a single rig capable of oil extraction in such circumstances can run as high as $900 million. Even as engineers grappled with the problem of capping BP's blown-out well, industry and government officials from half a dozen countries continued their assessment of prospects for mining the sea floor beneath the Arctic Ocean. This had, of course, only recently become plausible with the rapid melting of the ice covering the ocean's surface, a phenomenon that was itself caused in large part by the burning of fossil fuels.

Arctic sea ice reached its lowest volume in recorded history at the end of the summer of 2010. Not only had it melted back toward the pole to an unprecedented extent, but it was thinner than ever before; a top researcher described its current state as a "death spiral" that would end in an ice-free Arctic Ocean every summer. A German shipping company, meanwhile, made the first-ever commercial voyage through the Arctic's newly thawed "Northeast Passage," even as the worst wildfires in recorded history ravaged the Russian countryside to the south, fuelled by the hot, dry winds of a radically altered climate.

Further south in Pakistan, a monsoon of unparalleled ferocity submerged an expanse of land the size of Italy by mid-August. Around the same time, a Columbia University researcher, Richard Seager, urged residents of the American Southwest to begin preparing for the arrival of an era of "permanent drought" of Dust Bowl scale before the decade was out; Seager had used nineteen separate climate modelling computers to consider forty-nine different climate scenarios, and the perpetual-drought situation had been the near-term outcome in forty-six of them. And still the focus of the world remained on one oil spill in one benighted patch of tropical sea, as if stopping the leak and restoring some semblance of the ecosystem in those waters would be enough to put the status quo back on track. As if indeed the Gulf of Mexico weren't already scarred by a lifeless "dead zone" the size of New Jersey because of agricultural runoff borne there by the polluted Mississippi. As if one in 8 species of birds worldwide weren't threatened with extinction from climate change, as if 80 percent of the world's fisheries weren't already overfished, as if any sort of fishery could be deemed sustainable when every coral reef in the world was just a decade or two from terminal decline due to ocean acidification. As if, that is, we hadn't left business as usual for a rollercoaster sidetrack through catastrophic terrain some ways back. As if there was anything at all about the summer of 2010 that could be described as *usual*.

In the summer of 2010 the US government offered substantial aid to developing countries—India and China, in particular—to join it in the greatest expansion of shale gas drilling the world's ever seen. Like oil, natural gas was once something tapped in large subterranean pools by relatively straightforward drilling means. Shale gas extraction, by contrast, involves the pulverization of solid 400-million-year-old sedimentary rock. In the broad Marcellus Shale beneath the rocky hills of central Pennsylvania and upstate New York, the oil and gas industry pushed forward with plans to drill more than 20,000 new wells, promising to make every effort to ensure that the fracking chemicals it won't name will never leak into the adjacent drinking water supplies of cities like New York and Philadelphia. Throughout the summer of 2010 one shale driller, Anadarko, continued its protracted battle with residents and conservationists in central Pennsylvania over its plan to draw 720,000 gallons of clean water per day from the Susquehanna

River in Clinton County, home to five state parks and a state forest, to fuel its fracking operations.

In the summer of 2010 a Wyoming survey in a community surrounded by ongoing shale-gas operations reported that nine in ten of the residents questioned reported ailments consistent with exposure to toxic chemicals, including itchy skin, burning eyes, high blood pressure, memory loss, headaches and, in 80 percent of the cases, respiratory problems.

In the summer of 2010 the esteemed insurance firm Lloyd's of London and the Royal Institute of International Affairs issued a joint report arguing that peak oil was an emerging reality with "potentially catastrophic consequences" for governments that did not take dramatic action soon to build greater resilience into their energy supplies. The British government, though officially unfazed, had already begun secret talks on the subject of peak oil, revealing in leaked documents that it had learned from International Energy Agency (IEA) officials that the organization's predictions of a 2030 peak in oil production at 105 million barrels per day was "over-optimistic." One unnamed IEA official believed even 95 million barrels to be "impossible."

In the summer of 2010 two European nations discovered the outsized economics of modern nuclear energy. A new Bulgarian nuclear plant, originally expected to cost $5.8 billion, now bore a price tag of $11.4 billion, while French nuclear giant Areva revealed that the plant it was building in Finland would open three years late and cost roughly double its initial estimate. Nuclear companies the world over continued to tout themselves as the only realistic, affordable alternative to dirty fossil fuels.

In the summer of 2010, if not earlier, business as usual ceased to be. It carried on as it always had—or pretended to, *aspired* to, fought crazily to, with the same sort of panicked schemes that BP engineers were using to try to cap their spill throughout the summer—but it had become something else entirely. Business as usual had become a Leap all its own, staggering in scale and wildly ambitious in its technical complexity.

At its founding, this energy regime's business as usual was a simpler thing, more direct in its logic. Like this: An industrial economy needed energy. Lots of it. More and more. Fossil fuels were cheap and abundant and easy to extract, and oil in particular is energy-dense like no other fuel humanity had ever discovered, gathered in vast reservoirs and very easy to move around in quantity and put to a wide range of uses. Fossil fuels brought human industry to heights and scales unimaginable under the era of wood fires and manual labour they supplanted. It only made sense, under those circumstances, to seek out as much of the stuff as we could.

These are not the parameters of the conventional energy economy in 2010.

Business as usual has become this: There is no technical hurdle too great, no cost too high, no environmental impact too dire to oblige us to consider moving away from fossil fuels in any kind of hurry. If ancient stone must be turned to rubble, or the ocean turned to acid and coated with oil, so be it. Once we needed lots of energy, and fossil fuels provided it; now we need fossil fuels, because we refuse to seriously consider a world without them. We are investing our final years of abundant conventional energy in the idea that this failure of collective imagination is the best way forward. This is The Leap we are contemplating, the precipice from which we viewed the worst oil spill in human history in the overheated, fire-ravaged, drought-stricken, flood-ruined summer of 2010. We stand at this precipice, and our opportunities for getting onto another track diminish by the day. Our brightest possible future relies on making business as usual the leap not taken.

THE PIPELINE & THE SPIRIT BEAR

Here was another piece of business-as-usual news from 2010: in late May, Enbridge, an oil-and-gas pipeline developer based in Calgary, Alberta, filed a proposal with the Canadian government to lay two pipelines across 1,100 kilometres of northern Canadian wilderness, traversing half a dozen mountain ranges and the semi-sovereign territories of more than forty First Nations. One pipeline would carry 525,000 barrels of oil per day from northern Alberta's tar sands to a new terminal to be constructed at the port of Kitimat, a down-at-heel pulp town on the remote northern coast of British Columbia. A second pipeline would carry *condensate*, an oil by-product, back to Alberta's tar sands, where it is essential to the expensive, energy-intensive, environmentally costly business of upgrading the bitumen sludge mined from the region's soil into oil viscous enough to flow through the great pipe to the sea. Supertankers would come and go from the new terminal almost daily, carrying the oil down a narrow, treacherous fjord, then navigating tight passages between coastal islands and across the wind-ravaged Hecate Strait to reach the Pacific Ocean, thus to deliver their cargo to waiting ports in Asia.

The logic, by the standards of our leaping business as usual, was impeccable: Some of the world's most marginal and difficult-to-refine oil, made profitable because the dwindling supplies of conventional oil had pushed the price of a barrel so high, was to be piped across half a continent, then carried by mammoth ships through perilous waters and across an ocean, all to feed the industrial growth of booming China. Our last conventional fuel would stoke the engines of the developing world's roaring journey down the very same industrial path we'd taken.

Enbridge has dubbed the project "Northern Gateway." A glossy brochure outlining its benefits juxtaposes pictures of pristine mountain wilderness with construction scenes, rounding out the fantastical panorama with photos of busy workers wielding heavy machinery or posed behind banks of computer screens, as well as grinning bakers and restauranteurs and a Native boy playing a traditional drum. "We're building sustainable communities through jobs and investment," the accompanying text reads. A curious and rather proscribed use of the term *sustainable*, to be sure, but the brochure is most remarkable for a particular phrase it doesn't contain, the name of the place where the proposed pipeline would terminate: the Great Bear Rainforest.

At the end of the summer of 2010, I visited the Great Bear Rainforest for the first time, arriving by float plane from Vancouver to ply the inlets and channels of the region on a catamaran and wade on foot through its salmon streams. I had come at the invitation of a regional conservation group, which had brought a dozen of the world's best wildlife photographers and filmmakers to document the rainforest's awesome abundance of natural capital. I can report that the logic of Enbridge's pipeline looks very different from that vantage point.

The Great Bear Rainforest is the largest intact temperate rainforest remaining on the entire west coast of North America. Temperate rainforest once predominated from northern California to southern Alaska, but Great Bear represents the last substantial swath of it. On the ride up, I could see why. Flying low in a small plane, I tracked our journey from Vancouver north to the native community at Hartley Bay in a series of industrial scars. The coastal forests below were pockmarked with clear-cut patches and mismatched tree growth from several generations of logging. One cove contained an abandoned cannery from the heyday of British Columbia's fisheries a half-century earlier; another revealed a brand-new salmon farm, its livestock carrying the parasites and infections that were even now wreaking havoc on what remained of the wild salmon population. There were pulp towns and tugs towing logs, a handful of traditional fishing boats, islands here and there littered with outsized holiday homes.

There was evidence of a single relationship with Canada's wilderness, the one that has reigned since the first Hudson's Bay Company's trappers arrived on the continent four hundred years ago. Nature was a bounty to be harvested, a collection of resources to be exploited, a trove of riches to be looted. As we cleared the northern tip of Vancouver Island, the evidence of human industry receded rapidly, leaving only flat black sea and thick forest and the occasional BC ferry out of Prince Rupert far to the north. There was a stillness to the landscape, something almost forbiddingly wild. To fill the space, I fell into conversation with the float plane's pilot. I'd assumed he was a contractor hired by one of the conservation NGOs involved in the big photo shoot. Turned out he was a volunteer, a wealthy hobbyist who'd salvaged his plane — a Grumman Widgeon, a vintage amphibious craft built in the 1940s — from some abandoned oil-industry operation in Nigeria. He'd had the plane rebuilt part by part and now looked for excuses to take dramatic excursions from his summer home on Salt Spring Island, near Vancouver. His name was Julian MacQueen, and he'd made his fortune as the most prominent hotelier on Pensacola Beach in Florida.

At the start of the summer of 2010, in June, spilled oil from BP's Gulf blowout began washing ashore in front of MacQueen's hotels, cutting his business in half at the very peak of his season. (Unlike peninsular Florida, Pensacola relies mainly on tourists from neighbouring southern states who visit in the summer.) He'd spent the summer wrestling with BP's lawyers and forensic accountants over the scale of the damage, his best hotel filled mainly with journalists covering the spill. He became a bit of a celebrity, the face of blighted Pensacola's imperilled business community. He reckoned that was why he was the first and to his knowledge the largest claimant to date on Florida's Gulf Coast to have been paid out. As soon as he'd settled all that, he'd run off to his place on Salt Spring to relax. A neighbour soon mentioned a group needing some journalists ferried in and out of some isolated wilderness he'd never heard of. He had no idea until I told him that the ubiquitous snaking tentacles of the oil industry awaited us even at today's remote destination.

MacQueen dug out his iPad and opened a folder full of digital photos. As the Widgeon chugged along the mist-shrouded BC coast, he showed me pictures of white sand stained black and brown with oil, abortive makeshift cleanup efforts, Pensacola Beach packed defiantly with locals for the Fourth of July—the only crowd they saw the whole summer. "I spent twenty-five years building up a business and overnight it was gone," he told me. "I can't tell you the feeling of helplessness that I felt. It can happen like that. This is my life's work and I have 700 employees depending on me. I pay a million dollars in insurance every year, and the last thing on anyone's list was an oil spill."

We'd arrived by now in the heart of the Great Bear Rainforest. Uninhabited islands rose steep-sloped out of the water, crowned with towering cedars. Roiling streams poured out of the hills into secluded coves. Whaling vessels had once worked these waters, and cruise ships chugged through every so often, and Native Canadians had fished the region since long before it'd been named and charted on European maps, but much of the terrain was as close to untouched as the modern world ever gets.

Aside from Kitimat far up one of the deepest inlets, there are only two settlements in this core section of Great Bear: King Pacific

Lodge, a luxury eco-resort built on reclaimed US Army barges that operates in the summer and is then towed away to Prince Rupert for winter storage, leaving virtually no trace of itself behind; and Hartley Bay, the Gitga'at First Nation's primary settlement, a tidy village of 160 on a roadless promontory, accessible only by boat and float plane. We landed in Hartley Bay, with MacQueen piloting his plane down into the water in a series of tightly banked spirals.

We were met at the village dock by Ian McAllister, founder of Pacific Wild, the conservation group leading the publicity campaign against Enbridge's proposed pipeline. He pointed across the water to the northern tip of Gil Island, where the ferry *Queen of the North* had sunk just three years before. Later he would trace the proposed oil-shipping route for me on his catamaran—particularly the tight S-curve the supertankers would have to negotiate to loop around the south end of Gil Island each time they came and went. The smallest of these ships would be three times the length of the *Queen of the North*. Over the next few days, MacQueen would dig out his iPad again and again to show locals what a seacoast looked like in the wake of an oil spill.

The following morning, under skies that started misty and eventually cleared into a radiant blue, McAllister took us to see salmon streams on a handful of nearby islands. These streams are the living, teeming embodiment of biodiversity, impossibly rich in natural capital. Salmon are the keystone species in the Great Bear Rainforest—the most deeply interconnected link in the ecosystem's delicate web of relationships—and the shallow streams where they return en masse each year to spawn form the most crucial thread in the web. When studies attempt to place economic value on ecosystem services and return staggeringly large sums, they are inflated to a large degree by vital places like the Great Bear Rainforest's salmon streams, ageless locales from which so much of the earth's abundance is drawn.

These are just words, abstractions nearly as vague and arbitrary as GDP or net profit or replacement cost. None of them prepare you for the transcendent experience of standing knee-deep in water so thick with life the salmon can't help but bump into you, as you observe a death dance of such tenacity and precision it makes you dizzy. The salmon return at the end of their lives to the stream in which they were born. They force themselves upstream with relentless focus, over rocks and under fallen logs, flinging themselves bodily out of the water to clear waterfalls, shedding skin as they exhaust themselves to death from the outside in, all to find the spot where they will lay their eggs and then expire. It was long assumed that this was a survival-of-the-fittest contest to get to the safest spots the furthest upstream, but McAllister told me recent research has shown the salmon simply return, by some precise guidance system we've only begun to grasp, to places no more than a few feet from the exact spot in the stream where they hatched.

As they fight upstream, the salmon are easy marks for preda-tors. Which is why the banks of a Great Bear stream in spawning season resemble the aftermath of some grand bacchanal, the tall grass and forest floor littered with salmon carcasses and animal scat. Packs of wolves come first. They eat only the heads—thus to avoid some parasite in the stomachs of the salmon, it's believed— and so at each turn of the stream you find piles of salmon car-casses, their heads neatly severed and the bodies fully intact, providing a rich feast for birds. Bears arrive later in the season, after they've exhausted the local berry supply, gorging themselves on salmon until they reach such stuporous levels of excess that McAllister said you could sometimes walk right up to them and push them over without the slightest reaction. They eat more of the fish than the wolves do, but they are notoriously sloppy, spreading fish guts and bone and splatterings of flesh across the forest. The salmon remains and piles of nutrient-rich bear scat feed the plants and trees, which attract an awesome richness of bird and bug life, which attract bigger birds and river otters and wolverines, and so on in closed loops and interdependent circles of mutual enrichment that add up to exactly what we mean when we talk about the value of biodiversity.

I spent a long, meditative day wading in and out of salmon streams. We were visited by a couple of strolling black bears, and on the boat ride back to Hartley Bay a small pod of humpback whales passed by. But I only met some of the more exotic fauna that evening, on the laptop screens of the wildlife photographers who'd returned to the harbour after several days in the wildest parts of Great Bear. Here were coastal wolves loping along with salmon hanging from their muzzles, harbour seals and halibut, fin and killer whales, hulking grizzlies and the elusive, iconic "spirit bear." This last—officially known as a *kermode*—is a subspecies of black bear possessing a recessive gene that turns its coat a ghostly pale blond. The existence of the spirit bear was long thought to be a myth, and the Great Bear Rainforest is its only real home. Not surprisingly, it has become this singular ecosystem's most powerful icon.

Later in the evening, I was taken into the village to meet one of Hartley Bay's most revered elders, an octegenarian woman named Helen Clifton. We met in her living room, interrupted by a steady stream of grandkids trooping through to say good night. Clifton's father had been an Englishman married to a Gitga'at woman, and she'd grown up with feet in both worlds. She'd worked for a time in a cannery in Prince Rupert before settling with her full-blooded Gitga'at husband in Hartley Bay. She wore moccasins, a smart red sweater and traditional English jewellery.

There was a display case of Victorian-style dolls done up like little native girls in her foyer, a rack of caribou antlers over the fireplace, Gitga'at masks mounted in the rafters, a flatscreen TV mounted on one wall.

Clifton was well aware of the logic and priorities of places with much less connection to the wild than Hartley Bay. She was not opposed to change in general, but she was vehemently opposed to Enbridge's pipeline plan and the prospect of seeing supertankers in the ancestral waters of her people. She told me a story about her late husband's first encounter with a spirit bear by way of explanation for her opposition.

Her husband, Clifton explained, had been a lifelong hunter, taught by his father from early childhood that animals couldn't be left to suffer. You aimed for the head, and you never left a wounded animal in the forest. His father had told him as well about the mythic spirit bears living on the nearby island of Princess Royal, *a bear in the woods that looks like a ghost.* Clifton's husband made it to his fifties thinking this was a fairy tale his father told to remind him to be cautious.

He went deer hunting one day, and he came upon a bear in the forest. It reared up on its hind legs in front of him. "It seemed to just grow and grow until it was 8 feet tall," he later told his wife. Its coat was a ghostly white.

With a hunter's instinct, he raised his rifle and fired. The bear cried out, an unholy screech, eerily human, like a woman in pain. And then the bear ran off.

The hunter was wracked with guilt. "What my father told me," he thought. "It's real. And I didn't believe my father."

A dutiful son, the hunter went after the bear, looking for drops of blood, telltale signs of a badly wounded spirit bear on the forest floor. He found nothing. He went home to his wife.

"So he comes back home"—this is how Clifton remembers it, decades later—"and he says, 'Guess what I saw.' And he said, 'You'll find it hard to believe, because I never believed it all my life.' And he told me about this experience with a bear. 'Oh, why didn't you kill it,' I said. 'We would've had this white bear fur.' And he said, 'You foolish woman, that's your white blood talking.' So we both had to laugh. He didn't say that in an insulting way, just because, he said, 'It was only meant for me to see that it was real. Now I have to do something about it to protect it.' And so he told his people they are not to shoot that animal no matter what. 'It's there. I saw it. And nobody is to hunt it. We don't need it for nothing.'"

Clifton's husband did not stop hunting. He never doubted that the Gitga'at and everyone else needed to draw on nature's bounty to live, but he understood there were limits. You could not take *everything*.

I remembered then something Ian McAllister had said as we returned to Hartley Bay at sunset that afternoon. "You've got every major oil company in the world and the world's second largest oil reserve looking to diversify its markets, and the only thing in their way is that little community of 160 people." This was a slight exaggeration, inasmuch as McAllister's own conservation group and almost every single First Nations community along the 1,100-kilometre length of Enbridge's proposed pipeline were vowing to do everything in their power to stop its construction, to guarantee that business as usual would never include daily visits to the Great Bear Rainforest by supertankers laden with bitumen mined in Alberta's tar sands, bound under flags of convenience from far-off and indifferent lands to Chinese ports. In a less literal sense, though, it was an understatement.

This is the fundamental choice not just for the Gitga'at of

Hartley Bay, but for all of us as we contemplate the leap represented by business as usual today. We can have the pipeline or the spirit bears. There will be no sustainable system, however, that contains both.

The choice of the pipeline comes with its own solid logic and its own strident assertions—one of which is that you *can* have both. Enbridge points to its track record on safety and to super-tankers safely navigating the fjords of Norway. They promise to spare no expense in their environmental stewardship. Beyond this, they argue for the *necessity* of the pipeline. They promise 4,000 jobs in its construction, maybe forty or so permanent ones at the oil terminal in Kitimat, a town that just saw its last pulp mill close and needs every new opportunity that comes its way. Besides, bringing the pipeline to the larger port 120 kilometres north at Prince Rupert, which opens directly on the sea, would cost an extra CAD$500 million. And the world, more broadly speaking, needs oil. Gitga'at fishing boats run on it, and so do the vessels that bring just about every single useful thing to Hartley Bay that isn't locally caught fish or locally logged wood, and so for that matter do the float planes ferrying journalists into Hartley Bay to marvel at all the wonders of the rainforest.

Here is what struck me, though, viewing this prospect from the unique vantage of Helen Clifton's parlour in Hartley Bay. This was not an extension of business as usual into another underdeveloped place that sorely needed it. This was something else entirely. The scale of the risk was impossibly high, of a magnitude almost beyond measure. It began with the possibility of a super-tanker spill—which, if the Exxon Valdez disaster just a little north of Great Bear was any indication, would ruin the entirety of the spirit bear's habitat for generations and despoil British Columbia's coastal waters all the way south to Vancouver Island. It would mean the end of the salmon streams on which almost all the bio-diversity of the rainforest depend. Whatever place survived a spill of supertanker magnitude, it would not be the place we know now.

Risks of similar scale threatened the Enbridge pipeline all the way back to northern Alberta. The whole length of it ran through one kind of vital, biodiversity-rich ecosystem or another. And one of the stories of the summer of 2010 that will surely never appear in a glossy Enbridge brochure was the one about how three of its existing pipelines sprung leaks. The most severe of these, in an oil pipeline running across northern Michigan, poured more than a million gallons of oil into the Kalamazoo River in June. And then of course there is the eastern terminus of the pipeline: the Athabasca tar sands, that vaunted second largest oil reserve on earth. Also, by most measures, its most environmentally devastating, a voracious consumer of clean water and natural gas, the engine of the steepest part of the spike in Canada's carbon dioxide emissions over the last decade, its operations requiring the surface mining of vast tracts of pristine boreal forest and a lingering legacy of deadly toxic tailings ponds. Stretch Enbridge's value proposition westward at the other end—beyond the BC coast, to the Asian economies it would serve, multiplying their carbon footprints and deepening their oil addiction—and the risk mounts even higher.

Tabulate the full bill, ring it all up. Begin with an excess of greenhouse gases and an ecological mess at the supply end. Traverse hundreds of miles of delicate wilderness and the home-lands of fortysome First Nations that have never sacrificed their sovereignty to any colonial master. Carry on to the sea, to a super-tanker parade through the treacherous waters abutting the last healthy expanse of temperate rainforest in North America. Cross the ocean to arrive at the fastest growing greenhouse-gas furnace on the planet, and empty the boats' hulls onto the fire. The risks and externalized costs mount along every mile of this dubious value chain, and all of it simply directs more traffic along a fundamentally unsustainable track to the very precipice of a chasm it cannot cross.

No, this is not business as usual. This is a choice that would look familiar to the Easter Islanders who cut down the last trees on their depleted island to lever into place one last idol to a maddeningly indifferent god. They are called Moai, those great stone heads, and this is an Easter Island Moai sculpted in broad horizontal form, carved out of concrete and steel now instead of stone, a Moai reimagined in the shape of pipelines and supertankers— idols to the god of unlimited growth and limitless oil, whose promise of prosperity unending will surely come with just one more statue's construction.

This is the lesson of the summer of 2010, the clear choice between pipeline and spirit bear, between unsustainable and sustainable tracks, between a leap of blind faith in a twisted business as usual and a reasoned Great Leap Sideways.

OUR BRIGHTEST POSSIBLE FUTURE

There is another way to think of the summer of 2010, a news feed from a parallel reality on the other side of the chasm.

By the summer of 2010, wind overtook natural gas as the most abundant new fuel source on electrical grids across Europe. In the summer of 2010, a joint venture was formed to build the world's largest offshore wind farm, a 576-MW installation off the coast of Britain. In July and August of 2010 alone, Germany introduced 1,000 MW of new solar power onto its grid—a full gigawatt—and over the course of the year the German grid welcomed more new solar power than existed in all the world in 2005. Italy, meanwhile, emerged from out of nowhere to become the world's number-two market for new solar installations in the summer of 2010, and its solar power now vies with sunny California's to become the first to reach grid parity. California, for its part, approved construction of a new 250-MW solar thermal power plant in the summer of 2010, and venture capital firms in Silicon Valley and beyond poured billions into entrepreneurial cleantech schemes of a hundred different green hues on their way to an all-time record year of almost $8 billion in investments worldwide. A Danish joint venture headed by the biotech company Novozymes claimed it would drop the price of cellulosic ethanol fuel by 80 percent within a few years. The Chinese government introduced rebates for the purchase of EVs and vowed to produce a million emissions-free cars each year by 2015.

In the summer of 2010, while fossil-fuelled business as usual derailed catastrophically, the bustling traffic headed toward our brightest possible future raced faster and smoother than ever down the sustainable track.

Just weeks before the summer of 2010 officially began, I caught a glimpse of the choice I would come to see, by the end of the summer, as a choice between pipelines and spirit bears, in a half-empty office building in the middle of downtown Toledo, Ohio.

I'd come to the offices of Pilkington, one of Toledo's grand old glass firms, to talk about the potential for a Toledo solar boom with Stephen Weidner, who was in charge of developing new architectural products. Weidner was a career glass engineer, cautious as engineers often are, guarded in his enthusiasm for the industry's expansion into solar power. Sure, it might one day be a huge industry, but right now it was future tense and mostly a cottage-scale, lab-test sort of enterprise. It could not restore Toledo to its auto-industry heyday any time soon, and who knew if the whole business—the whole town, the whole world—would go that way.

Any real exciting potential directions for Pilkington? I wondered.

Well, Weidner admitted, there was one thing he was pretty jazzed about.

He led me down a hallway, along a row of half-empty cubicles, turning abruptly into one and re-emerging with a little decorative desktop gadget. It had a small solar panel mounted on one side and a fan the size of a hockey puck on the other.

"Is that a Dyesol cell?" I asked.

Weidner looked up at me, surprised. "Yeah, it is," he said. I explained how I knew what it was while we waited for the elevator.

A couple of years earlier, I'd been in Australia on a research tour and made a point of stopping in on the Canberra headquarters of a company called Dyesol. The company had recently signed an agreement with Corus, one of Europe's largest steel manufacturers, to investigate the feasibility of installing its solar cells on Corus's steel roofing material as it was being manufactured. (The company has since been purchased by Tata Steel.) There's a phase in the production line for Colorcoat roofing in which it gets tinted one colour or another, and Dyesol had developed a manufacturing process similar enough that it seemed highly plausible it could add its solar cells to the roofing in place of the colouring.

Dyesol's solar cells—produced by spreading a microscopically thin layer of dye made from a highly conductive metal called ruthenium over the extraordinarily large surface area created by a base layer of titania paste—were cheaper and faster to make than previous generations of solar technology, and they could generate current in extremely low light. In Australia I watched a small

Dyesol solar panel spin a bank of fans in a room with the venetian blinds closed to slits. By the time I met with Weidner in Toledo, Tata Steel had begun converting one of its old production lines in Wales to incorporate the Dyesol cells. Every year, the steelmaker produces 100 million square metres of its Colorcoat roofing—enough to re-roof every Walmart in North America— and within a few years it intends to start selling industrial quantities of the stuff with solar power built right into it.

In Toledo Stephen Weidner led me to a rear courtyard of the Pilkington tower to find a patch of sun. He located one and connected the wires on the little desktop apparatus, and its tiny fan began to spin furiously. Pilkington had recently entered into a joint venture with Dyesol to begin testing the viability of integrating solar cells into its glass production. It was small scale at present, but given the Toledo industry's long history with solar R&D and since Dyesol's own cells had always incorporated glass, it was a natural fit. On our way back up to his office, Weidner opened himself to the wider world of possibility. Almost everywhere you installed glass—curtain walls and roofs, interior walls, even ceilings—you could probably make Dyesol's solar cells work. Clean energy could be incorporated into everything we built, everywhere, effortlessly.

I left the meeting and hiked through Toledo's downtown, so fully abandoned at six o'clock on a Monday afternoon it felt like a stage set after production had wrapped. Lots of office buildings in need of new windows. New occupants. New jobs, a new industry, a way forward.

From the streets of Toledo, I couldn't even *see* two tracks. There was only the choice between the one headed toward our brightest possible future and nothing at all.

< ACKNOWLEDGEMENTS >

I LAUNCHED THIS LEAP of a book knowing full well I'd inevitably drag a great many others along for the ride. To those I've mentioned by name—here or in the text—and the many others I've surely forgotten to thank, I would like to extend my deepest gratitude. One name goes on the cover, but it takes a whole community to produce a book.

I would first like to thank the Canada Council for the Arts and the Alberta Foundation for the Arts for essential financial support. I'm grateful as well to the Government of Victoria (Australia), the Alfred Deakin Lectures and their wonderful curator, Robyn Archer, for enabling my Australian research, and to the Banff Centre and the Paul D. Fleck Fellowship program for providing a singularly inspirational workspace for the first phase of the writing.

I am thankful beyond words for the unwavering hand of my colleagues at Random House Canada during this turbulent time in the publishing game—in particular my editor, Craig Pyette, without whose wisdom and care this would be a much longer and weaker book; my publisher, Anne Collins, whose support over three books now is a testimony to the vital necessity of publishing houses; and Matthew Sibiga, who has turned the job of sales rep into something much more like production manager. My deepest thanks as well to my agents, David Kuhn and Billy Kingsland at Kuhn Projects, who turned a vague idea into a coherent project and brought it to market.

I owe my greatest debt of gratitude, as ever, to my resilient and ceaselessly supportive wife, Ashley Bristowe — my co-conspirator, travelling companion, sounding board, hawk-eyed copy editor, anchor and guide in writing as well as in life. I'm forever grateful as well to my children, Sloane and Alexander, for the inspiration they bring me every day, their tolerance of my odd work hours, and their patience as I dragged them (sometimes literally so) from one research site to the next. To Sloane, my apologies for not working our Legoland trip into this book, highlight though it was of the Danish research; and to Alexander, my eternal pride for being the first infant to see the world from the observation deck at Solúcar in Spain.

I would like to thank my parents, John and Margo Turner, and my father-in-law, Bruce Bristowe, for guidance, many kinds of support, and vital and timely grandparenting. Kelsey Thoms has my deepest thanks for keeping a chaotic household together throughout. Sara Simpson and John Johnston went above and beyond in more ways than I can count to keep me on track. Claire Cummings, Zoe Ferguson, Meike Wieblowski, Steven Drummond, Margaret Drummond, Brad Roulston, Jana Johnson, Jay Way, Bruce Manning, Alexis Bahry Mackenzie, Marlene Smith, and Sharon Monkman all provided generous support on the homefront as well. Tine Bihlet made the Danish research a joyous time for my children, and Anne Elsner did the same in Germany.

Special thanks to the staff, students and fellow parents at Lycée Louis Pasteur — a profoundly generous and welcoming community. And special thanks as well to Gillian Deacon, Gill

Irving and the Institutes for the Achievement of Human Potential, pro Leapers all. I'm also indebted to my inspiring colleagues and friends at Sustainable Calgary and CivicCamp Calgary—in particular Cheri Macauley, Noel Keough, Peter Rishaug, Byron Miller, Natalia Zoldak and Naheed Nenshi—for joining me to launch a Leap close to home.

In addition to those cited by name in the text, I would like to extend special thanks to many other colleagues for their generosity with their knowledge and expertise. In Australia, Brian Walker of CSIRO shared his research on resilience. Lars Gemzoe, Jeff Risom and Barbra Hald at Gehl Architects were enormously helpful on the subject of Copenhagenization. Jessica Engvall was an insightful guide in Helsingborg, Sweden. Nina Alsen provided timely assistance in Berlin. Tobias Homann, Thomas Grigoliet, Robert Scheid and Todd Buell at Germany Trade & Invest helped with the German research. Katrin Kuhnt and Christian Puschmann provided critical guidance to my research in Bitterfeld-Wolfen. Ana Cabañas Burgos and Valerio Fernandez Quero of Abengoa Solar were welcoming hosts. Jon Strunk of the University of Toledo (Ohio) found all the right sources for a whirlwind research trip, and Don Tormey of the Iowa Office of Energy Independence guided my way in Iowa. Karin Campbell and Andrew Pelletier of Walmart Canada lent their expertise to my research on Walmart's sustainability push. Ian McAllister, Norm Hann and Julian MacQueen provided essential support to my research in Great Bear Rainforest, and it never would have happened at all without the organization of the Great Bear RAVE by the International League of Conservation Photographers.

Paul Gipe of Wind-Works.org deserves more than these simple thanks for all he has done to document the rise and spread of feed-in tariffs, and Dave Hughes and Charlie Veron contributed to this book in ways well beyond those cited in the text. Juliet Burgess contributed her multitude of skills to the European research, and Wendy Schur provided assistance to my research on the Black Ball Line at the Mystic Seaport Museum in Mystic, Connecticut. Alex Steffen of Worldchanging.com was a valued colleague and wayfinder, and David Roberts of Grist.org has no idea how much his excellent work has helped mine. Sebastian Hanna of Chapters Indigo provided critical advice in the final stages of the book's production.

Like many nonfiction books, this one was wet-nursed by the magazine business. Evan Osenton at *Alberta Views*, Rick Boychuk at *Canadian Geographic*, Will Bourne at *Fast Company*, Jerry Johnson at *The Globe and Mail*, Jeremy Keehn at *The Walrus* and Tom Gierasimczuk at *Up!* all lent editorial guidance and editorial budgets to portions of this book's research.

A NOTE ON SOURCES

In order to avoid clogging up the text with footnotes and to keep the page count down, extensive source notes have not been included with this text. A full list of sources, annotated section by section, is available for download at http://www.randomhouse.ca.

< INDEX >